Iconomy: Toward a Political Economy of Images

Iconomy: Toward a Political Economy of Images

Terry Smith

ANTHEM PRESS

Anthem Press
An imprint of Wimbledon Publishing Company
www.anthempress.com

This edition first published in UK and USA 2022
by ANTHEM PRESS
75–76 Blackfriars Road, London SE1 8HA, UK
or PO Box 9779, London SW19 7ZG, UK
and
244 Madison Ave #116, New York, NY 10016, USA

British Library Cataloguing-in-Publication Data
A catalogue record for this book is available from the British Library.

Library of Congress Cataloging-in-Publication Data
A catalog record for this book has been requested.

ISBN-13: 978-1-83998-435-8 (Hbk)
ISBN-10: 1-83998-435-X (Hbk)

This title is also available as an e-book.

Dedicated to

W.J.T. Mitchell,
"Tom" to his many friends

CONTENTS

LIST OF ILLUSTRATIONS

ACKNOWLEDGMENTS

My thinking on these matters owes many debts to many people over many years. Outstanding among these are W.J.T. Mitchell and Nicolas Mirzoeff. Anna Rubbo, Nancy Condee, and Susan Bielstein were crucial to an earlier attempt to think about architectural iconomy before and after 9/11. For their advice during pivotal points in writing the chapters in this book, I thank McKenzie Wark, Leo Hollis, Mark Ledbury, Howard Morphy, Ian McLean, David Hay, and Bridget R. Cooks. An invitation from Jacob Lund, editor of the *Nordic Journal of Aesthetics*, was essential to the plotting of Part I. The work of colleagues at the European Graduate School—notably that of Jean-Luc Nancy, Judith Butler, Peter Szendy, Benjamin Bratton, Fred Moten, and Christopher Fynsk—has helpfully oriented, and disoriented, my approach to these topics. My colleagues at the University of Pittsburgh provided their usual supportive context, with Alison Langmead being particularly helpful to this project. During the Spring semester of 2022, students in my graduate seminar on "Image Economies: Past and Present"—Kathryn Carney, Diana Flatto, Mara Hassan, María Cecilia Llorens, Janina Lopez, Tiffany Sims, and Vuk Vuković—subjected these ideas to close examination. I also thank Theodor Ringborg, whose PhD I had the pleasure of examining while immersed in these deliberations, and Nicole Scalissi, whose dissertation I had the privilege of advising at an earlier moment.

I wish to thank Ilhan Ozan and Diana Flatto for their invaluable research assistance and Diana especially for her work in obtaining images and permissions.

For making available images of their work, I thank the artists and photographers whose work is illustrated and the following: Alamy Banque d'Images, Buku-Larrŋgay Mulka Art Centre, Yirrkala; Roslyn Oxley9 Gallery, Sydney; Classical Numismatic Group, Inc.; Centers for Disease Control and Prevention, Atlanta; *Fabian: The Australian Fabians Review*; Magnum Photos; AP Photo; Reuters; Getty Images; *The New York Times*/Redux; The White House;

Mitchell-Innes & Nash Gallery, New York; Gladstone Gallery, New York; Biennale of Sydney; Gavin Brown's enterprise, New York.

At Anthem Press, I thank commissioning editor Courtney Young, my editor Megan Grieving, the academic advisors, and the readers, for their astringency and flexibility, as well as Sreejith Govindan and all those at the Press and Lumina Datamatics who contributed to the making of this book.

And, as always, my family.

INTRODUCTION: EPIDEMIC IMAGES

I began writing these chapters while in quarantine in Sydney, having flown there from the United States on May 25, 2020, anticipating my usual three months stay. The strict lockdown conditions due to the pandemic meant that for the first 2 weeks I was confined to a hotel room, no argument, no exceptions, no problem. I had resolved to devote the coming days to revisiting an idea I have, for decades, taken as a given but never had time to think through: that the visual imagery so pervasive in contemporary life might exhibit definable structures, elusive and changeable but consistently so, just enough for its histories to be written and its emerging shapes perceived. I already had a name for this economy of images: *iconomy*, a simple combination of the Greek words for "icon" and "economy." Like several others who have used this term before and since, I foolishly thought that I had coined it. I was thinking about how certain buildings, then dubbed "iconic architecture," stood as symbols of cities within a worldwide chain of such images, how they operated within tourist economies and broader public imaginaries. The other side of this seemingly benign coinage became apparent at a moment when widespread trauma was occasioned by a war of images, when many of these buildings became targets. My response to 9/11 was *The Architecture of Aftermath*, published by the University of Chicago Press in 2006.

But the broader logic within which the contest of images is fought kept on eluding an analysis fitting its growing importance. I carried with me to Sydney a small cache of books, among them Guy Debord's *The Society of the Spectacle*, the *locus classicus* for any thinking about the nature of image economies under capitalism. It would, I figured, be a familiar place from which to start over. Decades of thinking about these issues in the company of many others doing the same was my greatest resource. There was also Google Books, my University Library access to e-books and articles, and the many files I had on my laptop. As the plane took off, the prospect before me was a few weeks, with minimal distractions, to think more about iconomy, this plausible but fugitive idea.

While I was in the air over the Pacific Ocean, asleep, something occurred at a street intersection in Powderhorn, Minneapolis, that quickly proved to be of enormous consequence. As part of a routine arrest for suspected petty theft, a White police officer placed his knee on the neck of a prone, shackled Black man who pleaded, in vain, for his life. On my arrival in Sydney, media was awash with stories about the killing of George Floyd, most featuring the cell phone video of it happening in real time. The murder, and its instant electronic propagation via the posted video, precipitated an extraordinary eruption of protests on the streets of cities across the United States then around the world. Iconomy ceased to be an abstract idea, the name of a theory about the image flow. Here it was, at maximum intensity, right here on the screens in my world: on my cell phone, my laptop, on this huge hotel television monitor, and inside my head. Soon, I learned of the mass protest marches occurring in Sydney, on streets and in a park on the other side of the city, a mile from where I was, demonstrations that I would have joined, despite the COVID-19 risk, were I able to leave my confinement. All I could do was watch and write. So, I did both. And continued to do so during the following months as I tried to gauge the value for critical thought and political action of theorizing image economies as iconomies.

Etymology and Iconomy

"Iconomy" combines "icon" and "economy," words with deep etymologies and long, usually separate, histories. *Oἰκονόμος* is a Greek composite word derived from *οἶκος* ("house; household; home") and *νέμω* ("manage; distribute; to deal out; dispense"), giving "economy" its most literal meaning, that is, household management. In Greece, during the fourth-century BC, this was the basic meaning of the term, as codified by Aristotle and his followers, underscoring other levels, from the personal, through the political (of the *polis*, the city), that of the managers and, at the top, that of the king, ruler, or, in rare cases, elected leader.[1] In 1374, Nicole Oresme, Aristotle's French translator, explained this usage:

> The second division is called economics, from Greek *ycon*, meaning image or conventional sign; and from *nomos* meaning rule or law; and from *ycos*, meaning science. For by means of economics the master of the house is able to establish conventions or rules or ordinances for governing his family and himself with respect to his family.[2]

In modern times, the broader meaning has come to prevail. "The economy" now routinely designates a society-wide system of resource allocation dedicated to the production, distribution, consumption, and exchange of goods and services to meet the needs of those living within it. The scope can be reduced to sections within a society or expanded to include the economies of nations in a geographic region, and further, in our contemporary condition, to encompass the world or global economy. The study of patterns of behavior within this system ("economics") is routinely divided into microeconomics, which focuses on the differing values of various goods and the behavior of individuals, families, companies, or other collective entities as producers and consumers, and macroeconomics, the study of large-scale factors that affect the national, regional, or world economy. The adjective "economical" usually connotes appropriate, even cautious—or, in its rational version, calculated, efficient—behavior within such a system.

"Economical" is, however, among the words least likely to capture the immense, and immensely volatile, traffic in images that—it is now equally routine to affirm—has become the definitive mode of exchange in contemporary societies. Intense visual presence, clamorous competition, and incessant diversification leading to massive overproduction are the most evident features of contemporary commodities. Social media is simply the most obvious and widespread vehicle of this saturation. Images seem to have become the primary commodities produced and consumed in contemporary economies. Images, too, are its primary currency. Substituting *εἰκών* or *eikṓn* ("image," "resemblance") for *οἶκος*, while retaining *νέμω*, gives us a word for this very contemporary phenomena: *iconomy*.[3]

There is, however, much that is misleading about making such a simple substitution, especially if one were to do so on the basis of such simplifications about the nature of modern and contemporary life. Several problems arise, as I will show. But I will also argue that a step of this kind is necessary, if taken with some restraint, if exercised from historical and critical perspectives, and, therefore, with careful but also bold attention to the politics of so doing.

In the first part of this book, I will interrogate some ideas about the necessitous relationships between images and economies, conceptions that have shaped our inheritances and that remain in currency. They take various forms, among them: myths, allegories, metaphors, edicts, narratives, theories, and world pictures. They are, in turn, Indigenous, ancient, medieval, modern, and contemporary. Part I tracks key conceptualizations of the relationships between images and economies, from Yolŋu Dreaming stories and Plato's Allegory of the Cave through Byzantine iconoclasm, Marx on commodities, Benjamin on the reproducible arts, and Debord on spectacle, up to contemporary theories of iconomy. It shows that each of these were or are propositions about the kind of political economy required by their place and their time.

This sequencing is largely a coincidence of selection: my treatment of them does not amount to a complete history. Several key figures receive scant reference: among them, Aby Warburg and Marshall McLuhan. Rather, I set out some landmarks, evoke aspects of their original contexts, but mostly read them from contemporary perspectives. I interrogate what they said for what they can offer to a political economics of images today.

Part II engages directly with image economies as they are currently constellated within public political spheres. Its chapters are studies of what David Levi Strauss calls "Iconopolitics."[4] It begins during the summer of 2020, when the usual business of the iconosphere[5]—depicting everyday life, selling commodities, enacting governmentality, and showing natural forces undergoing global warming—was displaced by three imageries of total emergency. Graphic imagery of the coronavirus and its national and global spread, plus film of its effects in hospitals, at testing sites, and on crowds, masked and not; the events staged by Donald J. Trump across a variety of mediums; and the cut-through impact of the cell phone video of a police officer kneeling on the neck of George Floyd as he died. The first announced information about the current and future state of the global pandemic. The second acted as the volatile epicenter of vast tracts of political and cultural agenda-setting, both in the United States and across its worldwide reach. The third brought to the boil a social struggle that is profoundly shifting relationships between the races, and those between citizens and police, in the United States and elsewhere. The ways in which these three constellations of images interacted—and cut through the other memes jostling for attention in the iconomy—continue to resonate today, even as they change, and change everything around them. Including, as we shall see, how artists and activists working in professional contexts and on the streets anticipate and respond to these events.

The chapters in this book are dispatches from inside the contemporary image wars, from positions at times at their many fronts, at others nearby, or at oblique angles. Yet always, I hope, from the distances necessary to critical implication. To achieve this kind of engagement with our contemporaneity, it is, I believe, necessary to both historicize and deconstruct its political iconomy. That is the goal of this book.

Notes

1 See Aristotle, *The Politics and Economics of Aristotle*, ed. Edward Walford (London: Henry G. Boyn, 1853). Aristotle understood images to be foundational to all perceptions, thoughts and judgements, viz.: "Images belong to the rational soul in the manner of perceptions, and whenever it affirms or denies that something is good or bad, it pursues or avoids. Consequently, the soul never thinks without an image."—*De Anima* (III, 7, 431a, 14–17).

2 Nicole Oresme, *Le Livre de yconomique d' Aristotle* [1374], ed. Albert Douglas Menut (Philadelphia: Transactions of the American Philosophical Society, 47. no. 5 (1957), 807–808). Cited Richard Allen Shoaf, *Dante, Chaucer, and the Currency of the Word: Money, Images, and Reference in Late Medieval Poetry* (Norman, OK: Pilgrim Books, 1983), 168–169. Oresme's "*yconomique*" is a Middle French spelling of "*œconomique*," now archaic.

3 Another common Greek word, *omoíōma*, evokes less the sense of an icon, more that of a likeness that is an effigy, a simulation, a mockup of some kind. When it comes to the contemporary spectacle as defined for us by Debord, Baudrillard, and many others, we might need, then, a word closer to *omoniomy*. If we wanted to evoke the constant foregrounding of the imagery of humanity within several image economies, *homoniomy* would be useful, but would likely be of diminishing range.

4 David Levi Strauss, *Co-Illusion: Dispatches from the End of Communication* (Cambridge, MA: MIT Press, 2020).

5 Here, I register my debt to the pioneering work of Arjun Appardurai, "Disjuncture and Difference in the Global Cultural Economy," *Theory, Culture & Society*, 7 (June 1990): 295–310; in *Modernity at Large: Cultural Dimensions of Globalization* (Minneapolis: University of Minnesota Press, 1996).

Part I

A BRIEF HISTORY OF ICONOMY

Chapter 1

A STRANGE IMAGE: SEEING THE DREAMING

> Glaucon: "It's a strange image you're describing, and strange prisoners."
> Socrates: "They're like us."
>
> —Plato, *The Republic*, Book VII, 515a

Plato's Allegory of the Cave is the most famous evocation within Western thought of what it is to know something, indeed, anything—from that which is immediately evident to everything that might be knowable. What kind of visual image does the allegory itself bring to our minds? W. J. T. Mitchell gives us the most useful answer: It is what he calls a "hypericon," that is, "a summary image [...] that encapsulates an entire episteme, a theory of knowledge."[1] No surprise that the allegory is right up there among his exemplars:

> Discursive hypericons such as the camera obscura, the *tabula rasa*, and the Platonic Cave epitomize the tendency of the technologies of visual representation to acquire a figurative centrality in theories of the self and its knowledges—of objects, of others, and of itself. They are not merely epistemological models, but ethical, political and aesthetic 'assemblages' that allow us to observe observers. In their strongest forms, they don't merely serve as illustrations to theory; they picture theory.[2]

He goes on to note Wittgenstein's concerns about the danger that a visual image—or picturing in general, indeed, any kind of representation—might short-change a complete understanding of complex phenomena and subtle ideas. Such disquiet is ancient. Indeed, as I shall show, it is the starting point of the cave allegory itself.

The allegory has attracted several interpretations, from the banal to the brilliant.[3] Most interpretations of its main meaning, however, have sedimented into contrasting pairs: between appearance and reality; seeing and knowing; superstition and objective knowledge; lies and truth; mystification and revelation; and the real and the ideal. It is an obvious starting point for our quest to trace some of the paradigmatic moments when images and economies have been thought together. The allegory vividly evokes two ways of world knowing, two kinds of spectatorial agency, two ways of managing (*oikonomía*), and two distinct regimes of truth (as Foucault came to name them)—both established first and foremost through the showing and seeing of images.[4] The two image economies stand in clear contrast to each other. Although one (the second member of each of the pairs just listed) is designated as superior, their pairing seems destined for perpetual impasse. As Plato's brother Glaucon says, the allegory is "a strange image." Socrates affirms that it is this uncanny strangeness that makes it so familiar.

When we read more closely, however, the allegory quickly exceeds interpretations that would lock it into contrasting, self-canceling pairs. There are, to start with, three settings, each primarily devoted to managing images in a distinctive way. There is the main part of the cave where the inhabitants, chained to their chairs, unable to move their heads, see only the shadows on the wall in front of them. They take these shapes, and the sounds they hear, as constituting the world as it is. They even compete to remember the shadows more or less clearly, to recall the order in which they usually occur, and somehow award and receive honors for their predictions. What prevails here is an image economy in its most basic form, as pure, passive consumption of whatever appears in front of your eyes.

In the second section of the cave, behind a low wall dividing it from the first, people (Socrates compares them to puppeteers) parade back and forth before a fire holding up "images of people and animals carved in stone and wood and other materials" while talking at will.[5] These icons (*eidolon*) cast the shadows seen by the enchained spectators. This is another image economy, a factory in which images are manufactured and displayed, even though perception of them is heavily mediated. While the fire is its source of energy, it is also partially lit by the sunlight coming down through a tunnel that connects the cave to the world above. This third domain is that of the Ideal Forms (*eidos*), usually interpreted as a literalized picture of the categories employed by a clear-thinking mind. As an economic sector, it is the warehouse in which prototypes and archetypes of thoughts and things are stored, in their most perfect arrangement, under the management of the Sun, which has generated them. The Sun is the source of light for this entirely rational system.

Each of these economies has created a condition in which a certain way of seeing the world has come to seem natural. Each worldview seems, for the most part, appropriate to the purposive functioning of its inhabitants. Each is an economy in its own right—until movement between them occurs, until they are experienced as linked and understood as relative to each other. At this moment, a fourth kind of seeing/knowing arises, a fourth arrangement of the elements occurs. The mysterious "someone" (the philosopher) who frees one of the prisoners already knows of these contingent economies and understands them to be valuable in ascending order, that is, as located within a larger system, governed by the Sun. The freed prisoner is first led past the dividing wall and shown the icon carriers and the fire, the mechanics producing what he now understands to be an illusory existence. (In Socrates' telling, he is blinded by the fire and passes through this section in a confused state.)[6] He is then led up the tunnel to the outside world, where the sunlight blinds him again. Soon, he begins to discern phenomena as shadows, and misreads reflections, but eventually comes to understand the world he is seeing as superior to that of the cave and as encompassing it. In a crucial pivot, he feels compelled to leave this world and return to explain it to his previous companions in the cave. Far from being welcomed, this would-be liberator is rejected—threatened with deadly violence by those who have flourished in the cave as it is if he persists in peddling his confused, implausible, utopian fantasies. At this point, a fifth relationship between seeing and knowing comes into view: the reality that humankind cannot bear too much Reality. The story reaches a climax in an odd mixture of farce followed by tragedy. The enlightened returnee foolishly tries to apply his newly found insight to the game of predicting the order in which the icons will appear. His double vision means that he fails miserably. The leaders among the shackled cave dwellers decide that his message is endangering their community and kill him.

Five ratios between seeing and knowing. These readings (some among several others, equally compelling) complicate the relatively simple configuration that comes to mind when we ask, as I did in the beginning, what kind of visual image does the allegory itself bring to our minds? Its symbolic form is a small stack of visual archetypes: a cave filled with flickering shadows below, a brilliantly lit array of ideal forms above, with blurred movement between them. What are these blurs if they are not figments of the movement in our own minds as we attach concepts to what we are being invited to imagine, and then, in memory, fix them in place by naming them? There is a reductive tendency here, the image becomes an icon of the generalizing kind, one that evokes a category which any instance will do to signify. But the allegory itself contradicts this tendency by its double trafficking up and out toward certainty, then back down into the domains of delusion, to end in ambiguity.

No surprise, then, that awkwardness attends almost all illustrations of the allegory, especially those which attempt to capture its several scenarios in one image. An illustration in the Parisian *Magasin Pittoresque* in 1855 shows the two basic levels but fails to show the passage between them (Fig. 1.1).

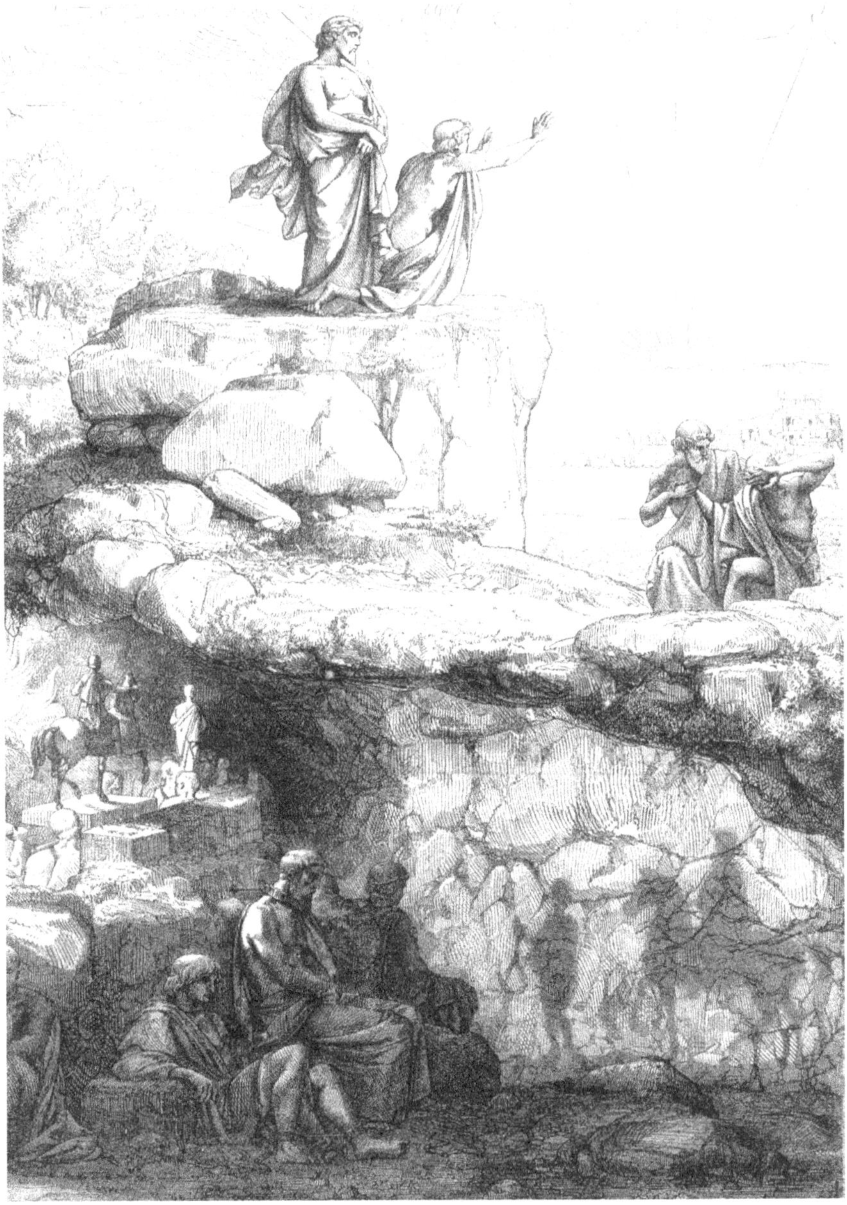

Fig. 1.1: Chevignard, *La Caverne de Platon*, *Magasin Pittoresque*, no. 23, July 1, 1855, lithograph. Pictorial Press Ltd/Alamy Banque d'Images.

Neoclassical in style and in narrative, it highlights the role of philosophy by depicting Plato himself bringing a Greek youth from delusion and blindness to a state of Sun-lit Enlightenment.[7]

This reminds us that the allegory is a very local story, based on actuality. In c.380 BC, Plato was writing in retreat, in his Academy, profoundly affected by the recent suicide of Socrates, his teacher, condemned by the people of Athens, who were fed up with his constant efforts to enlighten them.

Yet the Allegory of the Cave is not simply a parable about philosophy and its publics or lack of them. It is the centerpiece of one of the founding texts of political economy. Within the overall narrative of *The Republic*, it is located at a turning point. It comes at the end of lengthy discussions in which Socrates' interlocutors have been induced to envisage an ideal society, one that is led by a philosopher king, is policed by guardians, and made functional by workers. Plato envisaged three classes of people as necessary to form the ideal city: those whose souls are ruled by passions for wisdom or honor or money. The wise should rule, albeit reluctantly, the honorable should serve as military auxiliaries, and those who focused on money should perform economic functions such as farming for the city's food and making utensils, arts, and crafts (Book III, 434a–b). Karl Popper was right in pointing out the potential for racism in Plato's "myth of the metals" (Book III, 415a–c.), a eugenicist parable of these gold, silver, and bronze classes of people naturally and appropriately reproducing their qualities in their offspring.[8] But he was wrong to claim that Plato advocated racial purity based on inheritance. *The Republic* is explicit, and consistent, in requiring that birth be ignored when the person shows the qualities, or virtue, that fit the membership of another class.[9] We come to understand that the allegory is introduced as a dramatization of the challenges of educating people, against their natural inclinations, toward the building of a just society.[10]

Plato envisioned three social tiers, each with a kind of insight appropriate to its station, its duties, its daily life. The realm of Ideas is clearly the natural habitat of the philosopher king. The "natural" inhabitants of each part of the cave are less obvious. The icon carriers must be aware of the tunnel and of the occasional traffic up and down it, in which sense they are guardians preparing workers for their tasks. Yet their task is repetitive, making them more like workers. The enchained spectators, in their passivity, and their acceptance of their lot, would seem neither guardians nor workers. More like slaves. But when liberated and taken to see the Truth, they become guardians, among whose tasks is educating the citizens of the republic. Among the challenges they will face is rejection by most of those citizens.

When taken this literally, the allegory, like all poetry, begins to fray at the edges; the illusion reveals its mechanics; the backstage becomes visible; and the play loses its magic.

Nevertheless, when taken in its own spirit, the allegory artfully condenses the inevitability of friction between the three economies. Friction will arise, but not because Plato had in mind, as we might today, some missing element (such as religious revelation, democratic freedom, or authoritarian rule) to which all humans naturally aspire, the absence of which means that they will never achieve a coherent politics. It will arise because its constituent elements are incompatible.

The allegory itself has already shown the kind of role that the limits of representation will play in this impending shortfall. We have been told of shadows produced by imitations of those things and concepts, and told of shadows habitually, even willingly, mistaken for those things and concepts. Partial pictures are misread as standing for wholes. Bedazzlement and blinding occur before the Forms (of the Beautiful, the Truth, and the Good) reveal themselves. Insight is blunted when exercised in the real world: Its holder becomes less adept inside the cave where ignorance sets the rules of exchange. But the effort must be made: Education of the citizens, especially the philosopher kings and the guardians, depends on frequent exposure to beauty and frequent involvement in those arts—such as poetry, gymnastics (dance), and theatre—that build communality, share knowledge, and exercise justice.[11]

The remaining passages of *The Republic* expose several more, and more prosaic, reasons why ideal societies are so hard to establish. Philosopher kings are rare and are unlikely to be able to sustain their rule. Educating guardians in the complexities of their tasks takes too long and is too hard. Workers are likely to become dissatisfied with their lot. Given human nature, the ideal republic is a practical impossibility. It is, nevertheless, Socrates and Plato believed, a better social system than any other so far devised, or likely to be imagined. Therefore, aspiring to it, working constantly toward it, they urged, was the best of all available options.

There is a short coda to the allegory as I have outlined it. In a passage immediately following, rarely included in extracts, Socrates asserts that the person who has undergone the travails of release, revelation, and rejection has experienced these not merely as different kinds of seeing and bodily exertions but also as inner experiences, thus demonstrating that everybody possesses an already existing capacity to learn.

> As the eye could not turn from darkness to light unless the whole body moved, so it is that the mind can only turn around from the world of becoming to that of Being by a movement of the whole soul. The soul must learn, by degrees, to endure the contemplation of Being and the luminous realms. This is the Good, agreed?[12]

There must exist, he says, not an "art" but a "craft," a mode of education, that would bring this about, and on a scale that would transform whole societies into just ones.

At the time, as Socrates learned to his cost, Athens did not agree. Toward the end of his life, Plato sailed off to make his republican pitch to the ruler of Syracuse. That, too, failed. But the outlines of his allegory persisted. It has echoed ever since, not least because it so successfully dramatizes the possibilities and the limitations of trying to orchestrate the core qualities that, Plato believed, were characteristic of human societies: the fear-filled passivity of the majority, the cynical pragmatism of some, and the passionate commitment of the few to coming to know the Good and to persuading the others toward rebuilding their communities in its image.

As we shall see, other views of social possibility and limitation give rise to different political economies. Most have different conceptions of the strengths and weaknesses of images when they are brought into such service. The Allegory of the Cave is one of the first invocations in Western thought to place seeing at the heart of the kind of knowing needed for the practice of politics. It condenses—in one strange, deeply theatrical, tortuous, almost impossible to visualize image—the truth that this work toward perfection must be undertaken with imperfect tools.

Dreaming, Seeing

Let me draw a contrast—not a binary of two Origin stories, but one comparison among several possibilities—between the Allegory of the Cave and certain Indigenous understandings of the relationships between seeing and knowing and of the generation and circulation of images. They are much older, longer lasting, and arguably more relevant to present concerns than those imagined and employed by the Greeks during the classical era. They do not amount to "economies" in the senses in which that term made sense in ancient, or, as we will see, medieval, and modern settings. But they have existed alongside these economies and were increasingly more impacted—indeed, endangered—by them. In our times, Indigenous cultures have made significant gains against the degradations of colonization, yet they remain everywhere threatened by them and, in many places, directly subject to the worst impacts of more general changes, such as those of global warming. Gains have been won through individual and collective persistence, and organized political resistance, but also partly through a strengthening of capacities for self-representation. Many of these capacities have developed over millennia. They existed long before the mainly Western image economies that will be considered in the rest of this book and will, perhaps, outlast them.

I introduce some examples from the practices of Indigenous peoples who today live relatively independently within the societies that colonized their lands and constrained much of their cultures. These examples will, I hope, act as a counterpoint to the following chapters, and remain resonant when I review in conclusion what we have learnt about the political economy of images.

Imaging the Dreaming

Indigenous cultures are grounded in stories of world making that are replete with instances of the vividly visualized interplay between Originary Beings, ancestors, humans, animals, natural forces, and things. These foundational activities are understood to be ongoing, an incessant eternal returning that pervades all aspects of life and death, always has, and always will. Imagining these events and places in ritual activity or for instruction and learning is not a matter of simply matching an inherited, stable sign with its material or mythical signified: It is to act within a complex exchange between mimesis and alterity, between what can be shown and the othernesses that can only be indicated.[13] Further, these acts of ostension are not dichotomous. Instead, they are layered, graduated revelations and learnings, divulged and acquired piecemeal over a lifetime, calibrated initiations into the specific Indigenous world picture from the perspective of the clan, tribe, or people, managed by elders with more and greater knowledge.

Visual images are a vital currency within these Indigenous educational practices, along with song, ritual performance, and journeying to and direct experience of a sacred place. Anthropologist Michael Jackson reports a metaphor often used by Walpiri elders, traditional owners of substantial tracts of the Central Desert in Australia, when describing the process of initiation into the truths of their *kuruwarri* (partially translated in the English word "Dreaming") that involve the ancestor Yunkuyirranu:

> The word *yama* connotes the shade of a tree, as well as the shadow, image, or likeness of a person. When, in the Dreaming, Yunkuyirranu visited the site that bears his name, he left something of himself there. This vital essence or *kuruwarri* is like the shadow of a tree. To stand in the shade of the tree where Yunkuyirranu once stood is thus to come under his influence, to be steeped in the Dreaming there. The understanding generated by this process is seen as a 'coming into being' (*pulka-jarrimi*), a kind of birth.[14]

Particular words, images, songs, performative acts, and places are understood to possess their own power, and, at the same time, the powers derived from their location within the narration of the founding journey of the Originary Beings and the subsequent passaging of ancestors. Ritual activity centers on evoking a sacred place at which sacred events occurred within the larger, longer, sacred story. Body markings, rock paintings, images painted on bark, canvas, or any other surface all serve the same purpose: to embody the power of the occasion when an event occurred within the Dreaming and to manifest its continuing presence now, as you look, listen, feel, and sense. For millennia, Walpiri and other desert peoples have used a symbolic repertoire of abstract and indexical signs, readily drawn in the sand for intimate instruction and used in more elaborate forms for sand paintings, centerpieces of ritual performance. Usually, the event is pictured as a figure or a sign while the ground carries the story. But each also, always, evokes the other. The shared iconography becomes an iconology.[15]

An essential difference between Plato's cave dwellers and actual Indigenous peoples is that while the former are subjected to images which deceive them into believing that their diminished darkness is their limit condition—a condition from only a few can escape—the latter may live in the light—graduated, of increasing intensity—of progressively revealed truths about their place as part of everything around them, including that which is not visible in their immediate surrounds and that which is far away. To the Yolŋu people of the coastal regions of North-East Arnhem Land in the Northern Territory of Australia, the interflow of fresh water from the inland rivers and salt water from the surrounding seas is a convergence of difference that is definitive of the dynamics of their *wangarr* (the Yolŋu word for the ancestral past; they reject "Dreaming" as a misleading translation) and their everyday lives. Every element in this world was created by one or more of the Originary Beings and continues to embody their spirits and those of the ancestors descended from them.

In some circumstances, elders will indicate aspects of their knowledge of this world to outsiders. Here is Dula Nurruwuthun, speaking in 1993 in support of a land rights claim that the Yolŋu people were making for the waters around Yirrkala. He names the Beings who created these waters and their modes of appearance:

> Firstly I will talk about Gapu-Dha-yindi, the place of the open sea [literally: water with open mouth]. It is Dhäpuyŋu [its Dhuwa moiety clan name], Wurramangarminy, Würrungurkur [power names for the Dhäpuyŋu clan]. Their sacred design has the tantalising taste of the Green Turtle.

> It has the pattern etched by the smell of the sea around Walirra [a body of water in Blue Mud Bay] and Garrawandhu [the surrounding rock island] and Mapindawurruyu [a reef and sacred place within that body of water]. Sacred art that has been etched by the sea where the ocean named Wulamba roars. The open sea Dhukthukpa [power name for this water body], Yidiŋimirri [esoteric name of the resting place of the ancestral shark], Barrawarlandji [the shelter of the knowledge of the shark]. Yes, the sound of the roaring waters is called Wuklumba. The wide open sea has a huge tail of waves. Water that roars. This water existed in ancestral times and the cycle continues. It is massive endless ancient infinity. We call this water Gapu-Dha-yindi.[16]

What is being named here are not only the natural phenomena as they may be perceived by any observer but also the processes through which they were created during the *wangarr.* He is beginning an incantation which, in a ceremonial song cycle, might continue for some time, days, even weeks. The passage just cited might be compared to the table of contents of a book, a sand painting to the score of a song cycle.

Phenomena that are literally invisible, such as underwater currents and reefs, as well as those which are seasonal, such as recurrent floodwaters and brackish mixtures of fresh and salt water, are included. Everything was generated by the activities of ancestors—for example, certain underwater currents and reed beds are understood to be the result of fires (*gamata*) set by them that continue to burn today. While this knowledge is, in general terms, shared by members of both moieties within the Yolŋu—the Dhuwa and the Yirritja—specific clans within each moiety have ownership, by descent, of specific portions of land and sea in the region. They have the responsibility to maintain the existence of these places. Detailed knowledge of their ancestral formation is vital to fulfilling this duty. Anthropologists Howard and Frances Morphy usefully suggest that the relationship between seeing and knowing in play here be itself envisaged as a practice of perceiving dual landscapes: the outer, visible, natural vista and the inner, invisible, mythical domain of the *wangarr.*[17] Neither register, however, is taken as static; both are understood to be incessantly regenerative.

Representations of these phenomena—in body markings for ritual, on sacred objects, or in paintings intended for internal use or for the instruction of the *balanda* (White people)—deploy a coded system of signs, or "designs," that are the property of specific clans, to be used only by those authorized to do so. Severe penalties punish misuse. Like the Walpiri, Yolŋu artists tend to picture events through the actions of a figure or design while the ground suggests the setting of the unfolding story. Each also, always, evokes the other; as with all Indigenous representation, iconography becomes iconology.[18] Like other artists, Yolŋu use a range of devices to register degrees of expressive intensity, notably through intricate cross-hatching and color contrasts to produce an effect known as *bir'yun* (to shimmer brilliantly) that signals the presence of the ancestral spirit in the image—and thus on the body, the ground, or the painting.[19] In recent years, certain Yolŋu artists have consciously developed techniques for manifesting without depicting the presence of apparently invisible ancestral forces, places, and events in their paintings. Djambawa Marawili in 2013: "I found a new way of representing *miny'tji* [sacred clan designs] called Buwayak [Invisibility] but it is still the same ancient design."[20] The elusiveness of every image—its irreducible being there as standing for something which is not there, along with its radical incompleteness, its calling up of a viewer, and of viewers—is being made explicit here, put to work as a key aspect of this art's invitation.

Such reflexive subtlety belies long histories of racist projections by Europeans and others that view Indigenous peoples as ignorant primitives or noble savages, which treat their communicative modes as simplistic and instinctive.[21] The ancestral stories are a complex inheritance. Ambiguity, misrecognition, deceit, and arbitrary behavior by the powerful are as present within Indigenous belief systems as they are in those of any other humans. To the Yirritja clan within the Yolŋu, the activities of Barama, the primary Originary Being, and Banatja, Galparimun, and Lany'tju, his emissaries, are foundational to all that has happened since. Their doings, including their arbitrary and unworthy behavior, are constantly evoked as the basis of belief, the ground for morality.[22]

The light to dark contrasts between truth and lies, revelation and deception, and reality and representation that construct the hierarchical binary of the cave allegory have a different currency within Yolŋu ideology, and in that of other Indigenous peoples. Caves feature frequently in Dreaming stories, as they do in the Australian landscape. They continue to serve as places of shelter and ceremony. They are among the many sites at which the operations of the Dreaming as an epistemology may be experienced by those with the knowledge to do so.[23]

Similarly, Yolŋu have been and are involved in exchange economies of several kinds. They have long engaged in continent-wide trading between tribes of desired items, including animal furs, and ochres for painting. Yolŋu participated in the regional trade in fish dominated for centuries by fishermen from Makassar, Indonesia. They have coexisted with British colonists, including Christian missionaries, since the early nineteenth century and, since the 1960s, with a large bauxite mine that has cleared much of their land. The sharing of Dreaming imagery, notably the Yirrkala Church Panels and the Bark Petition to Parliament, played important roles in negotiations with the mining company and the federal government.[24] The Buku-Larrŋgay Mulka Centre was established as an arts center in 1976. Firmly controlled by the local community, its record as a creative hub, its active circulation of artworks for exhibitions, and the constant sale of artworks to museums, galleries, and individuals, makes it among the most successful of several such centers in remote Indigenous communities across Australia. The Yolŋu are active participants in the market for art in Australia and supportive of their artworks being shown and marketed overseas. Such sharing of secular versions of their sacred knowledge through creating and selling works of art, an obviously modern kind of economic activity, has mitigated existential threats to these communities, which suffer high rates of infant mortality, disease, unemployment, and incarceration. Indigenous artists based in the cities have been profiling White racism for five decades.[25] While income from art sales has become vitally important to the remote communities, securing it does not mean that the traditional kinds of relationships to ancestral presence are surrendered. Rather, Yolŋu, like other Indigenous peoples throughout the country, have adjusted their established forms of life to incorporate elements of these modernizing, *balanda*-dominated economies.[26] This has not been easy and remains a precarious, high stakes gamble.

It also remains a political one. In 2021, Yolŋu artist Dhambit Munuggur activated *wangarr* narratives to launch a condemnation of the Australian Government's exclusionary attitude toward economic, political, and climate refugees from Asia, the Middle East, and Africa. "Stop the boats!" has long been a winning slogan for conservative parties. In contrast, the Yolŋu recall their descent from the ancestral beings who came across the waters from a mythical land (Burralku) in the north. The archaeological time frame, based on dating of the Madjedbede rock shelter in Arnhem Land, is more than 47,000 years. Yolŋu also affirm their historical links to other peoples of the region. These relationships are a vital aspect of Dhambit's *wangarr* and a frequent subject in her paintings.[27] The left panel of *Welcoming the Refugees/Scott Morrison and the Treasurer*, 2021, shows a boat full of refugees seeking asylum, arriving in the Arafura Sea north-west of Yirrkala, welcomed by an ancestral octopus and dolphins, and being greeted and integrated into the Yolŋu community (Fig. 1.2). In the lower sections of the right panel, Yolŋu hold a discussion and then perform a ceremony that culminates in placing the Australian Prime Minister, an active proponent of closed borders, and the federal Treasurer, who supports this policy, into a boat that they launch out to sea. The descending shark suggests that they will face

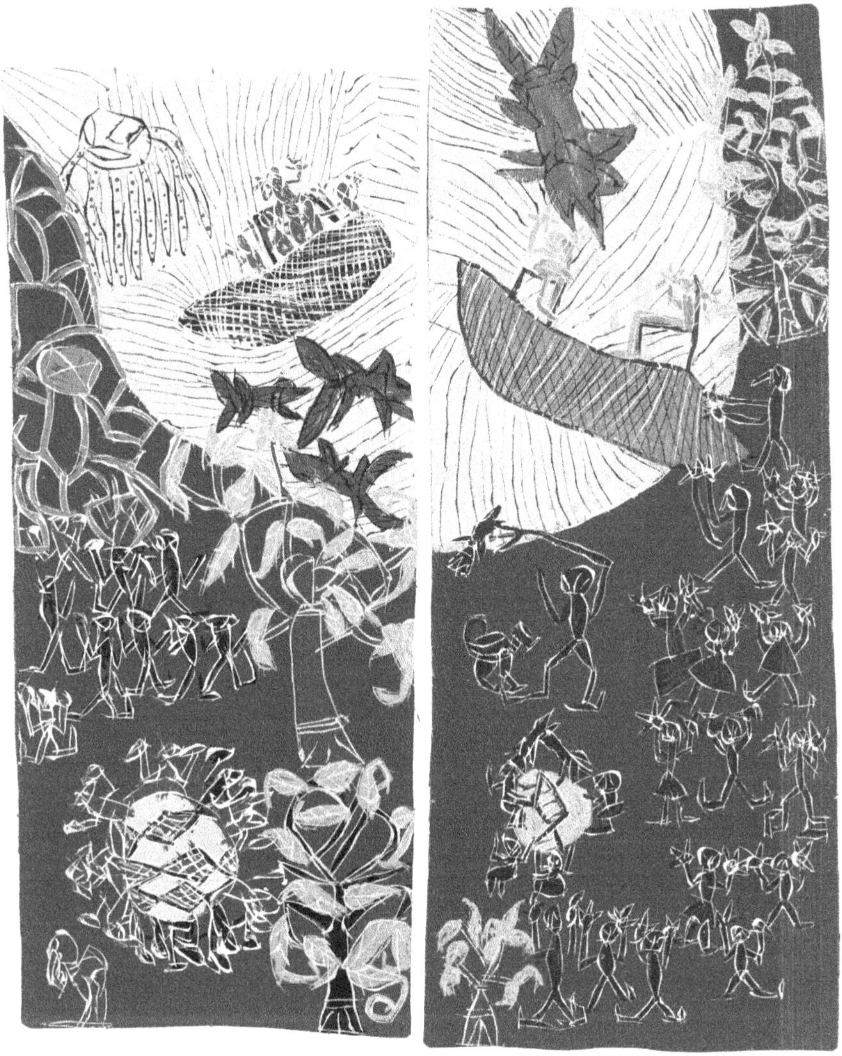

Fig. 1.2: Dhambit Munuggur, *Welcoming the Refugees/Scott Morrison and the Treasurer*, 2021, earth pigments and acrylic on bark, two panels: 241 × 108 cm; 260 × 102 cm. Courtesy of the artist and Buku-Larrŋgay Mulka Art Centre, Yirrkala, Northern Territory, Australia, and Roslyn Oxley9 Gallery, Sydney.

the same dangers as did the refugees and that their chances of survival are unclear. As the painting so vividly shows, they, like all living beings, are subject to the forces of eternal recurrence that cycle through this country, that govern this community, and which impact all who come into contact with it.

Notes

1 W.J.T. Mitchell, *Picture Theory: Essays on Verbal and Visual Representation* (Chicago: University of Chicago Press, 1994), 49. This idea is introduced in his earlier book, *Iconology: Image, Text, Ideology* (Chicago: University of Chicago Press, 1986), 5–6, 158.

2 Mitchell, *Picture Theory*, 49.

3 I am indebted to several including Martin Heidegger, *The Essence of Truth: On Plato's Cave Allegory and Theaetetus* (London and New York: Continuum, 2002); Hannah Arendt, "What Is Authority?" in *Between Past and Future* [1954] (New York: Penguin, 1977), ch. 3; Jacques Derrida, "Plato's Pharmacy" [1968] *Dissemination* (Chicago: University of Chicago Press, 1981); Luce Irigaray, *Speculum of the Other Woman* (Ithaca: Cornell University Press, 1985), 243–364; and Kaja Silverman, *World Spectators* (Stanford: Stanford University Press, 2000). For its focus on political economy, I wish to register here my debt to Roger L. Huard, *Plato's Political Philosophy: The Cave* (New York: Algora Publishing, 2007), which, however, takes a more optimistic line than I have been able to muster.

4 Michel Foucault, "The Political Function of the Intellectual," [1976] trans. C. Gordon, *Radical Philosophy*, no. 17 (Summer, 1977): 12–14.

5 Plato, *The Republic*, Book VII, 515a.

6 Plato, *The Republic*, Book VII, 515c and d.

7 Most illustrations are framed within prevailing contemporary ideologies. In Jan Saenredam's engraving made after Cornelis Cornelisz van Harlem in 1604, for example, the persuasion of the deluded is the focus, and the convincing is being done by members of a group of (mostly) Christian theologians. See https://www.britishmuseum.org/collection/object/P_1852-1211-120.

8 Karl Popper, *The Open Society and Its Enemies*, vol. 1, *The Spell of Plato* (London: Routledge, 1945).

9 See George Klosko, "Popper's Plato: An Assessment," *Philosophy of the Social Sciences*, 26, no. 4 (December 1996): 509–527; and Rachana Kamtekar, "Distinction Without a Difference: Race and *Genos* in Plato," in Julie K. Ward and Tommy L. Lott eds, *Philosophers on Race* (Oxford: Blackwell, 2002), 1–13.

10 Plato, *The Republic*, Book VII, 514c.

11 Notoriously, Plato's attitudes toward the arts are contradictory from text to text, and even within the same text, not least *The Republic*. Huard makes convincing attempts to locate what is widely seen as Plato's instrumentalist, censorious approach to the arts within its contemporary setting where, he suggests, these arts were taken as primarily public rather than private activities and thus evidently part of political discourse. See *Plato's Political Philosophy: The Cave*, 99–107, 143–159.

12 Plato, *The Republic*, Book VII, 517d. Heidegger hovers over this translation.

13 A classic study of this relation is Michael Taussig, *Mimesis and Alterity: A Particular History of the Senses* (London: Routledge, 1992).

14 Michael Jackson, *At Home in the World* (Sydney: HarperCollins, 1995), 153.

15 The classic study is Nancy Munn, *Walbiri Iconography: Graphic Representation and Cultural Symbolism in a Central Australian Society* (Ithaca, NY: Cornell University Press, 1973).

16 Dula Nurruwuthun, "Declaration," in Jennifer Isaacs et al. eds, *Saltwater: Paintings of Sea Country: The Recognition of Indigenous Sea Rights*, 2nd ed. (Yirrkala, NT: Buku-Larrŋgay Mulka Centre, 2014), 9.

17 See Howard Morphy, *Becoming Art: Exploring Cross-Cultural Categories* (Sydney: University of New South Wales Press, 2008), 89. For a detailed mapping of the traditional ownership of Yolŋu lands and waters, see Howard Morphy and Frances Morphy, "Tasting the Waters: Discriminating Identities in the Waters of Blue Mud Bay," *Journal of Material Culture*, 11, nos. 1–2 (2006): 67–85.

18 The major study of Yolŋu art is Howard Morphy, *Ancestral Connections: Art and an Aboriginal System of Knowledge* (Chicago: University of Chicago Press, 1991).

19 Morphy, *Becoming Art*, 82 ff.

20 Djambawa Marawili, "Remembering Saltwater," in Isaacs et al. eds, *Saltwater*, 117. In *Becoming Art*, Morphy shows several examples of this approach, which he names "emergent iconicity" (96ff.). See n. 17.

21 Despite the egregious hierarchy of the "myth of the metals," and notwithstanding the indelible contrast of a Sun-lit domain of the Good to a dungeon of flickering, misleading shadows, it seems unlikely that Plato's allegory was inspired by an instinctual, racist repulsion against savage barbarians living on the other side of the Mediterranean. Nor by a colonialist perspective of the modern kind. That was to come.

22 For a story about the conflicted relationships between these beings that pre-dates the recent revelation that Barama was the underlying being, see R.M. Berndt and C.H. Berndt, "Sacred Figures of Ancestral Beings of Arnhem Land," *Oceania*, 18 (1948): 314; cited Tony Swain, *A Place for Strangers: Towards a History of Australian Aboriginal Being* (Cambridge: Cambridge University Press, 1993), 199.

23 For an illuminating study of correspondences and differences between fundamental Yolŋu and Euro-American concepts, see Frances Morphy and Howard Morphy, "Locating 'Mind' (and 'Soul') Cross-Culturally," in Helen Bromhead and Zhengdao Ye eds, *Meaning, Life and Culture: In Conversation with Anna Wierzbicka* (Canberra: Australian National University Press, 2020), 249–272.

24 Terry Smith, "Marking Places, Cross-Hatching Worlds: The Yirrkala Panels," *e-flux Journal*, no. 111 (September 2020), at https://www.e-flux.com/journal/111/345649/marking-places-cross-hatching-worlds-the-yirrkala-panels/.

25 On this and related questions, see Terry Smith, "Country, Indigeneity, Sovereignty: Aboriginal Australian Art," in *Art to Come: Histories of Contemporary Art* (Durham, NC: Duke University Press, 2019), 156–197.

26 On Yolŋu adaptability, taking as an example changing forms of mortuary ritual, see Frances Morphy and Howard Morphy, "Relative Autonomy, Sociocultural Trajectories and the Emergence of Something New," *Insights*, 10, no. 9 (2017): 1–16. On the roles of art within Indigenous adjustment to external modernization Australia-wide, see Ian McLean, *Rattling Spears: A History of Indigenous Australian Art* (London: Reaktion Books, 2016).

27 See Ashley Crawford, *Artist Profile*, no. 53, 2020, at https://artistprofile.com.au/dhambit-mununggurr/.

Chapter 2

ICONOCLASH IN BYZANTIUM

Image economies are vital to religious observance, which is unimaginable without them. The major religions have constantly negotiated practices of worship that assign important roles to imagery of all kinds, from artifactual icons to mental images. No surprise, then, that the concept of iconomy arose in theological contexts, notably in interpretations of the iconoclastic controversies that embroiled the Christian church during the eighth and ninth centuries. In her essay, "The Face of Christ. The Form of the Church," Marie-José Mondzian (née Baudinet) examines "the iconic representation of Christ's face—the face of God's Son, also known as the Father's Economy."[1] Not for the first or last time, the Christian church split over the implications of representing the holy figures, dividing itself into iconoclasts versus iconophiles, with deadly consequences for those who lost the upper hand.

> For one camp, this economy was restrictive, for the other, it authorized the proliferation of an image whose paradigm should not be questioned. Economy, that is *oikonomia*, in Greek reads as *ikonomia*. To the Byzantine ear familiar with the iconoclastic debate, the law of the icon and the law concerning the administration of goods are one and the same thing. In either case, the supreme administrator, the great economist, is God the Father *who gave His essence to be distributed throughout the visible world through His own image*—the natural image of His Son.[2]

She notes that the iconoclasts of that era were rarely opposed to images as such, only those claiming to represent the Father, the Son, and Mary. Their argument from faith was that these beings were ineffable, that representations falsely circumscribed them, pictured them as if they were mortal while inducing worshippers to take this reduced image for the spiritual reality, that is, to treat images as idols, thus abusing clear injunctions against idolatry.[3] Meanwhile, on the secular level, iconoclastic churchmen and the emperors who supported them readily substituted imagery of useful saints and of themselves while maintaining the same overall relationships (i.e., the same general economy) between power and vision.

Inscription versus Circumscription

Nikephoros, the Patriarch of Constantinople from 806 to 815, was a key figure in these debates. Supported as a young scholar by pro-image empress Irene, and appointed as patriarch by emperor Nikephoros I, he was banished by the iconoclastic emperor Leo V for refusing to change his views.[4] Texts written in exile, known as the *Apologeticus major* and *minor* and the three *Antirhetikoi* or *Antirrhetics* (Diatribes), were his most influential.

Mondzian identifies several of his telling arguments. Two are pivotal to our inquiry. One goes to the nature of iconic representation, the other to the larger logic of image economies. In the first, Nikephoros accuses iconoclasts of failing to distinguish between inscription and circumscription in the delineation of "a face within iconic space." For the iconoclast, any representation of a holy figure circumscribes "divine infinity—the endless openness of the Word," thus their insistence on simple symbols, such as the cross. For the iconophile, in contrast, the delineation of holy figures such as Christ and Mary are resemblances, never a picturing. As Nikephoros puts it:

> And it is necessary to say where the term icon derives from and how it was formed according to its etymology, we say that it comes from the verb *eikô*, which has other meanings, but properly means: 'I am similar.' Thus the letter 'n' is added to the verb *eikô*, resulting in the word *eikon*, which signifies likeness. That is why the enemies of truth treat [the icon] that resembles Christ spitefully. From this verb, exactly from one principle and one root, the verb *eoike* is formed, which itself means 'to be (or to make) similar.' Because this is the case, who among the knowledgeable is not aware of the fact that the icon of Christ is different from Christ himself? Only that 'wisest' of all men, ignoring things that everybody knows, following his own personal impulses and personal instructors; if he had the least sense of conventional propriety, he should venerate and embrace this icon of Christ, at least on account of the relationship that Christ's icon has with the archetype, if for no other reason. [...] [because he insists on identity instead of resemblance] there will be as many Christs as there are icons. And so the sons will be multiplied, and the name of the Only-begotten will be removed. How should one feel about these arguments: criticize them for their impiety—or, rather, laugh at their folly?[5]

He is claiming that the icon is (in Mondzian's paraphrase):

> neither an essential identity nor a realistic reproduction (*homoiōma*). It is a *homoiōsis*, a formal resemblance that points to and stresses the direction of the gaze rather than indicating a place of recognition. The image of Christ is empty of His presence and full of His absence. [...] The incarnation of an absence, the flesh of the image is as supernatural as Christ's flesh after His resurrection.[6]

The result is that "Idolatry is averted because the eyes cannot find anything to 'graze upon' in this blessedly vacant object that respects the uncircumscribability of its model."[7] The contrast with what she calls "the sumptuary glorification of Christendom practised in Western art" is immediately suggested.[8]

Guile and Lies

Mondzian's second contribution to this inquiry is her mapping of how Nikephoros's defense of the sacred image became a strategy for the secular operations of the church, in parallel to the sacralization of the emperor. The individual worshipper's practice of seeing through the icon to the archetype, of accepting the simultaneity of an inferior material representation and a superior spiritual being, was systematized in the universal operations of the church and in the earthly operations of the Christian empire. Summarizing the argument of her major study, *Image, Icon, Economy; The Byzantine Origins of the Contemporary Imaginary*, she states:

> It was during this period that the church was compelled to produce an account of the theological status of the religious image that would nevertheless not be open to the slightest suspicion of idolatry. The solution arrived at was the dual doctrine of the *image, invisible* (and thus beyond the charge of idolatry), and the *icon, visible*, and thus perfectly fitted to be placed at the center of a pedagogical and political strategy serving the temporal power of the church. The foundations of this immense philosophical enterprise were laid in no less than the multifarious, interwoven strands of divine *economy*, God's overall plan for the salvation of humanity.[9]

The meaning of the word "economy" in play is plainly not the secular system of financial management familiar in modern societies, but the spiritual planning that, in several well-known New Testament verses, evokes nothing less than "God's plan for the salvation of humanity," the sum total of all of his deeds, not least the sharing and sacrifice of Christ, and the logic that unifies them. The divine plan is also understood to give its form to the operational framework for the organized, managed worship of Christ and Mary, to the church as a shared social institution and to Christianity as a daily individual practice: it is, precisely, how communities and individuals within them get their spiritual house in order. Post Constantine, the Christian spiritual economy becomes institutionalized on a society-wide basis, as an official church.

Such worship structured ritual behavior in sacred spaces but was also central to practices of everyday life based on belief in Christ's teachings about living—it became an *economy*, in the basic Greek sense of a conscious, sustained way of organizing one's home life. What connected these three economies (private, religious, state, each with both private and public dimensions, both on display to each other)? On a pragmatic level, the striking and distribution of coins. Imprinting the image of Christ on the obverse side of coins circulating through an empire suggested that Christ's modelling of the most desired economy of self and others—that is, Christian morality—was the model to be adopted within the domain ruled by the emperor, beginning with Justinian II from 685 to 695, whose image appeared on the reverse (Fig. 2.1). Mondzian:

> The power of the image is well known to the iconoclastic emperor who is quick to replace Christ's face with his own or his son's on the other side of coins, for the transmission of power also occurs dynastically at the human level. It is imperative for the Church that the image triumph. And triumph it did. For the Christian world, from that moment on, the theology of the face is the key to power.[10]

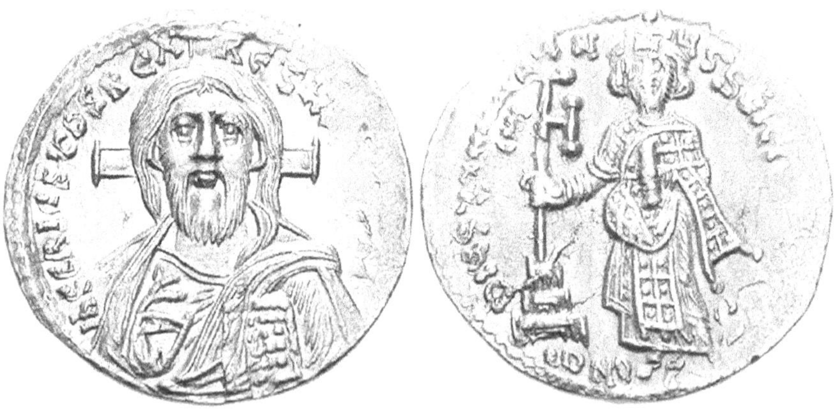

Fig. 2.1: Coin, Justinian II. First reign, 685–695. AV Solidus. 19 mm. Constantinople mint. Struck 692-695. Facing bust of Christ; cross behind/Justinian standing facing, holding cross potent on three steps. Classical Numismatic Group, Inc.

Nikephoros's "solution"—his modelling of a perceptual double-take—seems neat, even flawless, as a debating tactic. It was, in its historical reach, far more consequential. It authorized an elaborate charade that proved remarkably effective for centuries, returning to hegemony after frequent iconoclast eruptions. Its resilience, however, required constant maintenance, strategic dissimulation, and regular elaboration:

> [...] *oikonomia* is neither a disparate mosaic nor a fragmented term, but a type of intelligible edifice with coherent interweavings, or perhaps even a homogenous continent where the temporal power of the church is founded by the carnal, visceral, and providential economy of Christ, which leads us from the Word to the legitimacy of its icon, as well as to the strategic opportunity for guile or the lie.

Boldly, Mondzian offers this example:

> It is almost as if the long detour taken by the New Testament was only there to prove that God has a historical need for the Son, the Son for the church, and the church for temporal power, always and everywhere, in function of the same coherent and logical principle: the *oikonomia*.[11]

She goes on to ask: "Is it not significant that at each great convulsion of religious and political thought, the question of the legitimacy of the image was raised yet again?"[12] Her answer amounts to a set of further questions, as must all such answers when power is at stake:

> [...] *it concerns the nature of all images, and the impossibility of thinking and ruling without them* [...] Who, in the end, will be the master of the images? He who will be spiritually faithful to the natural image, he who will respect the natural image within the artificial image, or, finally, he who will continuously practice guile between faithfulness and unfaithfulness, in order to draw from that artifice all possible benefits?[13]

These are, as we say, good questions, precisely because they remain pertinent to the present and are likely to remain so. *The Byzantine Origins of the Contemporary Imaginary*, her book's subtitle, hints at their continuing resonance:

> Consideration of the image is still a sacred cause today only because the fate of thought and liberty are at stake in it. The visible world, the one that is given to us to see: is it liberty or enslavement? In order to

> be able to envisage a world radically founded on visibility, and starting from the conviction that whatever constitutes its essence is itself invisible, it proved essential to establish a system of thought that set the visible and the invisible in relation to each other. This relation was based on a distinction between the image and the icon. The image was invisible, the icon is visible. The economy was the concept of their *living* linkage. The image is a mystery. The icon is an enigma. The economy was the concept of their *relation* and their *intimacy*. The image is eternal similitude, the icon is temporal resemblance. The economy was the theory of the *transfiguration of history*.[14]

For her, as for the Byzantines, this transfiguration had begun with the appearance of Christ on Earth and would be complete only with his return. Meanwhile,

> Iconophilia has drawn us along in the wake of its violent adherences, but the voice of iconoclasm has never been killed, for all that. As for the idolaters, who were unanimously condemned by everyone—they still prosper and continue to offer us the most seductive pictures of our own desires to worship and destroy.[15]

It is remarkable that the logic at work in the double-take of Nikephoros repeats that envisaged in the Allegory of the Cave, albeit in reverse. Appearance and reality (in this case, the reality of the Christian Word), deception and truth, a signifier and a signified, are paired, as were shadows cast by icons and the ideal Forms in Plato's scenario. In both cases, the fundamental difference between these states is acknowledged, then flipped, the viewer being asked to know the icons as something other than what they appear to be, as passageways to a truth that cannot be seen. For the iconophile, the Truth of the Word can, with a sufficient exercise of faith, be experienced. In Plato's allegory, this option has been refused by cave-dwellers who prefer to remain idolators. It remains open, however, to the philosopher and, in a reduced version, to the guardians. For Nikephoros, the iconophiles parallel the philosophers and the guardians of the Church and the empire, while the iconoclasts become worse than the cave-dwellers in that they willingly destroy the icons which enable access to the image of the Truth while maintaining those of lesser value. They become, that is, idolators of the worst kind, those who choose to be so.

Other Religions and the Law

Faith of all kinds invites belief in immaterialities which are not visible, or tactile, or readily nameable—at least not completely so. Representations of some kind are required as intermediaries. Every organized religion finds it necessary to evolve procedures for managing the difference between symbols and what they symbolize. Image economies are formed, ruptured, and reformed. There are, for example, parallels in Buddhist spiritual practice to what we have seen in Christendom during the Byzantine era:

> Despite orthodox protestations, icons clearly played an important role even in a supposedly aniconic or iconoclastic school like Chan/Zen. According to the Zen scholar Mujaku Dochu, one can identify three kinds of 'spiritual images' (Ch. *lingxiang*, J. *reizo*, literally 'images [charged with] power,' *ling/rei*): those that protect the Dharma, those that fulfill a function in monastic life, and those that protect the individual after death.' Icons constitute thus an integral part of the spiritual economy (or rather, 'iconomy,' both from the same root ***oikonomia***) of the monastery. By the mediation that they establish in helping to 'make the invisible visible,' Buddhist icons, like their Christian counterparts, are at the same time seeable and seeing, passive and active. Their 'realism' is only the obverse of their supernatural quality.[16]

To both honor and avoid restrictions imposed by inherited law and custom, it becomes expedient to create domains of ambiguity—of the kind formulated by Nikephoros but present in all religions, including Judaism and Islam.[17] Not least because so many legal systems are based on religious moral codes, the management of images has a range of significant roles within them. These can take obvious forms, such as distinctive dress codes, the use of decorative insignia, and the creation of symbol-laden settings. Peter Goodrich maps these usages in his *Legal Emblems and the Art of Law*:

> It is in this context that we need to understand the legal use and meaning of images as the form of transmission and passage between *iconomy* and *oeconomy*, whereby the meaning of the icon is reiterated in the lawyer's devices, pictures, and emblems – *sacrae notae* all. The lawyers partake of the iconic and embody the images of the virtues in the emblems of law.[18]

But the image economies operative within the law, and in its social reach, are more deeply rooted than those of ritual performance. A foundational exploration of these issues, one that parallels Mondzian on religion in Byzantium, is Goodrich's *Oedipus Lex: Psychoanalysis, History, and Law* (1995).[19] To Costas Douzinas and Lydia Nead, mapping this complexity requires nothing less than a "legal iconology":

> The power of spiritual, edifying icons is celebrated and put into effect in the courtroom, in the wigs, the robes and the other performance and in the images of justice that adorn our public buildings. The law arranges, distributes and polices its own image through icons of sovereignty, tradition and fidelity, rationality and legality. The fear of idols is encountered in the renunciation of rhetoric in legal doctrine and theory, in the claim that reason alone without eloquence and passion can deliver justice, finally, in the regulation of artistic expression under the laws of public order, obscenity, copyright and libel. If the relationship between words and images is political, the law has been called upon to arbitrate the ancient quarrel.

From which this conclusion follows:

> It can be argued, therefore, that the modernist approach to the law–art relationship is deeply problematic. No radical separation exists between the two domains and not only dictatorial regimes develop policies on "obscene" images and "degenerate" art. On the contrary, intimate links exist between power, law and images at various levels. Historically, political powers have developed elaborate rules about visuality. Some refer to power and the law itself but, since at least the Byzantium, the law has organized a global regime of images, an economy of permitted representations or icons, an *iconomy*, and a criminology of dangerous and graven idols, or *idology*. At the philosophical level, the normative and the aesthetic have always influenced each other. In the same way that religious and imperial icons founded a speculum mundi on the absent image of God or King, modernist philosophy conceptualized the image of law through the key aesthetic category of the sublime. As a result of these links and influences a peculiar and historically changing combination of inonoclasm and iconophilia has developed which amounts to a complex legal administration of aesthetics and a related aesthetic organization of law. Its persistence indicates its structural and anthropological character. Law, imagery and their combination play a crucial role in the constitution of subjectivity. Too much emphasis has been placed in legal scholarship on law's effect on ideas and language and its operation through argumentation and logic.

> But the law has always had also a visual policy and understood the importance of the social bond. Their exploration is the task of a legal iconology.[20]

We will pursue these implications in the chapters to come.

Notes

1 Marie-José Baudinet, "The Face of Christ. The Form of the Church," in Michel Feher ed., *Fragments for a History of the Human Body* (New York, NY: Zone Books, 1989), 149.
2 Ibid.
3 See "Extracts from the Iconoclast *Horos* of Hieria," cited Marie-José Mondzian, *Image, Icon, Economy; The Byzantine Origins of the Contemporary Imaginary* [1996] (Stanford: Stanford University Press, 2005), notably 252 A-B on page 228, and 324 C-E on page 230. For an insightful elaboration of Mondzian's ideas, focused on the rulings established at the Council of Nicaea in 787, see John Panteleimon Manoussakis, "From Economy to Iconomy: The Legacy of Nicaea II," *Path, Journal of the Pontifical Academy of Theology*, 16 (2017): 149–162.
4 See Paul Julius Alexander, *The Patriarch Nichephorus of Constantinople: Ecclesiastical Policy and Image Worship in the Byzantine Empire* (Oxford: Clarendon Press, 1958), and Elizabeth A. Fisher, "Life of the Patriarch Nikephoros I of Constantinople," chapter 5 of Alice-Mary Talbot ed., *Byzantine Defenders of Images: Eight Saints' Lives in English Translation* (Washington, DC: Dumbarton Oaks Library and Collection, 1998), 25–40.
5 Nikephoros, "Extracts from the *Antirrhetics*," [818–820], cited Mondzian, *Image, Icon, Economy*, 238–239. The complete text may be found in J.-P. Migne ed., *Patrologica Graeca*, (Paris, 1860), vol. 100. See also Oksana Yu. Goncharko and Dmitry N. Goncharko, "A Byzantine Logician's 'Image' within the Second Iconoclastic Controversy. Nikephoros of Constantinople," *Scrinium, 13*, no. 1 (2017): 291–308. doi: https://doi-org.pitt.idm.oclc.org/10.1163/18177565-00131p20.
6 Baudinet, "The Face of Christ. The Form of the Church," 150, 151.
7 Ibid., 152.
8 Ibid. Curiously, this formulation frames Christendom within "Western art."
9 Mondzian, *Image, Icon, Economy*, back cover summary.
10 Baudinet, "The Face of Christ. The Form of the Church," 155. Iconclasts such as Leo II and his son Constantine V, object of Nikephoros's ire, removed the image of Christ, indeed all Christian symbols, from their coins, while retaining their own image. See Mondzian, *Image, Icon, Economy*, 158–159.
11 Mondzian, *Image, Icon, Economy*, 17.
12 Mondzian, *Image, Icon, Economy*, 5.
13 Mondzian, *Image, Icon, Economy*, 8. What she is calling the "natural image" here is that generated by God, to whom the "artificial image" embodied in the icon is a gateway, according to Nikephoros.
14 Ibid., 3.
15 Ibid., xiii.
16 Bernard Faure, *Visions of Power: Imagining Medieval Japanese Buddhism* (Princeton: Princeton University Press, 2000), 239, 278. See also Gregory P. Levine, *Daitokuji: The Visual Cultures of a Zen Monastery* (Seattle: University of Washington Press, 2005), 9.

17 See Kalman P. Bland, *The Artless Jew: Medieval and Modern Affirmations and Denials of the Visual* (Princeton: Princeton University Press, 2001). *Hiyal* is a controversial set of practices within Islamic jurisprudence (*Madhhab*), economics, finance, and trade to avoid violation of laws against usury.

18 Peter Goodrich, *Legal Emblems and the Art of Law: Obiter Depicta as the Image of Governance* (Cambridge: Cambridge University Press, 2014), 136.

19 Peter Goodrich, *Oedipus Lex: Psychoanalysis, History, and Law* (Berkeley: University of California Press, 1995).

20 Costas Douzinas, "The Legality of the Image," *The Modern Law Review* 63, no. 6 (2000): 815–816. Douzinas acknowledges his debts to W.J.T. Mitchell, *Iconology: Image, Text, Ideology* (Chicago: Chicago University Press, 1986) and Pierre Legendre, *Dieu au Mirroir* (Paris: Fayard, 1994). See also Costas Douzinas and Lynda Nead, *Law and the* Image (Chicago: University of Chicago Press, 1999).

Chapter 3

COMMODITIES AND CHAINS

Given the reverberations of Greek thought within the German Enlightenment, it will be no surprise to find the cave allegory echoing in the work of one of its most critical thinkers when he comes to consider the relationships between seeing, knowing, and acting in the world. Yet we might be surprised at the resonances of religious reflection—many of them sharing much with those of Nikephoros—in the thought of Karl Marx, a life-long opponent of organized religion. In a searching analysis of *Capital* as a literary text, J. Hillis Miller avers that "Marx's language in his analysis of commodities is permeated by a displaced theological or ontological terminology and figuration."[1] "Displaced," yes, but in the sense of having shifted from one (medieval) economy to another (modern) one, which it haunts. This is an action performed not by Marx himself but by the facts of the matter, as he explicitly states in a section entitled "The Fetishism of Commodities and the Secret Thereof":

> There it is a definite social relation between men, that assumes, in their eyes, the fantastic form of a relation between things. In order, therefore, to find an analogy, we must have recourse to the mist-enveloped regions of the religious world. In that world the productions of the human brain appear as independent beings endowed with life, and entering into relation both with one another and the human race. So it is in the world of commodities with the products of men's hands.[2]

Volume 1 of Capital is subtitled *A Critique of Political Economy* and is devoted to an extended analysis of the "The Process of Production of Capital." Its first chapter, on commodities, begins from this observation: "The wealth of those societies in which the capitalist mode of production prevails presents itself as 'an immense accumulation of commodities,' its unit being a single commodity."[3] The chapter defines the nature of commodities, and how they are produced, exchanged, and consumed in societies dominated by the bourgeoisie. Marx shows that crucial to these operations is the distinction between the value

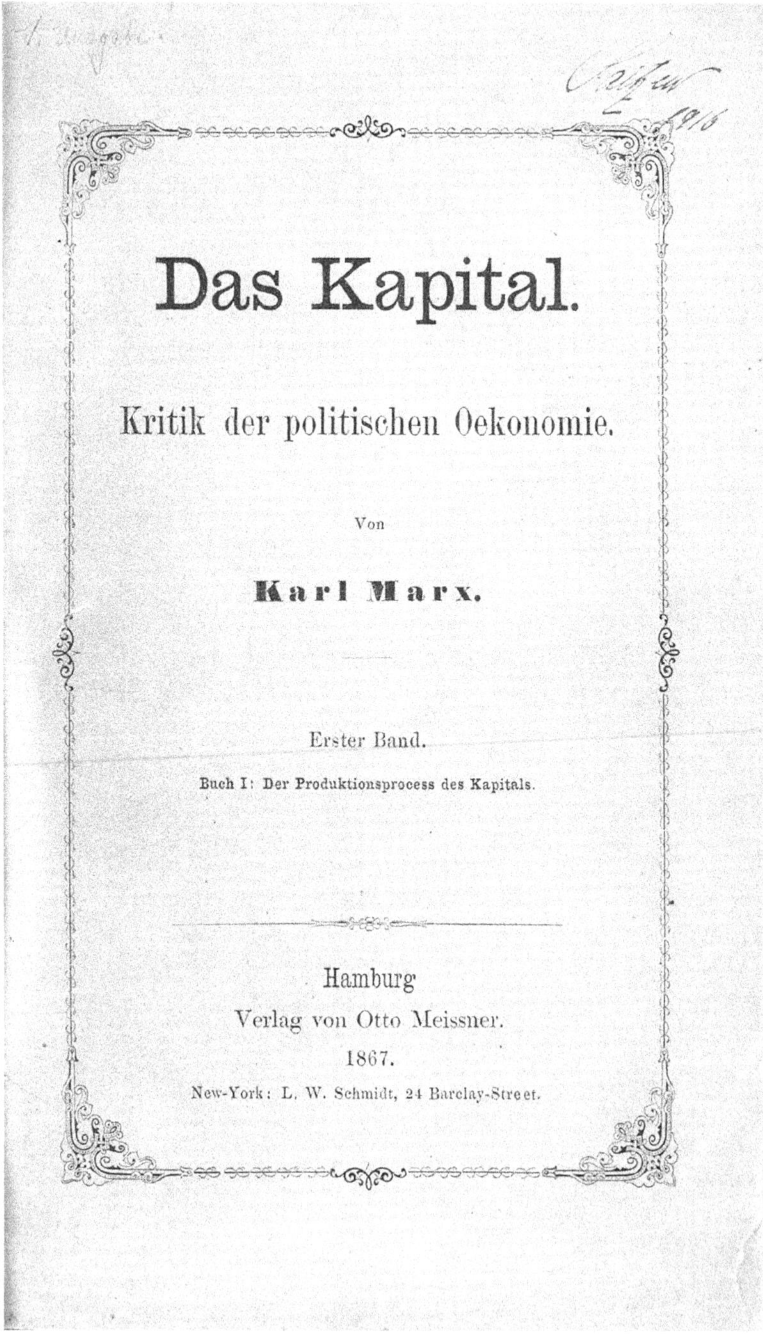

Das Kapital.

Kritik der politischen Oekonomie.

Von

Karl Marx.

Erster Band.

Buch I: Der Produktionsprocess des Kapitals.

Hamburg

Verlag von Otto Meissner.

1867.

New-York: L. W. Schmidt, 24 Barclay-Street.

Fig. 3.1: Karl Marx, *Das Kapital, Kritik der politischen Oekonomie*, vol. 1. Frederick Engels, ed. [1867] (Chicago: New World, 1906).

that inheres in an object produced by labor for a purpose, which he calls "use-value," and that which comes into operation when it is exchanged, which he names, variously, "exchange-value" or simply "value." What links these two values is an unstated, hidden, secret relationship: a modern, secular fetishism, akin to the worship of cult objects in primitive societies, gods in the ancient world, and icons in the Middle Ages:

> A commodity appears, at first sight, a very trivial thing, and easily understood. Its analysis shows that it is, in reality, a very queer thing, abounding in metaphysical subtleties and theological niceties. So far as it is a value in use, there is nothing mysterious about it, whether we consider it from the point of view that by its properties it is capable of satisfying human wants, or from the point that those properties are the product of human labour. It is as clear as noon-day, that man, by his industry, changes the forms of the materials furnished by Nature, in such a way as to make them useful to him. The form of wood, for instance, is altered, by making a table out of it. Yet, for all that, the table continues to be that common, every-day thing, wood. But, so soon as it steps forth as a commodity, it is changed into something transcendent. It not only stands with its feet on the ground, but, in relation to all other commodities, it stands on its head, and evolves out of its wooden brain grotesque ideas, far more wonderful than 'table-turning' ever was.[4]

"Table turning," Marx explains in a footnote, was a fantastical performance, common in China, involving movement of the tables by unseen spiritual forces which thereby declared their powerful presence.[5] But what are these strangely begotten "grotesque ideas"? Marx continues:

> Whence, then, arises the enigmatical character of the product of labour, so soon as it assumes the form of commodities? Clearly from the form itself. […] A commodity is therefore a mysterious thing, simply because in it the social character of men's labour appears to them as an objective character stamped upon the product of that labour; because the relation of the producers to the sum total of their own labour is presented to them as a social relation, existing not between themselves, but between the products of their labour. This is the reason why the products of labour become commodities, social things whose qualities are at the same time perceptible and imperceptible by the senses. In the same way the light from an object is perceived by us not as the subjective excitation of our optic nerve, but as the objective form of something outside the eye itself. But, in the act of seeing, there is at all events, an actual passage of

> light from one thing to another, from the external object to the eye. There is a physical relation between physical things. But it is different with commodities. There, the existence of the things *quâ* commodities, and the value relation between the products of labour which stamps them as commodities, have absolutely no connection with their physical properties and with the material relations arising therefrom.

At this point, the passage cited above occurs:

> There it is a definite social relation between men, that assumes, in their eyes, the fantastic form of a relation between things. In order, therefore, to find an analogy, we must have recourse to the mist-enveloped regions of the religious world. In that world the productions of the human brain appear as independent beings endowed with life, and entering into relation both with one another and the human race. So it is in the world of commodities with the products of men's hands. This I call the Fetishism which attaches itself to the products of labour, so soon as they are produced as commodities, and which is therefore inseparable from the production of commodities.[6]

Few have improved upon Chapter 1 of *Capital* as a forensic exposition of the hocus-pocus spun by commodification within capitalism. It is interesting that, in these passages, Marx goes straight to human perception, the action of seeing something, to a plain description of its operations, for his metaphorical contrast. And that he goes to religious mystification for this metaphorical parallel.

The Linen and The Coat: A Dialectical Dance

Marx, of course, maintained a resolutely secular view of religion, as we know from such latterly famous statements such as "religion is the opium of the people."[7] In *Capital*, these sentiments are plainly stated in passages such as this:

> Christianity fits bourgeois society: The religious world is but the reflex of the real world. And for a society based upon the production of commodities, in which the producers in general enter into social relations with one another by treating their products as commodities and values, whereby they reduce their individual private labour to the standard of homogeneous human labour – for such a society, Christianity with its *cultus* of abstract man, more especially in its bourgeois developments, Protestantism, Deism, &c., is the most fitting form of religion.[8]

At the same time, Marx was not averse to evoking the widespread, shared experience of religious belief to strike metaphoric gold in his long and rather dry exposition of the economics of commodity production and exchange.

> As a use-value, the linen is something palpably different from the coat; as a[n exchange] value it is identical with the coat, and therefore looks like the coat. Thus the linen acquires a value-form different from its physical form. The fact that it is value is manifested in its equality with the coat, just as the sheep-like nature of the Christian is shown in his resemblance to the Lamb of God.[9]

The earnestness of the Byzantine iconophiles is parodied here. As Hillis Miller drolly notes, few actually existing Christians have ever "looked like" Christ.[10] There is also, perhaps, the pathos of a more contemporary reference, Nikolai Gogol's 1847 short story *The Overcoat* or *The Cloak.* To further conjure the image of "embodied value," Marx draws more mundane parallels: "strutting about in a gorgeous uniform counts for more than when in mufti," and some anti-aristocratic ones: "A, for instance, cannot be 'your majesty' to B, unless at the same time majesty in B's eyes assumes the bodily form of A, and, what is more, with every new father of the people, changes its hair, its features, and many other things besides."[11] Status performance occurs within a socially understood symbolic language. Exchange value "converts every product into a social hieroglyphic."[12] Marx then ventriloquizes what commodities would say if they could speak:

> Our use value may be a thing that interests men. It is no part of us as objects. What, however, does belong to us as objects, is our value. Our natural intercourse as commodities proves it. In the eyes of each other we are nothing but exchange values.[13]

Do you, too, hear a Greek chorus here, sounding the voice of Fate, or a flock of angels murmuring as they go about their holy business of connecting mortals to the divinity, looking like chimera in the play of light inside a dark, smoky, and icon-filled church? In our time, such scenarios have become anachronistic: instead, we have become accustomed to constantly seeing and hearing advertisements in which branded products talk happily to each other, and to us, in their own voices or those of influencers, inviting us into their worlds, to the excitement of participation in imaginary microeconomies within a macroeconomy driven by pseudo-competition between brand-spanked commodities fed by the data it is sucking up in droves. Our (mostly) compliant condition is prefigured in the choir of commodities that Marx so vividly conjures. They seem to be making the same kind of self-satisfied sounds that Plato's cave-dwellers emit after they subdue the few among them who had been led astray by fantastical stories of another world replete with empty abstractions.

Nothing to Lose but Your Chains

Marx had a vision of a possible future quite contrary to the mercantile, industrializing, and imperialist capitalism that dominated his era: revolutionary socialism, with communist utopia as its goal. *The Manifesto of the Communist Party*, written with Frederick Engels and published in 1848, was unequivocal in its condemnation of bourgeois rule and in advocating for its revolutionary overthrow by the proletariat, in each nation and worldwide.[14] The seductive delusions of commodity culture are a recurring target:

> The bourgeoisie, wherever it has got the upper hand, has put an end to all feudal, patriarchal, idyllic relations. It has pitilessly torn asunder the motley feudal ties that bound man to his 'natural superiors', and has left remaining no other nexus between man and man than naked self-interest, than callous 'cash payment'. It has drowned the most heavenly ecstasies of religious fervour, of chivalrous enthusiasm, of philistine sentimentalism, in the icy water of egotistical calculation. It has resolved personal worth into exchange value, and in place of the numberless indefeasible chartered freedoms, has set up that single, unconscionable freedom – Free Trade. In one word, for exploitation veiled by religious and political illusions, it has substituted naked, shameless, direct, brutal exploitation.[15]

The mystifying image-world conjured by commodity economies is highlighted as an essential weapon in the bourgeois armoury:

> The bourgeoisie, by the rapid improvement of all instruments of production, by the immensely facilitated means of communication, draws all, even the most barbarian, nations into civilisation. The cheap prices of commodities are the heavy artillery with which it batters down all Chinese walls, with which it forces the barbarians' intensely obstinate hatred of foreigners to capitulate. It compels all nations, on pain of extinction, to adopt the bourgeois mode of production; it compels them

> to introduce what it calls civilisation into their midst, i.e., to become bourgeois themselves. In one word, it creates a world after its own image.[16]

What kind of world is this? The most oft-cited sentences of the *Manifesto* soon follow:

> The bourgeoisie cannot exist without constantly revolutionising the instruments of production, and thereby the relations of production, and with them the whole relations of society. Conservation of the old modes of production in unaltered form, was, on the contrary, the first condition of existence for all earlier industrial classes. Constant revolutionising of production, uninterrupted disturbance of all social conditions, everlasting uncertainty and agitation distinguish the bourgeois epoch from all earlier ones. All fixed, fast-frozen relations, with their train of ancient and venerable prejudices and opinions, are swept away, all new-formed ones become antiquated before they can ossify. All that is solid melts into air, all that is holy is profaned, and man is at last compelled to face with sober senses his real conditions of life, and his relations with his kind.[17]

The historically inevitable outcome is that, "like the sorcerer who is no longer able to control the powers of the nether world whom he has called up by his spells [...] the bourgeoisie forged the weapons that bring death to itself; it has also called into existence the men who are to wield those weapons – the modern working class – the proletarians."[18] An historical account of the rise of this class and its coming to revolutionary consciousness, assisted by the insights of disaffected bourgeois intellectuals, is followed by unequivocal proclamations of the political platform of the recently formed Communist Party.[19] The *Manifesto* concludes with these famous words:

> The Communists disdain to conceal their views and aims. They openly declare that their ends can be attained only by the forcible overthrow of all existing social conditions. Let the ruling classes tremble at a Communistic revolution. The proletarians have nothing to lose but their chains. They have a world to win. **Working Men of All Countries, Unite!**[20]

The philosophers have pointed out how to change this illusory world. The entire cave can now arise, throw off its chains, and see—in itself and its shared imaginary—the ideal forms of freedom.

Notes

1 J. Hillis Miller, "Promises, Promises: Speech Act Theory, Literary Theory, and Political-Economic Theory in Marx and De Man," *New Literary History*, 33, no. 1 (Winter 2002): 3.

2 Karl Marx, *Capital, A Critique of Political Economy*, vol. 1 [1867] (Moscow: Progress Press, 1996, based on first English edition of 1887, ed. Fredrick Engels, transl. Samuel Morse and Edward Aveling), at www.marxists.org/archive/marx/works/download/pdf/Capital-Volume-I.pdf, 48.

3 Marx, *Capital*, 27. The internal quotation cites a phrase from his own precursor to *Capital*, his essay *Zur Kritik der Politischen Oekonomie* (Berlin, 1859), 3.

4 *Marx, Capital*, 47.

5 In the German edition, he adds: "One may recall that China and the tables began to dance when the rest of the world appeared to be standing still – *pour encourager les autres* [to encourage the others]." This is glossed by the editors of *MECW* as follows: "The defeat of the 1848-49 revolutions was followed by a period of dismal political reaction in Europe. At that time, spiritualism, especially table-turning, became the rage among the European aristocracy. In 1850-64, China was swept by an anti-feudal liberation movement in the form of a large-scale peasant war, the Taiping Revolt."

6 Marx, *Capital*, 48.

7 Karl Marx, "Critique of Hegel's Philosophy of Rights" [1843], introduction in *Deutsche-Französische Jahrbücher*, February 1844; Joseph O'Malley ed., *Marx's Critique of Hegel's Philosophy of Rights* (Cambridge: Cambridge University Press, 1970), introduction, page 1, at www.marxists.org/archive/marx/works/1843/critique-hpr/intro.htm.

8 Marx, *Capital*, 31. This is the insight taken up by historian R.H. Tawney in his *Religion and the Rise of Capitalism* (New York: Harcourt, Brace & Company, 1926).

9 Marx, *Capital*, 36.

10 Although many have aspired to do so, not least Albrecht Dürer in his famous *Self-Portrait at the Age of Twenty-Eight*, painted in 1500. On Marx's savage irony, see Hillis Miller, "Promises, Promises," 3–4.

11 Both references, Marx, *Capital*, 36.

12 Marx, *Capital*, 49.

13 Ibid., 54. When Marx says on page 33 that "The [exchange] value of commodities is the very opposite of the coarse materiality of their substance: not an atom of matter enters into its composition," I am reminded of the statement by Nikephoros which Marie-José Mondzian cites as her epigraph to *Image, Icon, Economy; The Byzantine Origins of the Contemporary Imaginary* [1996] (Stanford: Stanford University Press, 2005): "Not only Christ but the whole universe disappears if neither circumscribability nor image exists."—*The Antirrhetics*, I, 244D. The same kind of mind is at work on a parallel problem.

14 Karl Marx and Fredrick Engels, *The Manifesto of the Communist Party* [1848] (Moscow: Progress Publishers, 1969), 98–13, at www.marxists.org/archive/marx/works/download/pdf/Manifesto.pdf.

15 Marx and Engels, *The Manifesto of the Communist Party*, 15.

16 Ibid., 16.

17 Ibid.

18 Ibid., 17–18.

19 Marx and Engels include a scornful rebuttal of those seeking to meld Christianity and Socialism: "Nothing is easier than to give Christian asceticism a Socialist tinge. Has not Christianity declaimed against private property, against marriage, against the State? Has it not preached in the place of these, charity and poverty, celibacy and mortification of the flesh, monastic life and Mother Church? Christian Socialism is but the holy water with which the priest consecrates the heart-burnings of the aristocrat."—Marx and Engels, *The Manifesto of the Communist Party*, 29.

20 Marx and Engels, *The Manifesto of the Communist Party*, 35. On page 67 of their translation, Morse and Aveling note that the ubiquitous slogan, "Workers of the World, Unite. You have nothing to lose but your chains!', is a popularisation of the last three sentences, not found in any official translation. Since this English translation was approved by Engels, we have kept the original intact."

Chapter 4

THE IMAGE IN THE ERA OF ITS TECHNICAL REPRODUCIBILITY

The revised translation of the title of Walter Benjamin's famous 1935 essay—from "The Work of Art in the Age of Mechanical Reproduction" to "The Work of Art in the Age of Its Technical Reproducibility"—signaled a shift in its use value for those interested in understanding the kinds of work that images do within capitalist modernity.[1] A more exact translation of "Das Kunstwerk im Zeitalter seiner technischer Reproduzierbarkeit," the new title also oriented English-language readers closer to Benjamin's major preoccupations in the essay, away from the cherry-picking within artworlds that had reduced its relevance for aesthetic inquiry to the commonplace idea that the widespread circulation of multiple photographs of individual works of art had caused them to lose the "aura" that they possessed when seen in their original niche in time and space.[2]

Underlying this banality, however, was a concept of consequence for understanding that capitalism was building a new kind of engine room, a society-wide apparatus. Benjamin's insight was a major update of Plato's pairing of deceptive shadows and ideal Forms, Nikephoros' icon/image double vision, and Marx's identification of the inner dynamic of commodification as the interplay of use and exchange value. Taking "art" to be the entirety of human visual representation, he introduced a distinction that constituted the next big step in thinking about image economies:

> Art history might be seen as the working out of a tension between two polarities within the artwork itself, its course determined by shifts in the balance between the two. These two are the artwork's cult value and its exhibition value.[3]

In modern times, icons produced during what were now seen as the primitive, ancient, and medieval eras were everywhere abstracted from their millennia-long grounding in ritual practices and valued as independent works of art. In Nikephoros' terms, they become images. Not natural, nor spiritual, but *aesthetic* images. Suitable above all for display among other images that have been similarly transposed. All classified according to their place within a transcendent History of Art. This transvaluation occurs in museums, as it does in the museumization of churches and other sacred places. These places, in turn, require new but secular forms of ritual behavior on the part of observers so that the image qualities of the displaced icons can be grasped. During the twentieth century, Benjamin argues, this dynamic is also—and politically more importantly—playing out on a society-wide scale, especially through the social workings of modern media such as lithography, photography, and film. Naming two of the great artistic innovators of his age—Picasso and Chaplin—he leaves us in no doubt as to whose art has the widest appeal and the greatest political potential.

> The technological reproducibility of the artwork changes the relation of the masses to art. The extremely backward attitude toward a Picasso painting changes to a highly progressive reaction to a Chaplin film.[4]

The political purchase of the essay is best known for the stirring slogan with which it concludes:

> '*Fiat ars—pereat mundus*' [Let art flourish—and the world pass away], says fascism, expecting from war, as Marinetti admits, the artistic gratification of a sense perception altered by technology. This is evidently the consummation of *l'art pour l'art*. Humankind, which once, in Homer, was an object of contemplation for the Olympian gods, has now become one for itself. Its self-alienation has reached the point where it can experience its own annihilation as a supreme aesthetic pleasure. *Such is the aestheticizing of politics, as practiced by fascism. Communism replies by politicizing art.*[5]

Benjamin had begun his essay with the reminder that Marx's analysis of the capitalist mode of production was undertaken when that mode was in its infancy, so that his account was less a contemporary description than a passionate prognosis of its likely growth and, he believed, inevitable self-destruction.[6] Writing nearly a century later, Benjamin wanted to show that a similarly transformational rupture of industrial production—from artisanal labor to machine manufacture on massive scales—was impacting production in one part of the more slowly changing superstructure, the visual arts, especially the form that most moved the masses, film. Perhaps the most perfect instantiation of his thesis about the aestheticization of politics,

Leni Riefenstahl's *Triumph of the Will*, had been released earlier in 1935. He does not mention it, preferring instead to point out the Dadaist subversion in Charlie Chaplin's films, which generate in their viewers "collective laughter" and "expert appraisal" of real-world situations—that is, a political consciousness of systemic inequity.[7]

> Our bars and city streets, our offices and furnished rooms, our railroad stations and our factories seemed to close relentlessly around us. Then came film and exploded this prison-world with the dynamite of the split second, so we can now set off calmly on journeys of adventure among its far-flung debris. With the close-up, the space expands; with slow motion, movement is extended [...] It is through the camera that we discover the optical unconscious, just as we discover the instinctual unconscious through psychoanalysis.[8]

Benjamin's essay, and Chaplin's *Modern Times*, released in 1936, complement each other as if they were twins (Fig. 4.1).

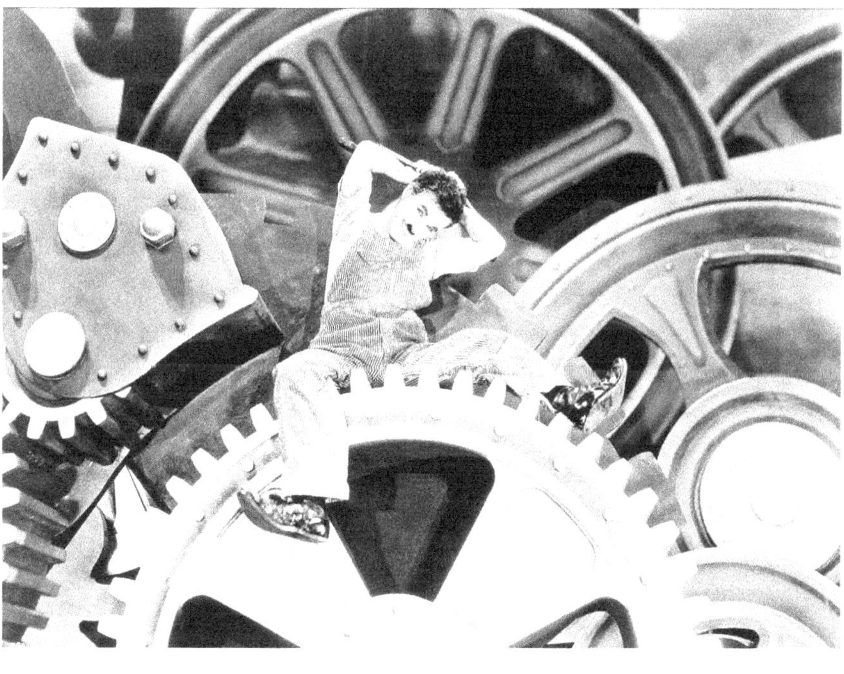

Fig. 4.1: Charles Chaplin, *Modern Times*, 1936. Film still. AA Film Archive/Alamy Banque d'Images.

The experience of film form as revelation of social reality illustrates his axiom: "*The function of film is to train human beings in the apperceptions and reactions needed to deal with a vast apparatus whose role in their lives is expanding almost daily.*"[9] The apparatus is mass production, mass consumption capitalism which strives to transform working conditions and everyday life to serve only its purposes. Yet its drive to monopoly and vast scale, requiring mechanization and reproducibility in every sphere, becomes counter-productive in many spheres, not least the communicative arts.

> On the one hand, film furthers insight into the necessities governing our lives by its use of close-ups, by its accentuation of the hidden details of familiar objects, and by its exploration of commonplace milieux through the ingenious guidance of the camera; on the other hand, it manages to assure us of a vast and unsuspected field of action.[10]

It is not only the case that new directors have emerged to rewrite the scripts for the actors carrying the icons behind the dividing wall in the cave. The mechanization of the modes of display, and updated processes of projection, have themselves changed what the shadows show. Despite their continuing efforts to deceive us, to entice us with visons of comfortably commodified lifeworlds and escapist fantasies, the apparatus cannot escape showing itself as an apparatus and thus expose the shadows as shadows. An epistemic leap has occurred. Chaplin's films, Fritz Lang's films, even Disney's Mickey Mouse, all screen imagery of the whole cave and the details of the lifeworlds of its denizens. Film has become moving imagery that moves those who see it to action, actions that might contribute to a vast collective, revolutionary transformation.

> Dealing with this apparatus also teaches them that technology will release them from their enslavement to the powers of the apparatus only when humanity's whole constitution has adapted itself to the new productive forces which the second technology has set free.[11]

Joel Synder glosses these passages in this way:

> The social function of film becomes its artistic functions. In evolving into a pure function, art will exhibit—reproduce—man his environment. In its revolutionary use, films will be made by workers, of workers, and for them. Film will show man in an environment re-made (re-produced) and managed by himself. [...] Art in this new definition is the sole means by which members of the revolutionary class can come to see themselves as shown by themselves.[12]

While "sole means" is an exaggeration of Benjamin's claims, art—in the expanded sense that he gives it—had indeed become a pivotal arena of political struggle. As he was writing, fascism had entered that domain with a reactionary policy, one that glorified total mobilization and a collective commitment to apocalyptical self-destruction. Today, similar celebrations of self-alienation threaten to undermine us as we confront, and too often deny, the unravelling of globalization and of modern geopolitics, while the impacts of human-induced global warming are evident everywhere. Almost a hundred years after Benjamin, the second part of this book will draw on his insights, and those of several others, to trace the contemporary aestheticization of politics and the politicized replies by several intersecting communities—artists of all kinds prominent among them.

Making the World Modern

For all of Benjamin's efforts to erase it, the gap between high art and popular culture remained rebarbative, in artistic practice, in its theorization, and in the wider world.[13] A more integrative account was needed, one that acknowledged this tension but understood it to be a minor variable, itself variable, within a larger ensemble—within, that is, the visual imagery of modernity, of the forces that were modernizing the world during the early and mid-twentieth century.

In *Making the Modern: Industry, Art, and Design in America* (1993), I set out to answer several questions about the forms taken by the base/superstructural relationships of modernity, especially in the United States, one of its major engine rooms. Among them: "Why does a certain variety of modes of visualization seem to play such an important role?" and "What place do specialist discourses, such as modernism within the visual arts, have in the broader imagery of modernity?"[14] I rejected any simple, deterministic equation between the Machine Age and Modernism of the kind prevalent in most general accounts of the art and design of the period. Instead, "an iconology of modernity" was charted, within which, I argued, all producers of imagery during this time worked:

> By the later 1920s the iconography of Modern America seems to coalesce into a limited, loose, but nonetheless flexible and effective ensemble of images. Its elements, so constantly repeated, varied, approximated, so rarely violated, are readily listed: (1) the industrial plant and manufacturing worker (for example, the River Rouge and the assembly-line worker); the agricultural site and the farm worker (the wheat silo and the sharecropper); (2) the vertical city and the crowd

> (almost always New York city and the Wall Street/Broadway crowd on the pavement); (3) the stylized product and the consumer (a burgeoning number of examples of great structural similarity).[15]

My gloss on these strands signaled my debt to Michel Foucault's brilliant dynamiting of historicism and ideological determinism by his focus during the 1970s on the dispersive structures of the micropolitics of power and the determinative contingencies of historical conjunctions.[16]

> This ensemble figures—in its internal relationships, its productivity, its dominance over other structures—a 'regime of sense' of considerable power. It indicates the presence of a visual order which organizes seeing in particular ways, despite the limited scope of its imagery and its structural fragility. It not only reproduces in visual terms what I argue is a new 'regime of truth' in the United States in the 1920s and 1930s—that is, a new corporations/New Deal consensus—but it was an active, constructive constituent of this regime and of the social formation on which it, in turn, was based. It grew from being an iconography—a repetition of images—to become an iconology [...] That is, these images and couplets, in their accelerating repetitions and predictable diversifications, secured increasingly ordered patterns of reading from those consuming them, while at the same time modifying other modes, even displacing them, until the new regime of seeing became itself the norm.[17]

While I now think I overplayed the political coherence of the "new corporations/New Deal consensus," I believe that the mapping of a visual imagery of modernity in the United States during those decades remains accurate. I traced the three major strands within this regime, beginning with the revisualization of manufacture as flow and assembly in the early Ford plants and culminating in the crowd-oriented spectacle of the New York World's Fair of 1939/40. This society-wide movement from base to superstructure (until the latter infused the base) was, I argued, the dynamic within which image makers of all kinds worked. The vertical/horizontal coupling in each of the three iconotypes, itself embodying a top–down distribution of power, was lateralized, recruiting image producers of all kinds while also affording them new forms of relative autonomy. For example, professional artists became trend-setting actors within each strand: Charles Sheeler, Georgia O'Keeffe, and Rockwell Kent were employed to create up-market advertisements for major manufacturers—respectively, the Ford Motor Company, Dole Fruit Company, and *Vanity Fair*—and to so in the style that they employed in their art.

On the government side, nationwide New Deal projects such as the Farm Security Administration employed several leading photographers—among them Walker Evans, Margaret Bourke-White, and Dorothea Lange—to record the impacts of the Depression and official efforts to alleviate it, and to do so by bringing to bear their sensibilities as independent artists, including their commitments to a critical realism as an artistic style. In some places, revolutionary political perspectives pitched themselves against these powerful regimes: notably, the visitors to Detroit, Diego Rivera and Frida Kahlo. A third strand offered less resistance: the streamline aesthetics evolved by self-styled "modernistic" industrial designers such as Raymond Loewy, Walter Dorwin Teague, and Norman Bel Geddes responded to a situation in which consumption was becoming itself a prevailing mode of production. John Vassos was one of the few who deployed streamlining critically. Each of the strands, along with their increasing interaction over time, helped to weave the shared sensibility that underscored the "regime of truth" then prevalent in the United States. Each strand also contained those who struggled to establish a different "politics of truth."[18] The third strand prefigured the next wave of consumerism, which grew from Postwar recovery. It also precipitated the next major step in the interpretation of image economies, Guy Debord's conceptualization of spectacle society.

Notes

1 Walter Benjamin, "The Work of Art in the Age of Its Technical Reproducibility: Second Version," in Michael W. Jennings, Brigid Doherty and Thomas Y. Levin, eds., *Walter Benjamin, The Work of Art in the Age of Its Technical Reproducibility, and Other Writing on Media* (Cambridge, MA: Harvard University Press, 2008), 19–55. The earliest instance of this shift known to me occurs in Joel Synder, "Benjamin on Reproducibility and Aura: A Reading of 'The Work of Art in the Age of Its Technical Reproducibility'," in Gary Smith, ed., *Benjamin: Philosophy, Aesthetics, History* (Chicago: University of Chicago Press, 1989), 158–174. See also Peter J. Hutchings, "In a Fishwife's Eye: Between Benjamin and Deleuze on the Timely Image," in Terry Smith, ed., *Impossible Presence: Surface and Screen in the Photogenic Era* (Sydney: Power Publications and Chicago: University of Chicago Press, 2001), 103, n3.

2 Benjamin, "The Work of Art in the Age of Its Technical Reproducibility: Second Version," 21-2.

3 Ibid., 25.

4 Ibid., 36.

5 Ibid., 42.

6 Ibid., 19.

7 Ibid., 20, 36, 52.

8 Ibid., 37.

9 Ibid., 26.

10 Ibid., 37.

11 Ibid., 26–27.
12 Synder, "Benjamin on Reproducibility and Aura," 171.
13 Even with avowedly Marxist aesthetics, quite opposite implications could be drawn from the same set of facts—as they were, during the same period, by Theodor Adorno and Clement Greenberg, among several others. See Theodor Adorno, "Letters to Walter Benjamin" [1935] and Benjamin's reply [1938], in Ernst Bloch et al., *Aesthetics and Politics* (London: New Left Books, 1977), 118–154; and Clement Greenberg, "Avant-Garde and Kitsch," [1939] in his *Art and Culture: Critical Essays* (Boston: Beacon Press, 1961), 3–21.
14 Terry Smith, *Making the Modern: Industry, Art, and Design in America* (Chicago: University of Chicago Press, 1993), 6.
15 Ibid., 7.
16 Announced in *Discipline and Punish, The Birth of the Prison* [1975] transl. A. Sheridan (New York: Vintage Books, 1977), the clearest statement can be found in "The political function of the intellectual" [1976] transl. C. Gordon, *Radical Philosophy*, no. 17 (Summer, 1977), 12–14. Art historians will recognize my debt to Erwin Panofsky, whose iconography to iconology method for interpreting Western art in the Renaissance tradition, charted in the introduction to his *Meaning in the Visual Arts* [1955] (Chicago: University of Chicago Press, 1982), I have socialized.
17 Smith, *Making the Modern*, 7–8.
18 Foucault, "The political function of the intellectual," 14. Jacques Rancière's "partitions of the sensible" and "aesthetic regimes" are glosses on Foucault's insights.

Chapter 5

SPECTACLE: ARCHITECTURE AND OCCLUSION

By the late 1960s, Guy Debord was able to confidently pronounce that

> The whole life of those societies in which modern conditions of production prevail presents itself as an immense accumulation of *spectacles*. All that once was directly lived has become mere representation.[1]

This axiom, the opening words of his tract *The Society of the Spectacle*, rewrites the famous opening lines of Karl Marx's *Capital* cited earlier: "The wealth of societies in which the capitalist system of production prevails presents itself as 'an immense accumulation of commodities'," while the next sentence echoes an even more famous line from *The Communist Manifesto*: "All that is solid melts into air."[2] Debord's axiom launches a section of his text entitled "Separation Perfected," the sentiment expressed in this second sentence: dwelling in the incessant, awe-inspiring exhibition of imagery that consumes us all, we have been separated from our natural modes of being. We live, instead, in a world of misrepresentations, enormously attractive but essentially deceptive images whose array we do not control, and which is managed against our interests. Sound familiar? The section ends with his second axiom: "The Spectacle is *capital* accumulated to the point where it becomes image" (Fig. 5.1).[3]

For all of their rhetorical exaggeration—*The Society of the Spectacle* is, before it is anything else, a polemic—Debord's statements remain relevant to the critical understanding of the exhibitionary economies that today persist—and, indeed, appear to prevail—as modern conditions of production turn into contemporary ones. Debord ostensifies his axioms as a series of self-generating statements, in the manner of Euclid's *Geometries* and Walter Benjamin's "Theses on the philosophy of history," but mostly by patching

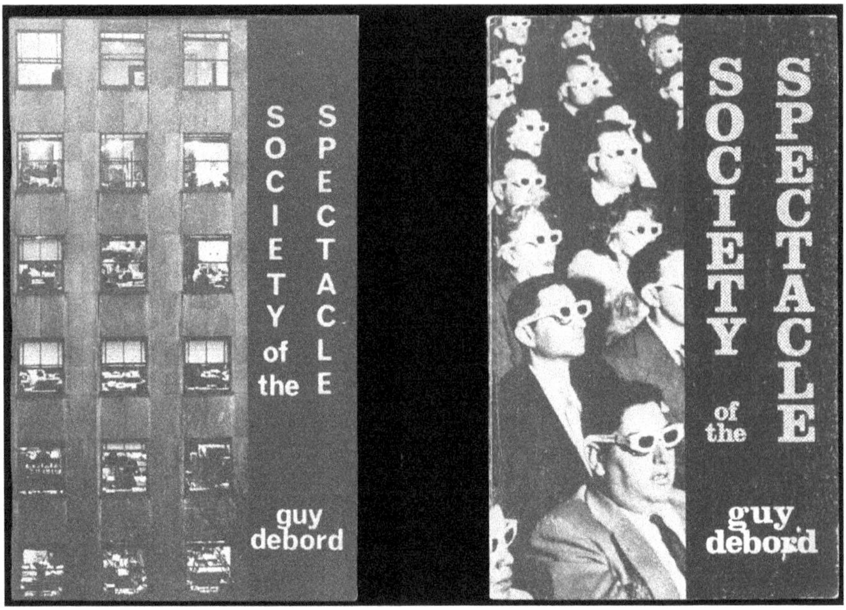

Fig. 5.1: Guy Debord, *Society of the Spectacle* (Detroit: Black & Red Press, 1970 and 2002).

and pasting from Marx on commodity fetishism and from then recently released early writings by Marx, notably his "Theses on Feuerbach."[4] This technique, a verbal collage, enables him to take several interesting tracks as he moves from the first to the second axiom. These tracks are not random. Each maps a historical trajectory into the present. For our purposes, his most relevant points concern the exhibitionary character of capitalism, which he rightly sees as fundamentally, and deceptively, *visual* in its operations—as, in a word, an iconomy. His word for these operations, however, is "spectacle."

> Since spectacle's job is to cause a world that is no longer directly perceptible to be *seen* via different specialized mediations, it is inevitable that it should elevate the human sense of sight to the special place once occupied by touch; the most abstract of the senses, and the most easily deceived, sight is naturally the most readily adaptable to present-day society's generalized abstraction.[5]

The prioritization of vision, Debord argues, does not mean that the spectacle is "a collection of images"—instead, it is "a social relationship between people that is mediated by images."[6] The core question then becomes: What is the nature of this mediation?

> Understood on its totality, the spectacle is both the outcome and the goal of the dominant mode of production. It is not something *added* to the real world—not a decorative element, so to speak. On the contrary, it is the very heart of society's real unreality. In all of its specific manifestations—news or propaganda, advertising or the actual consumption of entertainment—the spectacle epitomizes the prevailing mode of social life. It is the omnipresent celebration of a choice already made in the sphere of production, and the consummate result of that choice. In form as in content the spectacle serves as total justification for the conditions and aims of the existing system.[7]

This vicious circularity incessantly portrays itself as virtuous, as natural to human affairs, as historically inevitable, technologically necessary, and scientifically given:

> The fetishistic appearance of pure objectivity in spectacular relationships conceals their true character as relationships between human beings and between classes; a second Nature that seems to impose inescapable laws on our environment [...] the society of the spectacle is a form that choses its own content.[8]

Marx on the commodity resonates here; along with Engels on second nature. How do these relationships do their deceptive work? He now channels Benjamin: they do so by appearing to be a medium, an apparatus, or a technology:

> If the spectacle—understood in the limited sense of those "mass media" that are its most stultifying superficial manifestation—seems at times to be invading society in the shape of a mere apparatus, it should be remembered that this apparatus has nothing neutral about it, and that it answers precisely to the needs of the spectacle's internal dynamics.[9]

Our recent collective self-deception was to swallow the dream that the Internet is a mere technology for information transfer between people and people, people and machines, and machines and machines that is value free in its operations unless and until values are programmed into it. Even then, the dream goes on, we can choose to avoid the values that are inimical to free and open communication. Not so. Never was. No way, now that it has been substantially monetized and turned into a machinery for data collection and the surveillance of netizens.

In the final pages of his 1967 manifesto, Debord recognized that resistance which remained at the level of thought, discourse, and representation—however Situationist in form—was not enough:

> A critical theory of the spectacle cannot be true unless it joins forces with the practical movement of negation within society; and this negation, which constitutes the resumption of the revolutionary class struggle, cannot for its part achieve self-consciousness unless it develops a critique of the spectacle.[10]

We arrive at his final aphorism, his ultimate counter to spectacle's efforts "*to bury history in culture*":

> In the language of contradiction, the critique of culture manifests itself as *unified*: unified in that it dominates the whole of culture—culture as knowledge as well as culture as poetry; unified, too, in that it is no longer separable from the critique of the social totality. It is this unified theoretical critique that goes alone to its rendezvous with a *unified social practice*.[11]

Unified social practice was realized soon after on the streets of Paris during the period known as "May '68." Student and worker protests against conditions intolerable to each converged to become an insurrection with society-wide implications and effects. Situationist ideals appeared among the slogans and the goals. Debord and other members of the group were active in the occupation of the Sorbonne. The Gaullist state attempted to suppress the riots, to staunch the tides of change. Until it could no longer do so. For some weeks, the insurrection held, and revolution prevailed, until it was harshly repressed. But it joined a rising tide of similar insurrections in Africa and Central America, then soon throughout the world, moments where situations became, for a time, free to be themselves.[12]

Mediology

Debord's ideas on spectacle have attracted several critiques.[13] Régis Debray was one of the few critics who also offered a theory of the mediating purposes of images that is of parallel scope and purchase. Having recently returned for a period fighting with Che Guevara in Bolivia, and having survived imprisonment there, Debray scorned the revolutionary pretensions of the Situationists, whose subversive activities were confined to Strasbourg and Paris. Debray claims that Debord lifted his analytic framework from Feuerbach's *The Essence of Christianity* (1841), which—having seen through Nikephoros' faith-filled duplicity—argues that the religion was and remains an elaborate mystification, literally a circuit of bad faith. As well, Debray pinpoints the weakness in Debord's unthought presumption of a "generic nature" that is occluded by spectacle. He goes on to accuse Debord of turning the Marxian conception of ideology upside down: instead of working as a mix of deception by the powerful and self-deception by the powerless, it becomes a totalizing system that operates openly, in the full glare of its own prideful publicity. "The originality of *The Society of the Spectacle* was to bring together two banalities, overlaying the 1840s theme of alienation, absolutely unmodified, with 1960s objects—consumer society, culture, publicity."[14] More than recognizing the material character of ideology, operative within other coercive state apparatuses, as Althusser and others were to do so influentially in subsequent decades, Debord's idea of spectacle, Debray argues, turns everything and every relation into an ideological operation, the totality of which, despite its seeming variety, is essentially static.

> It is, at all events, presumptuous to claim that we have reached a general ethical system of sociology by means of a generic category that lumps together—by night when everything seems grey—theatre, art, galleries, film, museums, television, peep shows, virtual environments, silver-based photography, operatic set production and the front pages of newspapers. For man is not 'enslaved' in the same way to each of these spectacles, and each one of them has its way of conveying presence, crossing or creating distance and disembodying itself, its modes of enveloping its subject in space and time, its functions irreducible to one another and dependent on physical and mental universes—let us say 'mediaspheres'—which it is precisely a matter of clearly distinguishing between with the help of new theoretical tools.[15]

For Debray, these tools were his alternative theory of *mediology*, as outlined in *Vie et mort de l'image, une histoire du regard en Occident* (Paris: Éditions Gallimard, 1992). Mediology, he explains, is "the study not of the forms of media per se but of the mediations through which an idea or visual representation [*une imagerie*] becomes a material force [...] iconic efficacy, not the meaning but the power of images—what effects of amazement, imposition, or captivation the image has developed as a result of the techniques that have produced them and the cultural systems through which we perceive them."[16] This is not so far from Debord, except that he was working from inside the spectacle, exposing its egregious operations as a participant within them—where, he would claim, and show in his films, we are all caught.

What has Debord to say to us today? All of the factors he identified remain in play in the contemporary iconomy, even more so because, despite his assumption that spectacle was subject to entropy, it has not ceased to expand, although it has become increasingly volatile. It continues to shape public space in ever more pervasive ways but is riven by contradictory and random dynamics. Private consciousness, and alternative, critical conceptions of publicness—from the accommodating to the revolutionary—must negotiate within, and struggle against, the iconomy's insistent, totalizing but, in practice, unrealizable demands. As we shall see, "for" and "against" are not so readily defined as they were in Debord's day. But sometimes they are. And countering spectacle, en route to planetary worldmaking, remains the essential task.

Architecture in the Iconomy

Jean Baudrillard influentially took Debord's analysis one step further, arguing in books such as *The System of Objects* (1968); *For A Critique of the Political Economy of the Sign* (1972); *Simulacra and Simulation* (1981); and *Symbolic Exchange and Death* (1993) that political economy now included "sign value."[17] Benjamin's exhibitionary value operates, he argued, within what is primarily a semiotic system. Taking his own ideas to a self-referential extreme, Baudrillard went to argue that in postmodern societies "direct living" and "natural experience"—to which Debord still appealed as the basis for true community—had become impossible in a world consisting of hyperreal representations, that is, simulacra (primarily visual signs) of that which was once real.[18] These insights, while acute readings of the appearances and of the immediate experiences of contemporary life, mistake surface immediacy as the entirety of that life (having, of course, denied the distinction). The Gulf War did not take place: it was a media event. So, too, was 9/11. Insight into underlying causes is, by definition, blocked. Critique will always be absorbed, so it is pointless. Action for revolutionary change just feeds the monster. Capital is infinitely adaptable; humans are mired in mystification. Welcome to the desert of the irreal.

There were other ways of reading the role of imagery in events such as 9/11 and of parsing their political implications. In essays written in the early 2000s and in *The Architecture of Aftermath* (2006), I set out to chart some of them.[19] The targets on that day did not simply happen to be well-known buildings. The World Trade Center in New York and the Pentagon in Washington symbolized US economic and military power, while the likely targets of the third plane, the Capitol Building or the White House, symbolized the nation's governance. Images of these buildings had circulated in countless iterations throughout the world on multiple mediums, from official insignia through televised location shots, films, and tourist promotions to dollar bills. For much of the time, and in most circumstances, such symbolic connotations remain conventional and relatively benign, or, for those galled by the concentrated power which the symbols represent, untouchable.

Not so on 9/11. The attacks were an act of war within the iconomy. Osama bin Laden used icon-bearing airplanes (United, American) as weapons against the actually existing structures, the iconic architecture, upon which those city-signifiers ("icons") were based. While he may have had at the forefront of his mind the rhetorical and propaganda value of pursuing an updated version of the ancient practice of throwing one's troops against the walls of the enemy's citadels, the 9/11 attacks wreaked more than symbolic damage upon the US economy, military, and government. Financial losses were huge. A chaotic response by the Bush Administration deflated the myth of the United States as a "hyperpower." Inappropriate military overreach (the "War on Terror") led to failures on all fronts, not least 20 years of futile war in Afghanistan. In the years around 2000, Al Qaeda was producing not simply "media events" of the kind that had been generated for decades (by 1960, Daniel Boorstin was already labelling them "pseudo-events"[20]), it was conducting warfare, with icons as weapons. This was occurring within an image economy for which I, unaware of earlier usages, proposed the name "iconomy."

> In the new world disorder, the erection of powerful visual stereotypes seems, increasingly, to invite iconoclasm or defacement. This, in turn, invites us to speculate about just what image regime, what kind of *iconomy*, is coming into being.[21]

Insisting that we were dealing with much more than "the dense image manipulation that prevails in cultures predicated on conspicuous and incessant consumption," I remarked that "If anyone required a demonstration of the immediate but also far-reaching significance of the realm of visual culture—in its distinctiveness but also entanglement with the politics, economics, and ecologies of everyday life—surely 9.11.01 was it."[22]

The Image Complex

These resonances were subsequently explored by several others, including the pioneers of visual cultural studies, W.J.T. Mitchell and Nicholas Mirzoeff. Mitchell's 2011 book *Cloning Terror: The War of Images from 9/11 to the Present* deploys a method of image analysis he names, expanding Panofsky's more strictly art historical approach, "iconology."

> Images, from an iconological standpoint, are both verbal and visual entities, both metaphors and graphic symbols. They are, at one and the same time, concepts, objects, pictures, and symbolic forms. Some of them become operative forces in sociopolitical reality, attaining what is commonly known as 'iconic' status—widely recognizable, and provocative of powerful emotions. The figure of speech entailed in the phrase 'The War on Terror' was widely regarded as 'the most potent weapon in the battle for public opinion' waged by the Bush administration. The image of the Hooded Man of Abu Ghraib became a globally recognized icon 'more dangerous to American interests than any weapon of mass destruction.'[23]

The War on Terror campaign modelled terrorism as the sociopolitical equivalent of a painful, deadly pandemic threatening to invade the body of the nation and all citizens within it. The Hooded Man image made explicit the fact that the US state was miming this terrorist figure in its torturing of supposed terrorists. These mirrorings and several parallels in then new forms of communication, above all social media, led Mitchell to see cloning as the current "master metaphor or 'metapicture' of image-making itself."[24] In his *Watching Babylon, The war in Iraq and global visual culture* (2005), Mirzoeff develops a further set of similar readings, as does art historian Stephen F. Eisenman in his *The Abu Ghraib Effect* (2007).[25]

While image regimes were generating new metapictures (or "hypericons" as Mitchell elsewhere names them)—as they must to stay alive as compelling responses to their situations—the affective power of images has been measurably increasing. The thinking about images by each of these scholars find parallels in the methods being developed by the *Bildwissenschaft* project in Germany, led by Horst Bredekamp, in arguing that this change is occurring and that its logics require delimitating.[26] Historical perspectives are common to all these scholars, but they have been most extensively canvassed by Mirzoeff in his 2011 book *The Right to Look: A Counter-History of Visuality.*[27]

I share Mirzoeff's belief that, today, the current dominant regime, that of globalized, extractive, "Post-panoptic visuality," is being countered by what he calls "Planetary visualization"—that is, ways of seeing that bring together awareness of the vast scope and deep time of planetary processes (aka world picturing) with urgent action in the present in order to build small scale but worldwide coeval communality among humans, animals, and things.[28] This spirit inspires the intersectional protest movements, which announced themselves in the anti-globalization rallies in Seattle in 2000 and have surged, intermittently but insistently, since then. The interaction of this "activist imaginary" with larger image flows has been named "the image complex," a "political field" constituted by images.[29] These densely networked images surged again in 2020, especially since the posting of the video of the murder of George Floyd on May 25. Led by the imagery of Black Lives Matter, they have erupted frequently since then, their variety proliferating—from yellow umbrellas in Hong Kong, inflated rubber ducks in Thailand, to three fingered salutes from the *Game of Thrones* in Myanmar—their constancy increasing as people push back against oppressive regimes, both sides knowing that these are the end games.

Notes

1 Guy Debord, *The Society of the Spectacle* [1967] (New York: Zone Books, 1994), 12.
2 Karl Marx, *Capital, A Critique of Political Economy*, vol. 1 [1867] (Moscow: Progress Press, 1996, based on first English edition of 1887, ed. Fredrick Engels, transl. Samuel Morse and Edward Aveling), at https://www.marxists.org/archive/marx/works/download/pdf/Capital-Volume-I.pdf, 27; Karl Marx and Fredrick Engels, *The Manifesto of the Communist Party* [1848] (Moscow: Progress Publishers, 1969), at https://www.marxists.org/archive/marx/works/download/pdf/Manifesto.pdf, 16.
3 Debord, *The Society of the Spectacle*, 24.
4 Karl Marx, *Theses on Feuerbach* [1845] in Karl Marx, Frederick Engels, *Collected Works*, vol. 5, Marx and Engels 1845–1847 (Moscow: International Publishers, 1976), 5ff; Walter Benjamin, "Theses on the Philosophy of History [1940]," in Hannah Arendt ed., *Walter Benjamin: Illuminations* (Boston, New York: Mariner, 2019), 196–209.
5 Debord, *The Society of the Spectacle*, 17.
6 Ibid., 12. This remark prefigures later pages devoted to distinguishing his analysis from that of Daniel Boorstin, *The Image: A Guide to Pseudo-Events in America* [1962] (New York: Knopf Doubleday, 2012), who attributes the over-consumption of commodities in the United States, which he describes as a "too vast a technology of image-diffusion," to "too great an appetite for sensationalism on the part of today's public," thus, Debord believes, failing to see the systemic nature of spectacle itself (140–141).
7 Debord, *The Society of the Spectacle*, 13.
8 Ibid., 19.
9 Ibid.
10 Ibid., 143.
11 Ibid., 147.
12 Among many accounts, see Andy Merrifield, " 'Fulfilment was already there': Debord & '68," Verso blog, posted May 17, 2018, at https://www.versobooks.com/blogs/3821-fulfillment-was-already-there-debord-amp-68. The Situationists continue to inspire younger generations, for example, Tiernan Morgan & Lauren Purje, "An Illustrated Guide to Guy Debord's 'The Society of the Spectacle'," *Hyperallergic*, posted August 10, 2016 at https://hyperallergic.com/313435/an-illustrated-guide-to-guy-debords-the-society-of-the-spectacle/.

13 Thomas F. McDonough maps several of these in his introduction to a set of SI texts, "Rereading Debord, Rereading the Situationists," *October*, no. 79 (Winter 1997): 3–14. Debord reviews himself in Guy Debord, *Comments on the Society of the Spectacle* [1988] (London: Verso, 1998).

14 Régis Debray, "Remarks on Spectacle," *New Left Review*, 1/215 (November–December 1995), https://newleftreview.org/issues/I214/articles/regis-debray-remarks-on-the-spectacle. In aphorism 207 Debord famously says "plagiarism is necessary; originality requires it."

15 Ibid.

16 Ibid.

17 Jean Baudrillard, *The System of Objects* [1968] (London: Verso, 1996); *For A Critique of the Political Economy of the Sign* [1972] (St Louis, MO: Telos, 1981); *Simulacra and Simulation* [1981] (Ann Arbor: University of Michigan Press, 1994); and *Symbolic Exchange and Death* (London: Sage Publications, 1993).

18 Key publications from this phase include *America* [1986] (London: Verso, 1988), and *The Gulf War Did Not Take Place*, transl. Paul Patton (Sydney: Power Publications, Bloomington: Indiana University Press, 1995). For his exposition of these principles as they apply to imagery today, including a reference to the cave allegory, see his lecture "Violence of the Image," European Graduate School, 2004, at https://egs.edu/lecture/jean-baudrillard-violence-of-the-image/. For an insightful commentary, see Rex Butler, *Jean Baudrillard, The Defence of the Real* (London: Sage Publications, 1999).

19 Terry Smith, *The Architecture of Aftermath* (Chicago: University of Chicago Press, 2006).

20 Daniel Boorstin, *The Image: A Guide to Pseudo-Events in America* (1962) (New York: Knopf Doubleday, 2012).

21 Terry Smith, "The Political Economy of Iconotypes and the Architecture of Destination: Uluru, The Sydney Opera House and the World Trade Center," *Architecture Theory Review*, 7, no.2 (2002): 1–44, citing page 1.

22 Smith, "After Effects—Architecture, Iconomy, Contemporaneity," the introduction to *The Architecture of Aftermath* (Chicago: University of Chicago Press, 2006), 2.

23 W.J.T. Mitchell, *Cloning Terror: The War of Images from 9/11 to the Present* (Chicago: University of Chicago Press, 2011), xvii.

24 Ibid., xiv.

25 Nicholas Mirzoeff, *Watching Babylon, The war in Iraq and global visual culture* (New York and London: Routledge, 2005); Stephen F. Eisenman, *The Abu Ghraib Effect* (London: Reaktion Books, 2007).

26 On hypericons, see W.J.T. Mitchell, *Iconology: Image, Text, Ideology* (Chicago; University of Chicago Press, 1986), 6, and his *Picture Theory* (Chicago: University of Chicago Press, 1995), 49. On image affect, see W.J.T. Mitchell, *What Do Pictures Want? The Lives and Loves of Images* (Chicago: University of Chicago Press, 2005). On the *bildwissenschaft* project, see Horst Bredekamp, *Image Acts: A Systematic Approach to Image Agency* (Berlin: Walter de Gruyter, 2018).

27 Nicholas Mirzoeff, *The Right to Look: A Counterhistory of Visuality* (Durham: Duke University Press, 2011).

28 Ibid.

29 Meg McLagan and Yates McKee, "Introduction," *Sensible Politics: The Visual Culture of Nongovernmental Politics* (New York: Zone Books, 2012), 8.

Chapter 6

ICONOMY: WHAT'S IN A NAME?

> "The icon has been addressed as a manifestation of the divine 'iconomy,' that is, the most economical way to display the invisible in the visible world."
>
> — Boris Groys, *History Becomes Form: Moscow Conceptualism* (Cambridge, MA: MIT Press, 2010), 187.

We have already seen—in chapter 2—the first truly contemporary theorization of the central role of images in a political economy: Marie-José Mondzian's account of Byzantine iconoclasm, outlined in an essay of 1989 and set out fully in her book *Image, Icon, Economy; The Byzantine Origins of the Contemporary Imaginary* (1996). There, she exercised a characteristic restraint in hinting at but not coining the neologism "iconomy" as the general term for her subject. Writing during the first Gulf War, however, she does not refrain from asserting the current relevance of her project, not only in her subtitle but also in statements such as this: "From the specific standpoint of provoking belief or obtaining obedience, there is no great difference between submitting to a church council or to CNN."[1]

In 1992, Jean-Joseph Goux spoke of "a new 'iconomy'" to highlight the extraordinary financial values attaching to works of art in the contemporary art market.[2] In the same year, a more comprehensive contemporary theorization, entirely immersed in current problematics, was attempted. Arizona University graduate student Dion Dennis embarked on a project entitled *The Subject Under the Sign of the Market: Steps Toward a Political Iconomy*. In a 1993 essay, he defined it as follows:

> I define political iconomy as the processes, products and effects of information that commodify, deploy and circulate texts and images in a digitalized form. A viable political iconomy emerges in the social biography of commodities or 'thing effects' when the licensing of signs

> or information (icons) as commercial property becomes an integral part of market logic and activity. The conceptual birth of political iconomy comes from a critique of the global effects of recoding the personal, the social and the cultural as subsets of 'the Market.' When global redescriptions of all fields of social and cultural activity as but forms of the market become a major symbolic and political project (as happened in the 1980's) semiosis and political economy are no longer separate subjects of inquiry.[3]

Reading Foucault assiduously, reflecting on his experiences with personal computing and as a programmer for IBM, he became aware that technology was far from being a neutral "tool" and that commercialized data collecting was occurring on a massive scale, with the result that "a digitalized Panopticism has emerged."[4] Urgent questions are raised about "how subjectivities are produced and constrained under digital regimes of detail in the world of political iconomy."[5] It was becoming obvious that the "experience economy" was already answering these questions by figuring out ways to manage and monetize them.[6]

In 2016, in their introduction to *The Contemporary Condition* book series, Geoff Cox and Jacob Lund emphasized the importance of investigating "the significant role of media and information technology in the production and reproduction of contemporaneity."[7] They commended Benjamin Bratton's argument that the many, seemingly various, contemporary computational technologies are less "so many different genres of machines, spinning out on their own" but instead form a planetary-scale "accidental megastructure" consisting of several layers—user, interface, address, city, cloud, and earth—with multiple connections between them, which he names The Stack.[8] This is an insightful image, a strong candidate for the most recent world picture. It is also abstract—in fact, it is an abstraction of abstractions, a spatial metaphor of layered planes which, when diagrammed by Metahaven, gains much of its visual affect from its resemblance to a geological section or, more prosaically, the floors of a building or, more exactly, a stack of hard drives in a server farm. This is grounding of abstraction is intentional. The last term, "earth," is also the first, reminding us that this structure is located in the physical world with which its virtual workings always "blur." Imaging the conditions for the Stack-to-come (the "Black Stack"), Bratton poses these questions:

> Our experiment—indeed everyone's experiment for the coming decades—is tied to an ecologically ubiquitous computing, a gamble that in many ways underpins all others. The Stack-to-come should

> tilt the outcome of that impact towards a renewed modernity, but will it—in some configuration of *Clouds*, objects, tags, *Addresses*, *Interfaces*, sensors, algorithmic phyla—provide the lightness necessary to organize a restorative, subtractive, resilient modernity, or will its voracious energy appetite, toxic production footprint, and alienating visualization finally overwhelm all? [...] Will planetary-scale pervasive computing prove to be, in some guise, the integral media of real reindustrialization, allowing for light but powerful interfaces of governance and exchange, or instead, the final, most unsustainable machine consuming the remaining resources into its subterranean pits?[9]

Toward the end of *The Stack*, Bratton raises but downplays the implication that these machines, whichever direction they may lean, might eventually become indifferent to the priorities of their human masters. Gaia theorist James Lovelock has recently argued that, with innovation the driving force of planetary evolution, and with computational machines now generating most innovation and most likely to do so exponentially, the biosphere will promote cyborg interrelationships between machine and humans as a means of maintaining the balances that it requires to sustain it (that is, to sustain the life of its elements in overall productive equilibrium).[10] This is wishful thinking, an apolitical mush. *Bladerunner*, version 3, when even the replicants of the replicants happily, and mindlessly, embrace their redundancy.

I-conomy Inc.

If we can envisage the flow of images as having become, in contemporary conditions, a self-managing, externally negotiating system—an economy of iconicity, an *iconomy*—and if we recognize that this iconomy operates in a real world as disposed to contestation as it is to construction—thus generating the creation and sustaining of powerful *image regimes* as well as repeated *iconoclashes*—then how might we name all these relations as an area of research, analysis, and critique?[11] Several well-established disciplines actually undertake such work without naming it, except perhaps as topic, at most a subfield. Among the humanities are art history, cultural studies, museum studies, and history. Among the sciences are studies of visual perception, psychology, sociology, media studies, communications, behavioral science, and economics of culture. Assuming it be to a humanistic, social science—or, better, supplementing these, a post-human, deconstructive inquiry—some names have already been proposed. Names of the mode of inquiry mix with those for the object of study: "A science of seeing," "Word and image studies,"

"Visual culture," "Visual Studies," and "Image science (*Bildwissenschaft*)." If the iconomy is, or has become, a pervasive economy, an internally dynamic but also embedded system that is fundamental to human (and perhaps animal) societies, to machinic communication, and to natural reproduction, then why not follow Dennis Dion and name its study according to its object: *Iconomics*?

One good reason might be the ways in which the name has already been taken up for purposes inimical to what the world needs now. Google searches in print material most often turn up typed texts in which the "E" in the word "Economics" has been degraded, such that the machine misreads it as "I." (An interesting indicator that machines talking to each other are, like humans doing the same thing, quite capable of generating and multiplying misunderstandings.) A 1996 publication, *World Wide Web Yellow Pages*, a directory of terms to be found on the Internet at that time—as a print publication now wildly anachronistic—lists a redundant URL for a company named Iconomics that describes itself as "Your global illustration resource for graphics design via modem, mail, ftp, or floppy disc. Provides links to custom art, images, ordering, prices, and policy information."[12] This is likely an early iteration of Iconomics Inc., a Toronto-based software development and design company that has, its website claims, been "dedicated to implementing Enterprise Performance Management (EPM), Business Intelligence (BI) and Data Warehousing (DW) solutions since 1995."[13] Other businesses with the same or similar name since then include a short-lived development company, a public relations firm, a gaming mechanism within Minecraft, a web design and SEO company, a technology and business consulting group, and Iconomy: A Design Experience, a Johannesburg-based furniture and décor company.

It did not take long for the general economy to be defined as an *I*-conomy, making explicit decades of cultivation of individual consumers. This was led by market actors such as those just listed.[14] Recognizing that heightened consumer expectation has created "an Individual Economy—Iconomy for short," Notion, a venture capitalist group, has since 2009 invested in innovations that promote "What I want, where I want and when I want it."[15] By 2011, Urban Dictionary had this entry, more specific to finance capital:

> Iconomy is a state where certain 'financial tools' (derivatives/futures-options-cds etc), leveraged credit and uncontrolled increase of money supply, altogether sum up to a matchless value chaotically multiple of the total value of all fixed assets, properties and commodities reserves of the real economy.

Exemplified by credit default swaps, notorious as the immediate precipitators of the 2008 Global Financial Crisis:

> Credit expansion obtained by financial institutions creating virtual assets and investment potential in bureaucratically created financial tools, void of any real or productive value, is a prominent form of iconomy.[16]

In 2019, the name was adopted by The Iconomics, a Jakarta-based company offering a variety of business information and brand management services, with this mission:

> The Iconomics is established by professionals that have experience in integrated media. Our mission is to share business analysis and information to our readers. *We* want to take part in advancing the economy of Indonesia by delivering news and macro economy analysis. *We* are the media platform that people need. *We* do share good news to our readers but we also share reliable business forecast. We are the alternative media that give information that readers actually need to know.[17]

As its descriptor "Leading Disruption Economy" suggests, and its web presence shows, this enterprise is a pure product of imported, adaptive globalization. It also exemplifies every danger that adopting, despite qualifications and caveats, the word "iconomics" for the kind of thinking we need now might afford—not least, providing yet another professional service to rampant neoliberal globalization. Obviously, I do not propose its adoption in this form, or in any form susceptible to such usage. Rather, I see it as a placeholder for a critical project around iconicity that may name itself differently—if and when it does.

Digital Currency

The saturation of neoliberalism within most economies, so tellingly traced by Wendy Brown and David Harvey, can infect even those consciously opposed to its values.[18] Brazilian economist and sociologist Gilson Schwartz believes that "the challenges to economic theory at the beginning of the 21st century" are "summarized in a new theory of value as an icon—the Iconomy," especially in the case of digital currencies, which he understands as more than Bitcoin.

> No object of economy seems to implicate the dimensions of exchange, technology, and culture so reciprocally. When it comes to the emergence and emission of digital currencies in the field of culture itself (as with

> game and 'playable' fantasy worlds currencies), the phenomenon gains even more pertinence and seems to function as a source of inspiration and experimentation for new forms of ludic monetization with affective and effective impacts as powerful as those already verified in the creation, use, and circulation of the more 'conventional' money.[19]

When thinking of the iconomy as the general economy prevalent at present, however, he poses a set of pertinent questions:

> A new economy results from the accumulation of algorithms. What are its mechanisms to generate value, employment, income, capital and expectations? What icons, literacies and competences, as well as infra-structure determine and condition the development of these platforms? What are their local, territorial, regional and global effects? What rights are created and destroyed? What limits are overcome or replaced from the viewpoint of access to material comfort and sharing of immaterial heritage?
> Who are its protagonists within the entrepreneurial, governmental, social and political spheres?
> What is the children's and youth's insertion as the engines of this digital icon economy? How do new generations perceive themselves? And what social, economic and affective futures are being configured?
> What are the ruptures of the current order? What are the opportunities in the face of the evident destructive chaos and global massification of mass culture? How should university and research follow these transformations, benefitting cultural diversity through an interference in the mechanism of value representation itself?
> Cultural diversity is inseparable from monetary diversity. At a time when monetary, financial, and currency patterns are in global crisis, it is fundamental to perform a conceptual, technological, and socially innovative shift as academic networks and the business, governmental and civil society sectors come together with the purpose of generating and rebuilding infrastructures, contents, fraternity and diversity.[20]

An ongoing project on the outskirts of São Paulo, "with children and youth as protagonists, mapped out and mobilized by the *Youth Portal* and coordinated by the *City of Knowledge* together with the City Office for Human Rights and Citizenship of São Paulo," is testing possibilities for melding the values of iconomy and those of cultural diversity.[21]

We cannot expect one project on the edge of one city, however distinctive it may be, to be representative of every other micro instance and to model all possibility. But we can sense that the cave is now everywhere, and—if we were to compare, for example, the situation for an employee at Menlo Park, Calif., to that in the gravel mines of Uganda or the cobalt mines of the Congo—that the chains are now both self-applied and invisible to those who have while, at the same time, they are manacles ruthlessly applied, in sight of all, to those who have not.

Internet Imageworld

In today's globalized world, the most glaringly obvious fact about visual imagery is its quantitative increase. It is generated and reproduced in ever more varied ways on more and more platforms and is more widely disseminated than ever before. It is orthodoxy to claim that imagery, particularly visual imagery, was and continues to be a major driving force in the modernization of most societies, and that in most it has reached saturation point. Precisely such settling into orthodoxy is why we must pinpoint more precisely exactly how, why, and with which effects, this is occurring.

As of October 28, 2020, Instagram users had uploaded 50 billion photographs, at a current rate of 995 each second. About 500 hours of video are uploaded to YouTube each minute. Facebook users post 350 million photographs each day, at the rate of 4,000 per second, and there are 4 billion video viewings each day on the platform. About 4.5 billion photos and 1 billion videos are shared on WhatsApp. WeChat users send 205 million video messages each day. Across these sites, billions of people spend some hours each day on making, posting, and consuming images.[22] What was in the 1920s a first wave of mass image production and consumption, a wave that became a televisual tide in the 1960s, is now a constant tsunami, one that has become so familiar to so many that it seems normal.

In his *The Supermarket of the Visible: Toward a General Economy of Images* (2019), Peter Szendy makes this his starting point. Although his major focus is on film, he draws on Marx of the *1844 Manuscripts*, Mondzian on image economies, and Deleuze on cinema, to profile the largest economy, that is, the world. He asks a version of the same question we have been pursuing:

> Is there a market of the visible that would precede, that would exceed, the commerce of images in the supposedly strict sense of the word? Is there a bigger market, an arche-economy, of images, in other words, a super- or hyper-market of visibility that would be the counterpart (the "reverse") of the metacinema that for Deleuze is the world?[23]

That the Internet, initially a communication system internal to the US military, then offered as a free public good, as genuinely social media, has been thoroughly monetized is simply the most evident fact about its evolution. Yet, while the numbers about social media usage are overwhelming, and the ever-expanding, apparently chaotic, tsunami of imagery being exhibited on its platforms seems unstoppable, we should not be blinded to the new normalcy that is establishing itself inside the flow, against it, and alongside it—even as the flow rushes to fill every space, including those we can't see and those we might try to visualize. Its *horror vacui* voids every spatial metaphor we attempt to strike. Perhaps this, as much as the sheer impossibility of imagining the vast quantities of pictures now in circulation, accounts for the curious emptiness of those artworks that literally display its quantitative presence: Erik Kessels' *24Hrs in Photos* (2014), and even aspects of Thomas Hirschhorn's installation *crystal of resistance* in the Swiss Pavilion at the Venice Biennale in 2011.

But the Flood (Biblical metaphor) itself cannot resist analysis, least of all that which serves its inner normalcy by describing its rules of operation. The mistake is to take every instance as equally significant and potentially lasting, as if the world was an actual rather than a metaphorical supermarket of things and images, which constantly self-replenishes in ways as magical as the commodities themselves. In fact, the exclusionary violence driving the iconomy means that all but a few of its instant attractors prove themselves to be of any importance at all. In *The Rules of Contagion* (2020), Adam Kucharski surveys studies of Internet usage, which consistently show that "content rarely goes far without broadcast events to amplify it."[24] Almost all postings are not read by anyone or anything but the network that moves them; most are read by only one other user, once or twice; those that become viral do so mostly because media outlets or well-known personalities have boosted them.[25] Such extraordinary wastage means that effectiveness—for politicians, advertisers, and "influencers"—depends less on the inherent interest and relevance of the story than on the constancy of their posting of stories that might precipitate "cascades." It may be that Donald J. Trump's unprecedented online presence owed as much to his indefatigable energy as a poster as it did to his long-term status as a celebrity and to the importance of his position as the President of the United States. Similarly, online platforms must devote much of their design efforts to attracting users as often as possible (in the United States, cell phones are opened on average 80 times each day) and keeping them online for as long as possible. Constant, small-scale, and low-level connections are the basis of their cash flow. Perhaps, the true degradation of imagery these days is to be found here, especially when we recall Jean-Paul Sartre's premise that images are always a form of consciousness, initially unreflective but potentially richly reflective to the point of being essential to individual and social freedom.[26]

Ambient Imagery, Iconopolitics

In his *Ambient Screens and Transnational Public Spaces* (2016), Nikos Papastergiadis identified image saturation as having become, for many, a given, seemingly natural characteristic of their surroundings, at times blurring public and private, at others sharply dividing them.[27] The pandemic has induced heightened awareness of our conditions of confinement.

> Image saturation, the interweaving of commercial and emotional currents, images for and by machines, algorithmic curation, the networked 'trace' images—these are all factors serving to underscore the complexities of living in the age of the ambient image. Taken together, they indicate a need for a renewed exploration of how we learn to read the image, and for whom (or what) images are legible.[28]

A set of questions, some old, many new, have become urgent:

> What does the exponential growth in the means of production and circulation of images mean to the experience and interpretation of images? Do we even see an image as a single, discrete, framed entity that is isolated from billions of other images, or are the images always jostling, rubbing, folding and spilling with one another? Compounding this boom in the personal use of images is the advent of machinic technologies that make images from the capture and organization of existing images. There is much debate about whether AI will simply devour the personal image into bits for a big data world, or whether it can be aligned with human needs and thereby provide novel opportunities for creativity and freedom. The new digital media platforms have exacerbated tensions between commercial imperatives and the conditions of sociality. They have facilitated exchanges that operate on a scale and with such speed that they have exposed the limits of existing personal protocols, collective memories, and modes of public government. By aggregating and storing billions of private images, new companies have gained rights of access to unimagined domains. […] the consequences for the ambient image are far from certain.[29]

Yet, as we all saw, in May 2020 the video of the killing of George Floyd cut through the dazzling din of everyday emergency, standing out even among the regular stream of images of young black men brutalized by white police. It showed the deadly logic that underscored such imagery, which is usually glimpsed in short segments, if shown at all, or quickly scrolled past.

It showed, too, the necropolitics of all policing in divided societies. It precipitated a worldwide outburst of protest, amplified by the organized display of Black Lives Matter and similar imagery. Its ramifications continue to resonate. One is that it brushed aside the sense—widespread, paradoxically, in artworlds—that visual imagery in general is becoming inevitably more enervated.[30] The same recognition of the power of imagery is true for the spread of the COVID-19 iconotype and its associated visual messaging. These images may be about "bare life," but they are not weak. They remind us just how fragile a matter it is to live a full life, even to aspire to one. The imagery of racial injustice and of the pandemic is not simulated. In a so-called post-truth period, it is actually rooted in truth-telling about life and death.[31]

We are entering a domain that is mostly skirted by recent thinking about image regimes, including most of these discussed in this chapter. When describing the emergent digital economy as a political one, Dennis was thinking in Foucault's terms about inequalities in the relationships between individuals and others, and between them and organizations such as universities and search engine providers, rather than the politics of the public sphere. We have also canvassed several examples of iconomies within markets—financial, retail, and services. And earlier we noted the centrality of image economies within religious settings and to the operations of the law. Each of these claim to be fundamentally separated from the realms of public politics. Each of them is, in fact, thoroughly imbricated. So, we must ask these questions. What does an overtly political iconomy look like? How might political iconomics conduct itself as critical discourse?

Susan Buck-Morss identifies what has long been the central issue in an such enterprise:

> More than the sum of the merely empirical individuals of which Hobbes' Leviathan is composed, sovereignty is a transcendent category. The sovereign is an icon in the theological sense. He (or she) embodies an enigma—precisely the power if the collective to constitute itself. The sovereign figure as the personification of the collective demonstrates the power of the visual image to close the circle between constituting and constituted power, explaining why even when the illegalities of an individual sovereign are exposed, the faith of the believer is not shaken. As long as the circle appears closed, power remains intact; likewise, and conversely, as long as sovereign power remains intact, the circle appears closed. The closing of the circle demands a miracle, and the sovereign provides it.[32]

We return to a quintessential capacity of images, one that has consistently appeared in each chapter, that is, the power to register the absence while at the same time filling the present with the presence of that or whom the image refers or appears to resemble. It is a conjuring, not a merging of the object with its subject. There is always, we know, a difference waiting to make itself felt. But the power of the image depends on the agreement between us to defer that occasion, to suspend its possibility, and to give time for the transfer of desires to take place. For Plato, this exchange occurred between the cave dwellers and the shadows then, better, between the freed person and the Ideal Forms, above all the Form of the Good. In Byzantium, it was between the believer and the Holy Trinity/Emperor. For the Leviathan, it was the divinely ordained, dynastic sovereign, and his subjects. In authoritarian regimes, it is the dictator and the people. In democracies, the people elect their leaders but wrestle between the urge to confer on them quasi-mystical powers, thus surrendering their own sovereignty, or, in contrast, they take on the responsibility of treating their leaders and themselves as citizens with agonistic work to do in defining the collective project.

Due, in large part, to its proclivity toward overreach, but also because of fierce resistance to its degradations, capitalism as we have known it has arrived at its zombie incarnation, ready to haunt a future that could be even worse than the world it has afforded to date.[33] We cannot take its words or its images at their exhibited value. Iconopolitical critique requires us to trace historical trajectories, identify causes, and deconstruct operative structures, as always when we wish to see our contemporaneity more clearly.

It is to this that we turn in the second part of this book.

Notes

1 Mondzian, *Image, Icon, Economy*, 223.

2 Jean-Joseph Goux, "L'art et l'argent: vers une nouvelle 'iconomie'," *Art Press*, 65 (January 1992); "Art and Money; Toward a New 'Iconomy'," in *The Supermarket of Images*, ed. Peter Szendy et al. (Paris: Gallimard-Jue De Paume, 2020), 65–72. Within his career-long studies of symbolic economies, Goux has also explored the transition from aesthetic value established by reputation within artists' academies to value measured by sales of artworks during the Impressionist period. See his *L'art et l'argent. Le rupture moderniste. 1860–1920* (Paris: Bluson, 2011).

3 Dion Dennis, "License and Commodification: The Birth of an Information Oligarchy," *Humanity & Society*, 17, no. 1 (February, 1993), 52–53. Internal references are to his own unpublished paper, "Under the Sign of Saturn: An Exemplar of Political Iconomy," Arizona State University, 1992; and to Colin Gordon, "Government Rationality: An Introduction," in *The Foucault Effect: Studies in Governmentality*, eds.

Graham Burchell et al. (Chicago: University of Chicago Press, 1991), 1–52. And a not-so-hidden reference to Arjun Appadurai ed., *The Social Life of Things: Commodities in Cultural Perspectives* (Cambridge: Cambridge University Press, 1986).

4 Dennis, "License and Commodification: The Birth of an Information Oligarchy," 48.

5 Ibid., 53.

6 B. Joseph Pine II and James H. Gilmore, *The Experience Economy* (Boston: Harvard Business Review Press, 2011). See also Luc Boltanski and Eve Chiapello, *New Spirit of Capitalism* (London: Verso, 2005). More recent studies include Michel Volle, "Towards a Post-Industrial Iconomy," in *The Digital Era Revisited*, vol. 2, ed. Jean-Pierre Chamoux (London: Wiley, 2019).

7 Geoff Cox & Jacob Lund, *The Contemporary Condition: Introductory Thoughts on Contemporaneity and Contemporary Art* (Berlin: Sternberg, 2016), 25.

8 Benjamin H. Bratton, "The Black Stack," *e-flux journal*, no. 53 (March 2014), at https://www.e-flux.com/journal/53/59883/the-black-stack/.

9 Benjamin Bratton, *The Stack: On Software and Sovereignty* (Cambridge, MA: MIT Press, 2015), 356. The medieval/modern imagery of Fritz Lang's *Metropolis* (1927) echoes here.

10 James Lovelock (with Brian Appleyard), *Novacene: The Coming Age of Hyperintelligence* (London: Allen Lane, 2019).

11 On iconoclash more specifically, see Bruno Latour, "What is Iconoclash? Or Is There a World Beyond the Image Wars?," in *Iconoclash: Beyond the Image Wars in Science, Religion and Art*, eds. Bruno Latour and Peter Weibel (Cambridge, MA: MIT Press, for ZKM, Karlsruhe, 2002).

12 *New Rider's Official World Wide Web Yellow Pages* (Indianapolis, IN: New Riders Pub., 1996), 478.

13 See http://www.iconomics-inc.com/company.html.

14 For an illuminating account of iconomic operations within stock market discourse—specifically Federal Reserve Board Chairman Allan Greenspan's famous 1996 comment on "irrational exuberance"—see Michael Kaplan, "Iconomics: The Rhetoric of Speculation," *Public Culture*, 15, no. 3 (2003): 477–493. See also John Bloom, "Free Market in a Pop Iconomy," *The Genius of Money: Essays and Interviews Reimagining the Financial World* (Hudson, NY: Steiner books, 2009).

15 See "The Iconomy: What I Want, Where I Want and When I Want It," *Notion*, posted December 21, 2017, at https://notion.vc/resources/the-iconomy-what-i-want-where-i-want-and-when-i-want-it/. On iconomy as "brand aesthetics," see Martin Kornberger, *Brand Society: How Brands Transform Economy and Society* (Cambridge: Cambridge University Press, 2010).

16 Posted by bilwander, December 29, 2011, at https://www.urbandictionary.com/define.php?term=Iconomy.

17 See https://www.theiconomics.com/about-us/.

18 David Harvey, *A Brief History of Neoliberalism* (Oxford: Oxford University Press, 2005); Wendy Brown, *Undoing the Demos: Neoliberalism's Stealth Revolution* (New York, NY: Zone Books, 2015).

19 Gilson Schwartz, "Iconomy, Cultural Diversity and Ludic Monetization on the Internet of Things," in *Diversity of Cultural Expressions in the Digital Era*, eds. Lilian Richieri Hanania and Anne-Thida Norodom (TeseoPress: Buenos Aires, 2016), 74–75. See also Gilson Schwartz and Diego Vianna, "The Iconomy of Creative Currencies in the City of Knowledge: A Transmonetary Approach," 3rd International Conference on Social and Complementary Currencies, Salvador: Management School at the Federal University of Bahia, 2015.

20 Schwartz, "Iconomy, Cultural Diversity and Ludic Monetization on the Internet of Things," 80–81.

21 Ibid., 81. In such contexts, he and colleagues define iconomics as "the triadic structures that underlie local, national and global media ecologies. These are the 'I' or the individual (as citizen, consumer and person of passions); iconicity (memes, codes, symbols, and narratives); and economy (of supply/demand, scarcity/abundance, production, distribution and investment)."—Joanne Garde-Hansen and Gilson Schwartz, "Iconomy of Memory: Remembering as digital, civic and corporate currency," *Digital Memory Studies* (New York: Routledge, 2017), abstract.

22 Data drawn from statistics sites, such as that of Omnicore for Facebook at https://www.omnicoreagency.com/facebook-statistics/.

23 Peter Szendy, *The Supermarket of the Visible: Towards a General Economy of Images* (New York: Fordham University Press, 2019), 8–9. See also his lecture at the European Graduate School, August 9, 2019, at https://www.youtube.com/watch?v=d8mvqnMat3M and Emmanuel Alloa, Marta Ponza, Peter Szendy, eds., *The Supermarket of Images* (Paris: Gallimard/Jeu de Paume, 2020).

24 Adam Kucharski, *The Rules of Contagion* (London: Profile Books, 2020), 208.

25 Ibid., 181–182.

26 This is the main thrust of his *The Imaginary* [1940], see note 3.

27 Nikos Papastergiadis, *Ambient Screens and Transnational Public Spaces* (Hong Kong: Hong Kong University Press, 2016).

28 Sean Cubitt, Celia Lury, Scott McQuire, Nikos Papastergiadis, Daniel Palmer, Jasmin Pfefferkorn, and Emile K. Sunde, "Ambient Images," *Nordic Journal of Aesthetics*, nos. 61–62 (2021), 73.

29 Cubitt et al., "Ambient Images," 75–76.

30 These paradoxes are illuminatingly explored by Hito Steyerl, "In defence of the poor image," *e-flux Journal*, #19 (November 2009), at https://www.e-flux.com/journal/10/61362/in-defense-of-the-poor-image/.

31 See Terry Smith, "Truth in Transition: As the Decade Breaks," in *Fabricating Publics: The Dissemination of Culture in the Post-Truth Era*, eds. Bill Balaskas and Carolina Rito (Liverpool: DATA browser series, Open Humanities Press, in partnership with Exhibition Research Lab, Liverpool John Moores University, 2021).

32 Susan Buck-Morss, "Visual Empire," *diacritics*, 37, nos. 2–3 (Summer-Fall, 2007), 172. This article also provides the best available commentary on Mondzian's *Image, Icon, Economy*.

33 McKenzie Wark, *Capital Is Dead. Is This Something Worse?* (London: Verso, 2019).

Part II
ICONOCLASH

Chapter 7

THE SPIKE-CROWNED VIRUS

> World: "There is no way we can shut everything down in order to lower emissions, slow climate change and protect the environment."
> Mother Nature: "Here's a virus. Practice."
>
> —Anonymous.[1]

In the June 3, 2020, edition of the Sydney newspaper, *The Daily Telegraph*, Warren Brown's cartoon entitled "Recession" was published on the main editorial page (Fig. 7.1). The trope is Welcome in the New Year, but this mid-year message is bleak. The central figure is an unkempt man in pajamas, slippers, and dressing gown, representing readers confined to their homes by lockdown orders required to combat the pandemic, or, like many others, recently thrown into unemployment by its effects. He opens his door, not to a new-born baby in a ribboned bassinette, but to a Scrooge-like figure, dressed as an undertaker, who carries a wreath with the insignia "Recession." Resigned to his fate, the man admits the deathly messenger to his bleak house, which symbolizes not only the actual home of the average Australian but also the national economy. Both are already ravaged by several forces, each of them out of control. They come from a distance, but are intensely present, obliterating all signs of domesticity. In the background, the fires that raged across millions of acres of bush land throughout the early months of the year, despite the best efforts of the (mostly volunteer) Rural Fire Services. The spiky blobs of the coronavirus float everywhere. Meanwhile, a masked housewife spills her hoarded reams of toilet paper, the US President Donald J. Trump holds up a Bible, and a police officer beats a looter. "Come on in," the man says despairingly, "It wouldn't be 2020 without you [...]"

Some of these elements reflect the ideological orientation of the newspaper: The central figure is white, male, working-class, oppressed, and resentful; a looter rather than a black man or a protestor is shown battling the police officer. Others are specific to Australia: the raging bushfires, although much of California was in flames by June, so global warming in general is also evoked. Everything depicted is instantly recognizable as a visual signifier of the forces

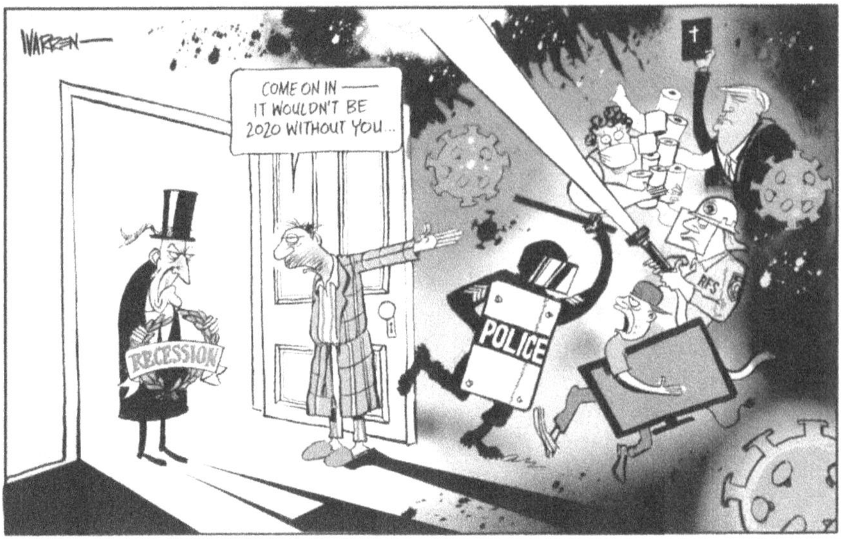

Fig. 7.1: Warren Brown, "Recession," *The Daily Telegraph*, Sydney, June 3, 2020.

that were most powerfully shaping 2020 in many places throughout the world and in the imaginaries of many of its peoples.

Skilled in acute condensation of the image flow, alert to its political implications, and sensitive to the moods of his fellow citizens, the cartoonist has grasped a larger truth, one that I will explore in the second part of this book. That three image regimes had pushed to the fore of personal and social imaginaries in many parts of the world. The imagery clustering around the coronavirus as it became a pandemic; the events staged by Donald J. Trump across a variety of mediums; and the anger and activism unleashed by the viral circulation of the cell phone video of the murder of George Floyd.

Doubtless, the meanings of these images that were most striking in 2020 and 2021 will soon fade, be displaced or, where media is tightly controlled, repressed. By the time you read this, a range of vaccines may have reduced the coronavirus to the bearable level of influenza in at least some parts of the world, Trump may have faded to the outer reaches of media attention, and, after constructive community building, policing may be somewhat demilitarized and incorporated within the nonviolent safeguarding of those communities—again, at least in some parts of the world. Other clusters of imagery, different visual figuring of other world-shaping forces—wars, natural disasters, technological transformations, visions of possibility—will resume their usual urgency. But viruses love to mutate, so pandemics will break out again, most likely on larger scales. Tribalist nationalism will not fade away, nor will the need to keep working to transform societies based on racism, inequality, and coercion toward those grounded in justice, equity, and freedom. Our journey through a history of thinking about images and economies in the first part of this book has shown that each of these values strives to articulate its goals, sustain itself, and resist competing forces, through forming, adapting, and maintaining visual regimes that have become increasingly prominent—at times, a leading factor—within other, more obviously political, means of ultimately achieving their ends.

So, with no claims based on hindsight, but open to insight, let us revisit the imagery that constellated and contested during 2020 and 2021, to discover what caused them to become epidemic and then pandemic. Let us apply an epidemiology to these image regimes, track how they became viral cascades, trace how they did their work and with which effects, to learn what to do about them when they recur in the same or similar guises. Which, we can be sure, they will. The outbreaks of 2020–2021 are a past that is not yet past. They made visible the operations of existing image economies, and then they reconfigured them. They also prefigured those to come.

The Spiky Blob

On December 31, 2019, the World Health Organization notified those who follow its website that a viral "pneumonia of unknown cause" had been announced by the Wuhan Municipal Health Commission. On January 9, 2020, Chinese authorities certified that the outbreak was caused by a "novel coronavirus." Two days later, as the first person died, these authorities released the genetic sequence of the virus. Human-to-human transmission, however, was denied until January 21, asymptomatic transference likewise until late February. On January 30, based on evidence accumulating in other Asian countries, the Director-General of the World Health Organization declared the outbreak "a public health emergency of international concern." It took until March 11 for WHO to make the assessment that COVID-19 could be characterized as a pandemic.[2] This is the beginning of what is now a very well-known, and still contested, story. Its unfolding as a visual regime is, however, less known, and is the subject of this chapter.

The most familiar image of the virus, the "spiky blob," appeared very early in this rapidly accelerating timeline. It was created by medical illustrators at the Centers for Disease Control and Prevention, Atlanta, on January 21, one day after emergency operations began in the United States (Fig. 7.2). Commissioned to imagine "an identity" for use in public communications, Alicia Eckert and Dan Higgins considered the usual options: illustrate the symptoms of the disease, its effects on the human body, or its means of

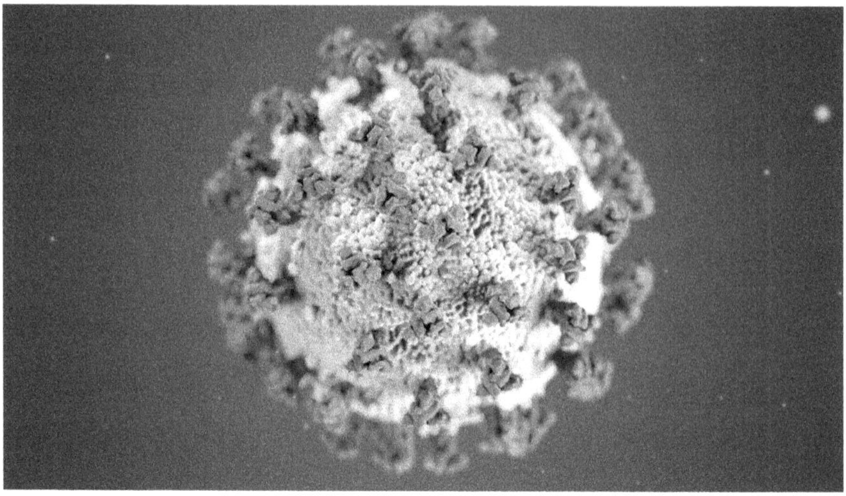

Fig. 7.2: Alicia Eckert and Dan Higgins, SARS-CoV-2, digital image, Centers for Disease Control and Prevention/Alissa Eckert, MSMI; Dan Higgins, MAMS, January 21, 2020.

transmission. None of these being firmly established or known in the case of SARS-CoV-2, they chose a single, still, stand-alone image based on the appearance of the virus when seen through microscopes, the kind of illustration known in the trade as a "beauty shot."[3] Many such images can be found in the RCSB Protein Data Bank, a repository shared by researchers in the field which collects research reports, including graphic visualizations, still and 3D, of the detailed chemical structures of proteins. Drawing on images of previous viruses, each of which is characterized by the proteins that cover its surfaces, and using Autodesk 3ds Max software, the CDC illustrators decided to highlight the proteins that elongate when the virus invades human cells (red, spike-shaped clusters like those on a crown), the envelope proteins that help the virus enter the cells (yellow crumbs), and the membrane proteins that give form to the virus (orange dots). A virus invisible to the naked eye is made legible by showing it doing its work at a nano level. One of our cells, its new host, is the gray blob. Shaping the cell as a sphere (unconsciously) elevates it to a world, suggesting an unspecific, indistinct, yet totally threatened totality—a global, planetary pandemic.[4]

A few weeks later, at Tsinghua University, Beijing, structural biologist Dr. Sai Li looked through a microscope at a frozen sample of thousands of coronaviruses magnified to more than one millionth of an inch. He could see the atomic structure, or "molecular assembly," of the viruses, their "detailed architecture" that he and colleagues were subsequently able to describe in full.[5] Using the same color range as adopted by the CDC illustrators, the Tsinghua team traced the proteins on the exterior of the virus as well as those that penetrated its core (Fig. 7.3). Subsequently, researchers elsewhere used similar imaging to picture the dance-like movement of the spike proteins, the virus's ability to fold its RNA genome into extraordinary shapes to enable these movements, as well as its capacity to generate novel proteins. Image making of this kind is a mode of thinking within a professional community that has developed its own iconography into an iconology, that is, an expandable set of specific images into an epistemology, a systematic language that generates knowledge about its signifieds. At the same time, they have created an iconosphere, a domain of

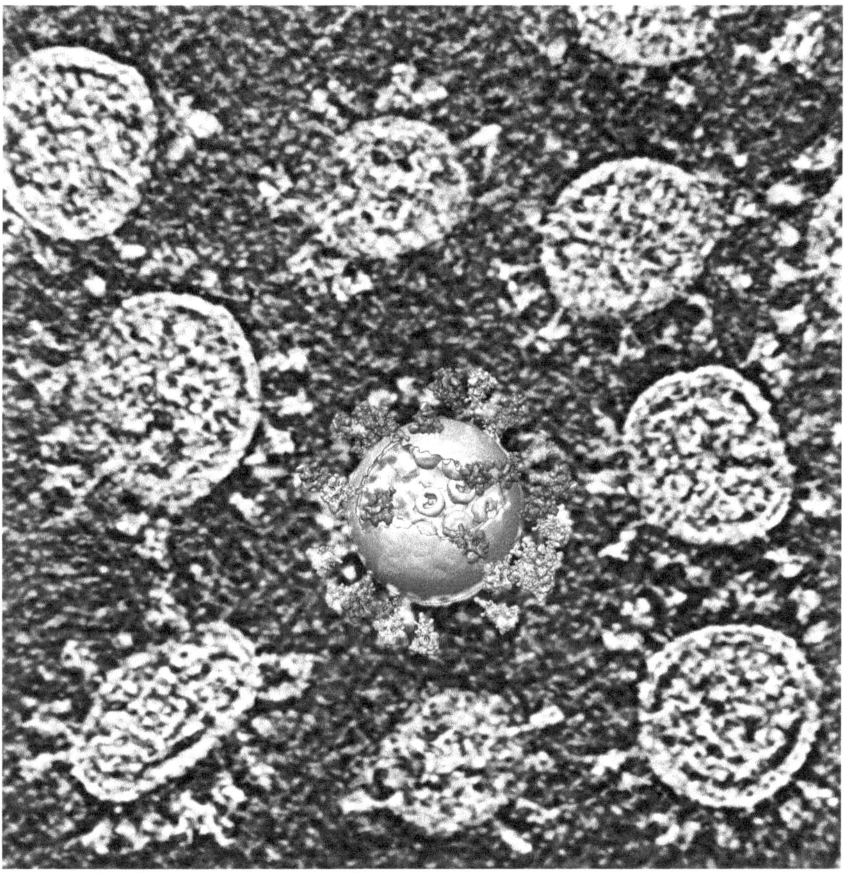

Fig. 7.3: Sai Li and others, Magnified representative intact SARS-CoV-2 reconstructed from cryo-electron tomograms, Tsinghua University, Beijing, January 2020. From "Molecular architecture of the SARS-CoV-2 virus," *Cell*, 2020; DOI:10.1016/J.CELL.2020.09.018

staggering but knowable complexity, in which graphic inference from material information used in experimental testing is shadowed by the beauty, and unspoken horror, of the materials in formation.[6]

Any successful vaccine would depend on triggering the body's immune systems into blocking one or more of these extremely complex and ever-changing movements. And doing so without negative side effects. Visualizing these processes is vital to devising preventions against the disease. At the National Institute for Heath, Bethesda, Maryland, Drs. Barney Graham and Josh D. McLellan applied ideas they had developed when researching the structures of HIV, RSV, an acute respiratory virus, and MERS, the Middle East respiratory syndrome. Meanwhile, researchers at the drug company Moderna had encoded a modified protein on strips of genetic material known as messenger RNA. This was the platform Graham and McLellan needed to carry their vaccine. On January 11, one day after receiving the genome sequence for SARS-CoV-19, a week before the NCDC illustrators began their work, two weeks before the WHO noted that the virus had become of international concern, and two months before the disease was pronounced a pandemic, the two scientists had designed a vaccine. It immediately entered trials, which were funded largely by the Trump Administration, its single success in managing the pandemic. Undertaken at "Warp Speed," approved in record time, it began to be distributed by Moderna and Pfizer in late December, 2020.[7]

The Spread

If the spiky blob quickly became the iconotype of the virus—the lead graphic on 24/7 news programming, in daily newspapers, magazine articles, and social media posts—it was soon amplified by photographic, film, and digital imagery of the impact of the virus on the health, daily life, economies, and politics of country after country as it spread around the world. Initially, this seemed as indiscriminate, relentless, and chaotic as the disease itself. Debate raged over the point of initial outbreak and thus the root "cause" of a zoonotic transmission that had actually been millennia in the making. Set shots of the live animal food market at Wuhan were matched to those of the Institute of Virology in that city. A bat from the market? A leak from a botched experiment at the Institute? A bioterrorism agent developed in the United States and somehow planted in the unidentifiable "patient zero" in Wuhan? Meanwhile, responses to the virus created their own sensational news. By February 28, Amazon was obliged to remove from its distribution system over 1 million products that falsely claimed to prevent or cure the virus. It also took down tens of thousands of overpriced health products such as unwearable masks, ineffective disinfectant wipes, and misleading advertising such as claims that vitamin C was effective against the virus.[8] Cue multiple images of masks of all kinds, from N95 particle filter respirators to high-end fashion accessories and freebees made by your local community artist.

While the virus itself remained invisible, the vehicles of its transmission seemed to be potentially everywhere: any surface, each touch, some liquids, every cough, particles, droplets—maybe though asymptomatic transfer from someone who has no idea that they are infected! At first alarming, this quickly became normal. As scientists began to learn more about the virus and its preferred modes of transmission (answer: human to human), myths about both abounded. COVID was caused by 5G mobile networks or mosquito bites, it could be spread by shoes, houseflies, and by swimming, it did not thrive in hot weather and cold weather, and it could be cured by hot baths, hydroxychloroquine, and garlic. Cue photographs of each situation and video clips of advocates of such misinformation, the most prominent and consistently erratic among the latter being the US President Donald J. Trump.[9]

As health authorities and governments struggled to manage the growing emergency, infographics became an important tool for providing basic information in accessible, at-a-glance formats about the symptoms, avoiding infection, sanitizer safety, mental health issues, isolation strategies, and staying informed as conditions and knowledge of them changed.[10] Augmenting the imagery of spiky blobs, attempts to regulate the tempo of the public panic about the pandemic were made through announcements by heads of government and public health officials, broadcast on mass media, and posted to social media. Press conferences, nationally televised addresses, and daily postings on notice boards and on virtual media conveyed information about the incidence of the virus in one's locality, its spread within one's country, region, and elsewhere, and the relative success or failure of mitigation efforts. Maps of the continents and oceans were crisscrossed with lines tracing transmissions and glowed red with hot spots. They were surrounded by numbers of the infected in regions, nations, and cities, figures that spun wildly upwards, like those of jackpots on gambling machines. Constantly updated charts of infection rates and deaths in states, counties, and cities matched weather reports on most media.[11]

Presidents, prime ministers, governors, and mayors called frequent press conferences to issue instructions about rules of confinement, while directors of national disease control centers, doctors in prominent hospitals, and epidemiologists explained what they were learning about the nature of the virus and issued appeals to wear masks, wash hands, keep social distance, and get tested if you have the slightest symptom. The nature and effectiveness of these messages varied from place to place. In China, the omnicompetence of the Party was (as always) the main story, personified in recurrent imagery of President Xi Jinping in face masked, active interventionist mode. In the United States, national messaging was split between the evasive glosses offered by mask-defiant President Trump during interminable press conferences and the calibrated expertise of Dr. Anthony Fauci, the director of the National Institute for Allergy and Infectious Diseases. Elsewhere, attempts were made to promote national unity through shared participation in metaphorical acts with supposedly ancient resonances: Three weeks into a hastily called and increasingly porous nation-wide lockdown, Prime Minister Modi asked all Indians to turn off all electricity and light candles and lamps at 9 pm for nine minutes.[12]

The massively unequal impacts of COVID-19 throughout the world during the early months of 2020 quickly laid bare the dependency of even the most "developed" countries on their precariat, in particular the role of underpaid, often migrant workers in protecting and serving those infected and those confined by quarantine rules. As these impacts became known, the most common metaphor was both visual and medical: that the virus worked like an X-ray, revealing not only hidden normalities but also the pathologies in the social body. By contrast, literal images of the effects of the virus on human bodies were rarely broadcast (most are internal, and privacy laws restrict publication without consent), although more were posted on social media (against its grain of positive self-messaging). Yet, news reports soon led with videos of fast-filling hospital wards, of people (faces pixilated) in IC units smothered with equipment to aid their breathing, of harassed nurses and doctors, clad head to toe in often makeshift PPE, and of long lines of people waiting to be tested (most glued to their cellphones). During the early months of 2020, a society-wide sense of mutuality prevailed in many places. A sense of sacrifice for the sake of shared survival was paramount. Reports of assistance to the elderly and those at risk abounded. Rituals arose spontaneously: In many cities, medical workers on their ways home from work in the evening were applauded by grateful citizens. In Northern Italy, where the virus struck early and hard, neighbors in lockdown performed for each other on their balconies and at windows. Musicians in separate apartments played their parts in shared performances. COVID choirs sang together using Zoom as their platform.

On the other hand, the panic induced by pandemics also appeared just as quickly and ran as deep. Some questioned the alacrity with which governments declared states of emergency, imposing wide-scale restrictions on freedom of movement, thus reducing everyone to a state of "bare life," as if each of us was the worst enemy of the other.[13] Panic buying of personal protection equipment and of "essential" supplies became itself endemic. Cue film of supermarket shelves empty of toilet paper rolls, plastic water bottles and containers of sanitizer. Voiceover: "There is enough for everybody. Be calm.

The supply chains are working. Give them time to catch up." Subtext: Until there is not, they aren't, and we have run out of time.

The willingness of central banks to print money to shore up national and international economies and to maintain the powers that be in place, exposed again (as it did in 2008) the neoliberal fiction that the operations of "free markets" are at the heart of democratic societies. By contrast, the community-level responses in most countries showed that timid but deeply desired steps toward genuinely free sociality are possible, when the threat of the return of fascism or of no society at all becomes sufficiently real. The paradoxes of this situation are graphically summarized in Sam Wallman's poster "We're All In This Together," which also served as the cover image for the December 2020 issue of the magazine of the Australian Fabian Society (Fig. 7.4).

Early in the outbreak, the role of media—so much of it cloned into partisanship and mired in misinformation—in reporting on the phenomenon was already a cause of concern.[14] Nevertheless, some media rose to the occasion. An example is the coronavirus issue of *Time Magazine*, "What to Do When the World Stops," published on March 19, 2020.[15] In March, the International Center for Photography, New York, long-time home base for "concerned photography" in the United States, issued a call for imagemakers around the world to post and tag their experiences of living through the pandemic. The website filled quickly and an exhibition was selected, for the venue and online.[16] Meanwhile, several professional photographers developed photo-essays that are at once informative records and moving documents. A striking collection of these constitute The COVID-19 Visual Project, A Time of Distance, "an ongoing permanent archive of the coronavirus pandemic: effects, struggles, and glimmers of hope," which collects well-crafted images of the recent transformations of everyday life, the emptying of urban environments, sheltering in place, economic impacts, the chaos of hospital emergency zones, the rushed death rituals, "nature's rebound," and "the new normal" (Fig. 7.5).[17] Professionals such as Magnum photographer Alex Majoli contributed to collaborative projects of this kind while also continuing normal assignments such as illustrating an essay on the deathly march of the virus through Sicily for *Vanity Fair*.[18] Similarly, Yonas Tadesse profiled for *The Guardian* newspaper and website the courage and dedication of the coronavirus taskforce at the Ekka Kotebe Hospital in Addis Ababa.[19] By contrast, it is no surprise that *Vogue* magazine treated the subject through the lens of their favorite photographers passing their time in isolation, nor that they spent the time photographing themselves.[20]

Social media was of course saturated with imagery of the pandemic, as we all live within its parameters, and the point of platforms such as Facebook and Instagram is to share the details of our lives as events worth seeing. #coronavirus and #COVID-19 collect vast quantities of this content every

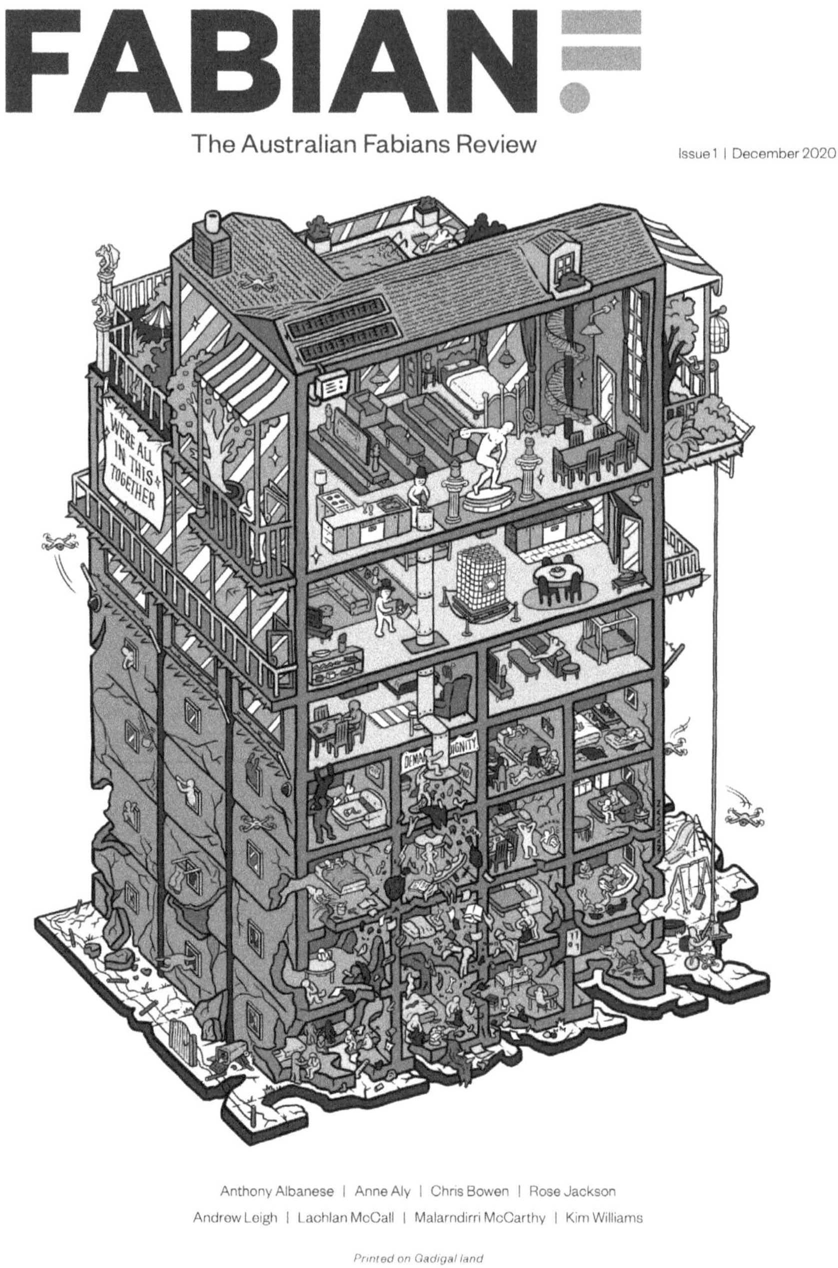

Fig. 7.4: Sam Wallman, "We're All in This Together, 2020," poster and front cover image for *Fabian: The Australian Fabians Review*, issue 1, December 2020.

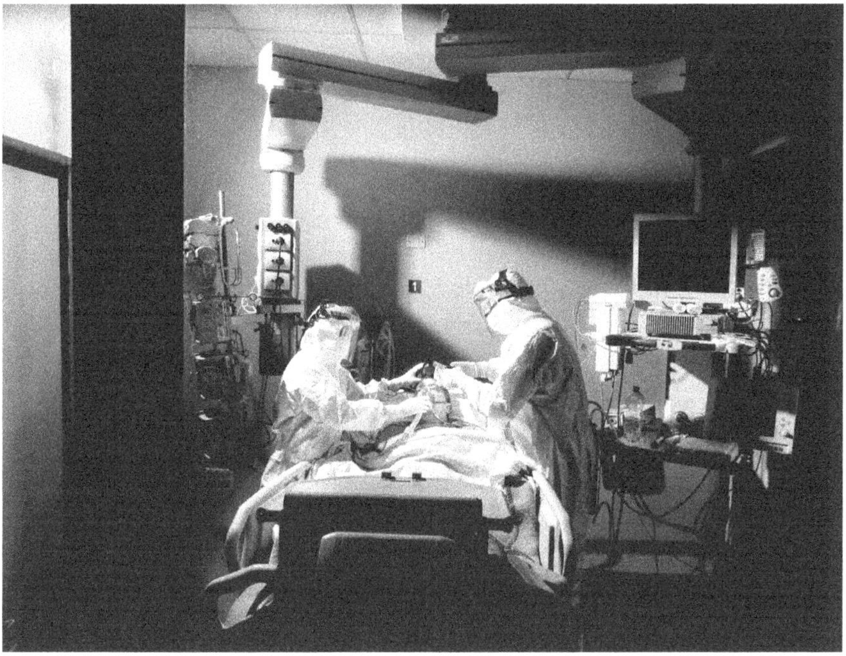

Fig. 7.5: Alex Majoli, The COVID-19 Visual Project, A Time of Distance, Scene #1112, Caltagirone, Gravina City Hospital, Italy, 2020. ©Alex Majoli/Magnum Photos.

second from all over the world. Among these images are photographs of street art murals that picture the virus, often by combining the spiky blob with an art icon, or both with a safety slogan.[21]

We will see in the following chapters that the pandemic is precipitating structural shifts in the contemporary image economy. If making (versions of) one's private life (quasi) public is the driving force of social media, the lockdowns and other public health restrictions necessary to control the pandemic have obliged the working lives of many to migrate to shared virtual platforms. So, too, with participation in public events. Isolated from each other at home (if we have that privilege), we communicate via images of each other and imagery of what we need to share. We spend more time than ever before with visual images of the lives of others. Information about the world comes to us primarily in ways shaped by its digital transmission. As we have seen in this chapter, picturing the pandemic has generated a fresh range of imagery, carried by inherited, recent, and new technologies. It is as yet unclear how transformatory of the iconomy, in parts or as a whole, these changes will prove to be. Meanwhile, some good questions are being asked, including this one: "Which (new) categories of ephemeral images and image stereotypes have emerged that allow for reflection on our pandemic reality, depict it, comment on it, or even co-determine it?"[22]

COVID Injustice and Justice

The unfolding of the pandemic shaped the other two constellations we will trace—the imagery of racial injustice and of Donald J. Trump—in quite specific ways. In the United States, African Americans became infected and died at disproportionate rates and were more impacted economically. George Floyd was one of those so infected and effected. Nancy Fraser makes the link explicit:

> By the time the protests erupted in May 2020, it was already clear that Americans of color, and Blacks in particular, were disproportionately contracting and dying from Covid. They got worse health care and had a higher rate of underlying conditions, linked to poverty and discrimination, and associated with bad Covid outcomes—asthma, obesity, stress, high blood pressure. They faced greater risks of exposure, thanks to frontline jobs that could not be performed remotely, and to crowded housing conditions. All this had been reported in the Media. And it resonated, lending new meaning to the phrase 'Black Lives Matter'.

She notes that since the founding of BLM in 2014

> [...] there's been a great deal of organizing, including consciousness-raising and reading groups, forming a new generation of militant anti-racist activists, especially young activists of color. That was the context, the atmosphere in which reports of the racialized impact of Covid were received and processed. On top of that came George Floyd's murder by the Minneapolis police, captured for all the world to see in that enraging and heartbreaking video. And so the fuse was lit.[23]

Roxane Gay explains the negative mutuality of the three clusters we have been following:

> Eventually, doctors will find a coronavirus vaccine, but black people will continue to wait, despite the futility of hope, for a cure for racism. We will live in the knowledge that a hashtag is not a vaccine for white supremacy. We live with the knowledge that, still, no one is coming to save us. The rest of the world yearns to get back to normal. For black people, normal is the very thing from which we yearn to be free.[24]

COVID confinement meant that, on a purely pragmatic level, the video of Floyd's murder was seen by more people, who paid it much closer attention, because they had more time to view a long video of the kind of occurrence that they would usually see, distractedly, flashing by in their constant information-flow. Likewise, the long periods of staying home meant that more people decided to get out onto the streets to support such a legitimate cause, one so great that it overrode their fear of infection: Thus, wear a mask while protesting against racial injustice. In mirror reversal, most followers of Donald Trump followed their leader in taking pride in not wearing a mask while demonstrating their support for him, his policies, and actions at his rallies and in their own marches and manifestations. They created a swirl of super-spreader events.

Salvation by Vaccination?

In September 2020, political scientist Adam Tooze posed a serious world question, the biggest one at the time: "The question is whether nation states, politicians, science, business, and the public at large can organize themselves in such a way as to deliver high-quality vaccine at affordable prices to all of the world's 7.8 billion inhabitants."[25] Cue images of medical scientists in laboratories, liquid being inserted into phials, machines dripping the vaccine into small purple, blue, white (Pfizer, Moderna, and Oxford Astra Zeneca), and red (Sputnik and Sinovac) capped cannisters as they speed by on conveyer belts, to be packed into boxes for freezing and then transported to hospitals, establishing shot of a hospital, a patient being calmly inoculated, the swab, the bandage, and the smiles all round. Voice over: The developed nations are prioritizing their citizens, despite the protestations of the World Health Organization, despite many of them (with the then unexceptional exception of the United States) having signed on to the COVAX initiative, which pools funds and information from 172 countries with the goal of providing "worldwide equitable access to safe and effective vaccines."[26]

Although nothing else seemed more urgent in December 2020 than containing the pandemic, a broader perspective was necessary then, as it is now. Tooze continued: "COVID-19 is bad. But it is not, after all, the proverbial 'big one'—other, far more lethal diseases are easily imaginable. We are certain to face more such global challenges, not just in public health but in climate policy as well [...] we must reckon with the blowback that will come from our comprehensive and destabilizing transformation of the natural environment [...] Seen in these terms, the race to develop a vaccine is a test run for the political economy of the future."[27] Exactly.

Lockdowns and several other extraordinary precautions, such as border closures, "flattened the curve" in several countries and contained the spread in a few, such as Aotearoa/New Zealand, Taiwan, Singapore, Vietnam, and Australia—for a time. Meanwhile in Russia, Turkey, and Britain, where, like the United States, national leadership prioritized economic growth over public safety, the situation remained out of control. If the virus itself spreads at every opportunity, as viruses do and have done so with such frequency in recent decades that we may have entered "an era of pandemics," human responses to it have been an equally characteristic mix of opportunism and obduracy.[28] Vaccines against the coronavirus were developed in record time. Developing equitable systems for their distribution, however, are unlikely to be established without major changes in the dispositions of power within and between the nations of the world. World government, anyone? Meanwhile, the virus mutates, using the unvaccinated to generate new variants that are less susceptible to existing vaccines. Delta is overwhelmed by Omicron. Omicron generates sub-variants. A minority opposed to vaccinations and to mandates of the governmental kind rage in protest.

A paradox has emerged as we have tracked the emergence and the unfolding of COVID imagery: SARS-CoV-19 is invisible to the naked human eye; its transmission between humans is invisible when asymptomatic but all too evident to the senses when it is not. In most societies worldwide, the pandemic's effects and efforts to combat them have become the main topic of public discourse, the primary preoccupation of citizens, and the main challenge to governments. COVID imagery became viral within iconomies everywhere (Fig. 7.6).

Throughout his term as the President, sensing that in some deep way the pandemic threatened the feel-good factor that he felt was essential to his political success, Donald Trump consistently downplayed the threat posed by the virus. During a visit to the Centers for Disease Control in Atlanta on March 6, 2020, he returned again and again to the low numbers of deaths relative to infections, compared to those impacted by influenza, and relative to other countries.[29] A photograph taken at a press conference held during his visit shows him among scientists, officials, and the state governor, wearing a KEEP AMERICA GREAT cap, and holding with evident discomfort a printout of images of the virus (Fig. 7.7) What had brought about a state of affairs in which the broadcast opinions of this man counted as much within the contest for world attention as did signs of the rapidly spreading ravages of the virus itself?

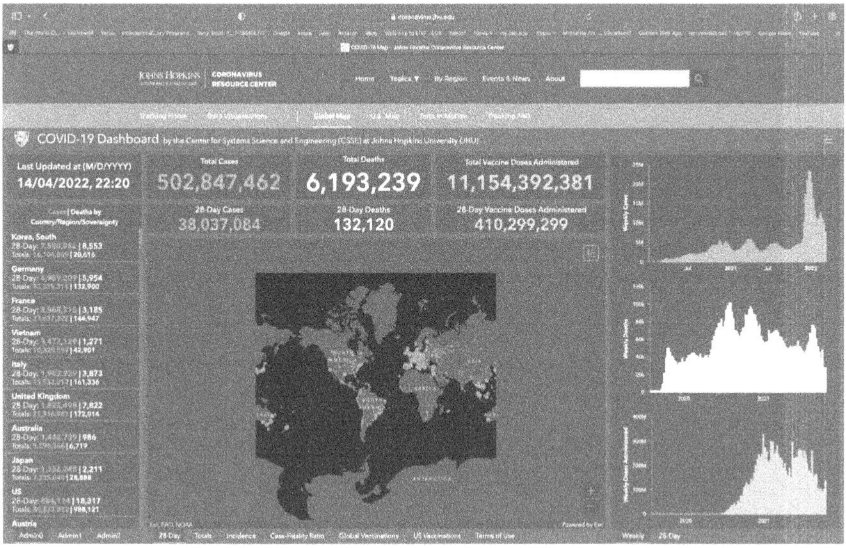

Fig. 7.6: Screenshot of Coronavirus Resource Center, Johns Hopkins University, "COVID Dashboard," April 14, 2022, at https://coronavirus.jhu.edu/map.html.

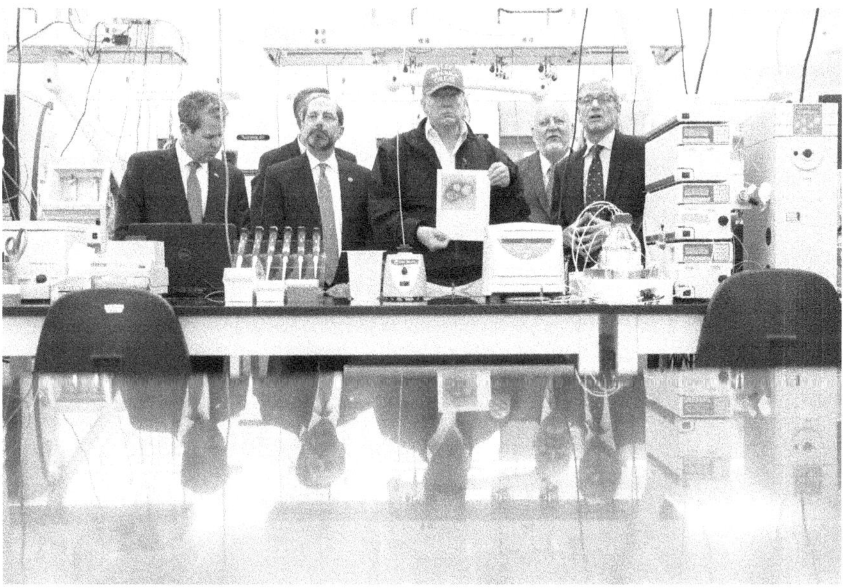

Fig. 7.7: President Donald J. Trump at the Centers for Disease Control Headquarters, Atlanta, GA, March 6, 2020. Alex Brandon/AP Photo.

Notes

1 Cited David Leser, "Trunk Call," *Sydney Morning Herald, Good Weekend*, 30 May 2020, 15.

2 See World Health Organization, "Timeline: WHO's COVID-19 Response," at https://www.who.int/emergencies/diseases/novel-coronavirus-2019/interactive-timeline#event-42. For a narrative of the early response to the virus in China, see Chris Buckley et al., "Behind the Curve: 25 Days That Changed the World: How COVID-19 Slipped China's Grasp," *New York Times*, December 30, 2020, at https://www.nytimes.com/2020/12/30/world/asia/china-coronavirus.html?action=click&module=Top%20Stories&pgtype=Homepage. For basic information on viruses such as SARS 1, MERS-CoV, and SARS-CoV-2, see, for example, Layal Liverpool, "Coronavirus," *New Scientist*, updated November 20, 2020, at https://www.newscientist.com/term/coronavirus/. For a vivid account of the impact of the disease in the United States, see Lawrence Wright, "The Plague Year," *The New Yorker*, January 4 & 11, 2021, posted December 28, 2020, at https://www.newyorker.com/magazine/2021/01/04/the-plague-year.

3 Cara Giaimo, "The Spiky Blob Seen around the World: How C.D.C. Medical Illustrators Created the Coronavirus Pandemic's Most Iconic Image," *New York Times*, April 1, 2020, https://www.nytimes.com/2020/04/01/health/coronavirus-illustration-cdc.html.

4 While the CDC image was designed to concentrate public attention around an enemy to be defeated, the imagery shared by scientists through the Protein Data Bank has similar visual parameters. See the RCSB website as of December 9, 2020, at https://www.rcsb.org/news?year=2020&article=5e74d55d2d410731e9944f52&feature=true. Without context, the image might read as a very poor attempt at a birthday cereal package for the visually impaired, or an equally tasteless rendering of the unconscious fear of red revolutions breaking out from the gray matter of ordinary life.

5 "Molecular Architecture of the SARS-CoV-2 Virus," *Cell*, vol. 183, issue 3 (October 29, 2020), at https://www.cell.com/cell/fulltext/S0092-8674(20)31159-4?rss=yes.

6 See Carl Zimmer, "The Coronavirus unveiled," *New York Times*, October 9, 2020, at https://www.nytimes.com/interactive/2020/health/coronavirus-unveiled.html?action=click&module=RelatedLinks&pgtype=Article. On the modern history of medical imaging, see Lorraine Daston and Peter Galison, *Objectivity* (New York: Princeton University Press, 2010).

7 Described in detail in Wright, "The Plague Year."

8 "Coronavirus: Amazon removes overpriced goods and fake cures," *BBC News*, February 28, 2020, at https://www.bbc.com/news/technology-51675183.

9 See World Health Organization, "Mythbusters," posted November 23, 2020, at https://www.who.int/emergencies/diseases/novel-coronavirus-2019/advice-for-public/myth-busters.

10 A good example of such a site is Australian Government, Department of Health, "COVID-19 coronavirus in pictures," *healthdirect*, at https://www.healthdirect.gov.au/coronavirus-covid-19-in-pictures.

11 Traced by Isaiah Bertagnolli, "Some Thoughts I Had While I Was on My Computer during Quarantine," Cultural Studies Common Seminar, University of Pittsburgh, Spring 2020, "What Is a World Question? Before and in COVID-19," https://www.culturalstudies.pitt.edu/sites/default/files/2a%20BERTAGNOLLI%20A%20COVID-19%20Diary.pdf.

12 See Nikhil Titus, "Tracing a Nation by Candlelight," Cultural Studies Common Seminar, University of Pittsburgh, Spring 2020, "What Is a World Question? Before and in COVID-19," https://www.culturalstudies.pitt.edu/sites/default/files/3.%20TITUS%20Tracing%20a%20Nationa%20by%20Candlelight.pdf.

13 The commentary by Giorgio Agamben and Sergio Benvenuto early in the pandemic, including Agamben's revised opinion, may be found at "Coronavirus and the Philosophers," *Journal of Psychoanalysis*, February and March 2020, at http://www.journal-psychoanalysis.eu/coronavirus-and-philosophers/. A richer set of reflections may be found at *Critical Inquiry*, "Posts from the Pandemic," at https://critinq.wordpress.com/. Helpful historical and analytical perspectives soon surfaced. See, for example, David Barnes, Merlin Chokwananyun, and Kavita Sivaramakrishnan, "Pandemic Syllabus," *Public Books*, July 13, 2020, at https://www.publicbooks.org/pandemic-syllabus/. See also Verso's Coronavirus pamphlet series: Grace Blakely, *The Corona Crash*; Andreas Malm, *Corona, Climate and Chronic Emergency*; Dean Spade, *Mutual Aid*; and *The Care Manifesto* by The Care Collective (all London: Verso, 2020).

14 See Martha Powell, Future Sciences Group, "What Role Can Media Play in Managing the COVID-19 Outbreak?," Infectious Diseases Hub, March 3, 2020, at https://www.id-hub.com/2020/03/05/role-can-media-play-managing-covid-19-outbreak/.

15 *Time Magazine*, "What to Do When the World Stops," March 19, 2020, at https://time.com/5804786/coronavirus-issue/.

16 See "#ICPConcerned: Global Images for the Global Crisis," March 2020 Ongoing, at https://icpconcerned.icp.org/.

17 The COVID-19 Visual Project, A Time of Distance, 2020-ongoing, at https://covid19visualproject.org/en/chapters.

18 Alex Majoli, "The Eye of the Storm," *Vanity Fair*, March 26, 2020, at https://www.vanityfair.com/news/2020/03/coronavirus-in-italy-scenes-from-the-eye-of-the-storm.

19 Yonas Tadesse, "On the Frontline against COVID in Ethiopia—A Photo Essay," *The Guardian*, posted September 7, 2020, at https://www.theguardian.com/world/2020/sep/07/on-the-frontline-against-covid-19-in-ethiopia-a-photo-essay.

20 *Vogue*, April 28, 2020, at https://www.vogue.com/article/photographers-artists-coping-quarantine.

21 See Sarah Cascone and Caroline Goldstein, "Street Artists around the World Are Spreading an Urgent Message: Stay Home," *Artnet*, March 30, 2020, at https://news.artnet.com/art-world/coronavirus-street-art-1814961.

22 See Steffen Haug and Ursula Ströbele, "Digital Realities: Political imagery and mediatized nature in times of COVID-19," Conference December 15–16, 2021, Zentralinstitut für Kunstgeschichte, Munich, CFP, at https://www.zikg.eu/aktuelles/veranstaltungen/2021/workshop-digital-realities/#Since.

23 Nancy Fraser, "American Interregnum," *New Left Review*, Sidecar, April 20, 2021, at https://newleftreview.org/sidecar/posts/american-interregnum?pc=1331.

24 Roxane Gay, "Remember, No One Is Coming to Save Us," *New York Times*, May 30, 2020, at https://www.nytimes.com/2020/05/30/opinion/sunday/trump-george-floyd-coronavirus.html.

25 Adam Tooze, "The World is Winning—and Losing—the Vaccine Race," *Foreign Policy*, September 19, 2020, at https://foreignpolicy.com/2020/09/19/the-world-is-losing-the-vaccine-race/.

26 World Health Organization, "172 Countries and Multiple Candidate Vaccines Engaged in COVID-19 Vaccine Global Access Facility," posted August 24, 2020, at https://www.who.int/news/item/24-08-2020-172-countries-and-multiple-candidate-vaccines-engaged-in-covid-19-vaccine-global-access-facility.

27 See Dipesh Chakrabarty, "The Era of Pandemics? What Is Global and What Is Planetary about COVID-19?," *Critical Inquiry*, In the Moment, posted October 16, 2020, at https://critinq.wordpress.com/2020/10/16/an-era-of-pandemics-what-is-global-and-what-is-planetary-about-covid-19/.

28 Tooze, "The World is Winning—and Losing—the Vaccine Race."

29 See Cameron Peters, "A Detailed Timeline of All the Ways Trump Failed to Response to the Coronavirus Crisis," *Vox*, posted June 28, 2020, at https://www.vox.com/2020/6/8/21242003/trump-failed-coronavirus-response.

Chapter 8

TRUMPMANIA

The descent of Donald J. Trump, accompanied by his wife Melania, down the escalator into the lobby of the Trump Tower in New York on June 16, 2015, to announce his candidacy for President of United States marks the beginning of what became—by its own outlandish gambit and, arguably, by any objective measure—the most visible icon, the biggest BRAND, and the most intensely debated, era-defining force in all media throughout the world in the five years that followed (Fig. 8.1). The moment when this extraordinary phenomenon began to shrink can be dated with equal precision. On November 5, two days after the 2020 Presidential election, as votes were being counted across the nation and the prospect that he might lose office became real, President Donald J. Trump gave a press conference in the White House briefing room that was timed to capture attention on the evening news broadcasts of the major TV networks (Fig. 8.2). As his misstatements, distortions, and outright lies about the election process mounted, and his accusations of fraud against his opponents grew strident, ABC, CBS, and NBC cut away to anchors who rebutted his claims, directly characterized them as lies, and went on to other news. MSNBC did so within one minute, and even at Fox News, his most committed media backers (to the extent of having become a de facto propaganda department during his Presidency), the White House correspondent noted that there was no evidence to back up the president's claims of electoral fraud.[1]

This moment had been prefigured on other media. *The Washington Post* had been running a fact-checker column devoted to Trump since the early days of his candidacy. In the month leading up to the election, the volume of false or misleading claims averaged by 50 a day, more than 20,000 in total since he began campaigning. On May 27, two days after George Floyd died, Twitter labelled as "unsubstantiated" a Trump tweet that Mail-In ballots to the upcoming election would be "substantially fraudulent." The company did the same for a few subsequent tweets that published false information about the pandemic and, by November 4, immediately after election day, joined the growing chorus of media tagging the President's statements about

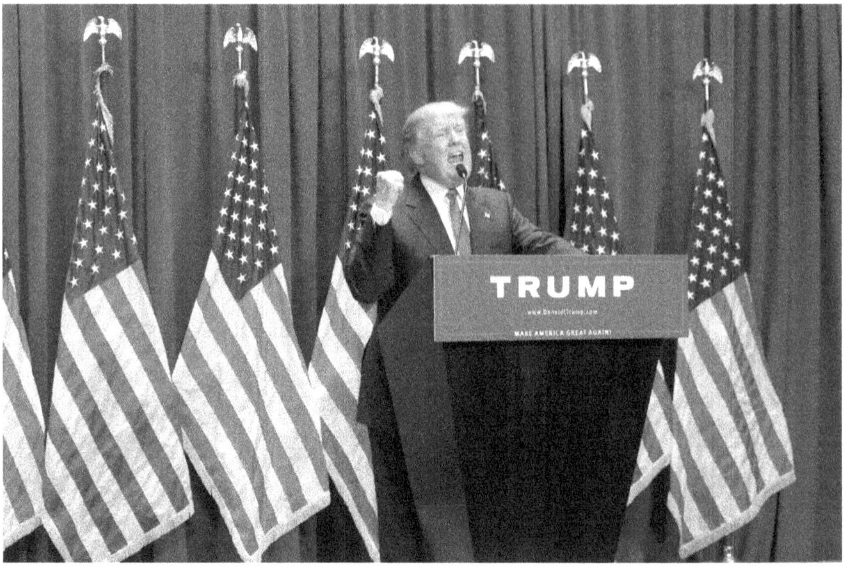

Fig. 8.1: Donald J. Trump announces his candidacy for President of United States, Trump Tower, New York, June 16, 2015. Photo: Brendan McDermid/Reuters.

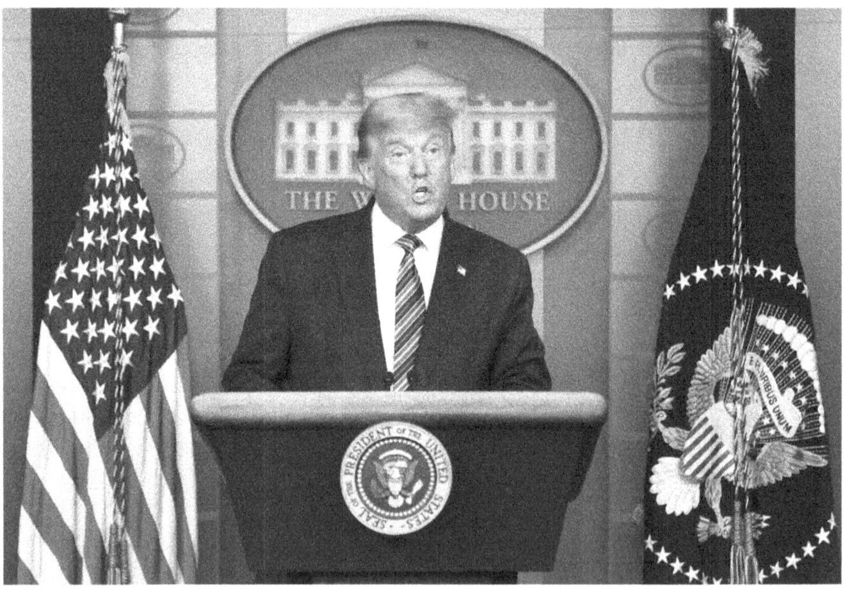

Fig. 8.2: President Donald J. Trump denies election loss, White House Briefing Room, Washington, DC, November 5, 2020. Photo: Brendan Smialowski/AFP/Getty Images.

the results as fraudulent themselves. Cartoonists around the world drew variations on the theme of a cry-baby deprived of his toys. CNN commentator Anderson Cooper used a more original, blimp-deflating image to sum up Trump's "sad and truly pathetic" performance:

> That is the most powerful person in the world, and we see him like an obese turtle on his back, flailing in the hot sun, realizing his time is coming. But he just hasn't accepted it, and he wants to take everybody down with him, including his country.[2]

The riotous invasion of the Capitol Building on January 6, 2021, was proof that, even on his way out, Trump had the power to precipitate at least one seemingly apocalyptical event of this kind. Was it a one-off Insurrection of the Idiots or a premature premonition of the Civil Wars to come?

For decades before his election as the president, Donald J. Trump had devoted much of his energy to establishing himself as a celebrity. He understood early on that his skills at self-promotion outshone those he had as a businessman and were indeed the basis on which he could grow his father's fortune. His most successful enterprises were those that capitalized on his name to leverage funds from others: family, friends, banks, investors, and, from 2016, followers and voters. Within real estate, the pinnacles were the Trump Towers and Hotels, eventually in several cities worldwide. Within entertainment media, from 2004 to 2015, he played a successful businessman in *The Apprentice*, a reality television series in which contestants competed for positions within Trump organizations. It is a staple of spectacle culture that celebrities are "famous for being famous." An assiduous publicity-seeker, always ready with an off-beat, "colourful" story, Trump's notoriety in conventional media expanded since he joined Twitter in 2009. Before announcing his presidential candidacy in 2015, he had issued over 22,000 tweets. After that, up to January 8, 2021, he posted over 34,000 more.[3] Like most other users, he used Twitter and Facebook to share information, announce events, retweet, or share posts he liked, and comment on media memes and cultural issues. He also, controversially, used these platforms to introduce policy changes, fire officials (up to and including the Secretary of State), praise and threaten foreign leaders, attack individuals with whom he disagreed, celebrate supporters, keep Republican politicians in check, comment on political events of all kinds, and, in a preponderance of messages, assess the nature of news coverage of his Presidency. On the day of his election defeat in November 2020, Donald Trump had 88.8 million followers on Twitter, 35 million on Facebook, and 24 million on Instagram. As for a traditional print medium such as books, in December 2020,

NPD Bookscan noted that during the previous four years, more than 1,200 unique titles about him had been published, compared to 500 on Obama's first administration.

The central figure in a geopolitical hegemon, US presidents naturally attract enormous attention, at home and abroad. But an analysis published in February 2017, one month after he took office, estimated that "it is likely that no living person has ever been as famous as Mr. Trump is right now. It's possible that not even the most famous or infamous people of the recent or distant past—say, Barack Obama, Osama bin Laden, Bill Clinton, Richard Nixon, Michael Jackson, Muhammad Ali, or Adolf Hitler—dominated media as thoroughly at their peak as Mr. Trump does now."[4] Such judgements are of course unmeasurable, but the impact of the Trump brand can be more exactly assessed. Data gathered by mediQuant, which measures worldwide coverage of a topic that is not paid advertising in all media, showed that in 2017, Trump's mentions not only outshone those of any other figure but those of all other famous figures combined. The sheer quantity of social media today, along with its proclivity toward self-amplification, exaggerates into enormous prominence stories that might otherwise trend then peter out. Trump's ability to manipulate this media, his thirst to constantly supply it with stories that precipitate cascades of others, and his instinct for stories that surprise and shock, that have irresistible news value and that feed algorithms disposed to emotive contestation, make him (and his media team) a key agent in this enterprise of promoting a self-promoting contagion.[5] The analyst concluded: "The new president doesn't simply dominate national and political news [...] He has taken up semipermanent residence in every outlet of any kind, political or not. He is no longer just the message. In many cases, he has become the medium, the ether though which all other stories flow."

A more exact analysis might insist that it was a heavily mediated constellation of Trumpian *imagery* that became both message and medium, a visual image regime in its own right. Its components, constantly repeated, were set out for all to see in his June 2015 announcement speech. In a blue suit, with white shirt and red tie, Trump stood (as Presidents commonly do) at a lectern, a panoply of folded US flags behind him, and presented himself above all as an anti-politician. At that point, he stood as an independent, not as the Republican that it suited him (and the GOP) to soon become. Attacking professional politicians as corrupted do-nothings, he promised to "clean up the [Washington] swamp." As an ardent economic nationalist, he railed against capitalist globalization and in favor of local manufacture, using the slogan "Make America Great Again." As a foreign policy isolationist, he opposed the network of international alliances established since World War II known as the Washington Consensus or "rules-based order," preferring transactional relationships that placed "America First." Acting out his television persona, he spent most of the speech sketching examples of how he would easily solve all the issues facing the country and the world by "the art of the deal," of which he was the supreme master. Likewise, there was nothing subliminal in his embodiment of white suprematism. Mexican immigrants were described as drug-dealing criminals and rapists. Every Obama initiative was trashed. Seven years into the presidency of an African American, Trump represented himself as the spokesperson of those who had had enough of the slide into multiculturalism, of those who feared that the rising demographic tide of otherness would soon engulf them. To these voters, Trump's primary qualification was that he was—as you can see at a glance—not Black.

Being White is, at its roots, the state of not being Black. In a blistering analysis of the place of race in the 2016 election, Ta-Nehisi Coates points out that

> Donald Trump arrived in the wake of something more potent [than earlier icons of blackness]—an entire nigger presidency with nigger health care, nigger climate accords, nigger justice reform that could be targeted for destruction, that could be targeted for redemption, thus reifying the idea of being white. Trump truly is something new—the first president whose entire political existence hinges on the fact of a black president. And so it will not suffice to say Trump is a white man like all the others who rose to become president. He must be called by his correct name and rightful honorific—America's first white president.[6]

In his inauguration speech on January 20, 2017, Trump presented himself as a Phoenix rising from an apocalyptical landscape of postindustrial ruin, the "American carnage" from which he vowed to raise up those who supported him. A few days later, adviser Steve Bannon spelt out the constituents of what became known as Trumpism in a speech to the Conservative Political Action Conference. There were five. America First exceptionalism: "we are a nation with a culture and a reason for being"; "national security and sovereignty" (the Wall on the US–Mexican border, and immigration bans); "economic nationalism" (withdrawal from trade partnerships, aggressively self-interested transactions within a world of competing interests and clashing civilizations); "deconstructing the administrative state" (rescind regulations, private enterprise actors to take main governmental roles); and fighting the "corporatist, globalist media," mouthpieces of the manipulative elites that have betrayed the American people.[7] This mixture did not amount to a policy platform: nor could it be, as the components are contradictory, pathways to impasse. Rather, Trump presented himself as the voice of a substantial constituency of voters—at the time unacknowledged by any political party—who were so disenchanted that they would abandon their party allegiances or their disengagement from voting in exchange for this one shot at fucking up "the system" that was fucking them over.

Such a reaction has not been unique to the United States. The recent resurgence of conservative values, reactionary attitudes, right-wing political movements, and religious fundamentalisms throughout the world is the result of factors that, in every instance, are resolutely local in cause, form, and effect. Each can claim its reason for being, each can rationalize its irrationality, and each can argue a coherent case for the priority of an idealized past over the chaos of the present. The Trump–Bannon package built on the radical evangelism that became prominent in the "culture wars" of the 1980s, on the polarizing tactics of Newt Gingrich as House Speaker in the 1990s, and on the fiscal conservatism pushed by the Tea Party since 2009, each of which expanded the base of committed Republican Party voters while at the same time narrowing their vision of democratic possibility. The shock doctrine, crony capitalism of the Bush–Cheney regime modelled the roughish authoritarianism that this base recognizes as the right kind of leadership. Rogues are no longer exceptional figures; rogue states are no longer aberrant. Sovereign nations of all kinds—various kinds of democratic state, one-party autocracies, family feudalisms, and dictatorships—are behaving more and more like rogue states; and leadership of them is increasingly falling into the hands of rogues.[8] Understood as vast social movements, and as warring sovereignties, these rogues and rogue states seem to be calling for a global Last Judgment as they fight to maintain conditions that, in effect, will guarantee the death of life on our planet. At the same time, and in the same gestures, these rouges fantasize that they, and those like them, will be exempt from a fate deserved by everyone else.

Notes

1 Maggie Haberman and Michael J. Grynbaum, "Trump Lies in the White House and Networks Pull the Plug," *New York Times*, November 5, 2020, livetracker.

2 See SkyNews, November 5, 2020, posted to YouTube at https://www.youtube.com/watch?v=nQUGuQogGEg.

3 Sarah Lyall, "A Hundred Days without Trump on Twitter: A Nation Scrolls More Calmly," *New York Times*, April 17, 2021, at https://www.nytimes.com/2021/04/17/us/politics/trump-twitter.html. Trump's 56, 571 tweets are archived at https://www.thetrumparchive.com.

4 Farhad Manjoo, "No Relief as Media Obsesses on Trump," *New York Times*, February 23, 2017, B1, at https://www.nytimes.com/2017/02/22/technology/trump-news-media-ignore.html.

5 For a detailed analysis of contagions of many kinds—pandemics, economic, social, and political—see Adam Kucharski, *The Rules of Contagion* (London: Profile Books, 2000).

6 Ta-Nehisi Coates, "Epilogue," *We Were Eight Years in Power, An American Tragedy* (New York: One World, 2018), 344.

7 See https://www.nytimes.com/2017/02/24/us/politics/stephen-bannon-cpac-speech.html.

8 See Noam Chomsky, *Rogue States: The Rule of Force in World Affairs* (London: Pluto Press, 2000); Jacques Derrida, *Rogues: Two Essays on Reason* (Stanford: Stanford University Press, 2005).

Chapter 9

INCIDENT AT POWDERHORN, MAY 25, 2020

Is Darnella Frazier's cellphone video of the murder of George Floyd by a White police officer on a street in Powderhorn, Minneapolis, on the evening of May 25, 2020, just another among countless visual images of such arbitrary killings of Black men, and of some Black women—such as Breonna Taylor, to say her name—that today regularly circulate through social media, mass media, and collective memory?[1] Seasoned observers intone that such images at first attract intense emotional reactions of varying sorts, and, from those moved to grief and anger, especially those close to the deceased and those from the locality, deeply felt declarations of eternal remembrance. Then, like points of light in a galaxy, or, perhaps more accurately, graves in an infinite cemetery, they disappear into what might be called the national palace of social amnesia—or, if they had international currency, into the no-place of world forgetting (Fig. 9.1).

Videodeath Comes to Powderhorn

The videodeath of George Floyd may be different. As it went viral, it shocked even those numbed by the normalities of structural violence. Within hours, protests erupted in Minneapolis. Within days, they had spread to cities across the United States. In less than a week, in cities, suburbs, and country towns around the world, people marched against this murder, against racial repression in the United States, and, increasingly, against racism and other forms of unfreedom in their own communities. In cities and country towns throughout Australia, for example, thousands marched to protest this killing, the killing of Blacks in the United States, and the national shame of Indigenous deaths in custody. The incarceration rate for Indigenous Australians is over 10 times that of non-Indigenous Australians.[2] Between 1987 and 1991, an extensive Royal Commission into Aboriginal deaths was held and made several recommendations to alleviate an already dire situation. Since then, 470 have died, among whom 40% did not receive the medical care required.[3] No police or corrections officers have been convicted of any wrongdoing.

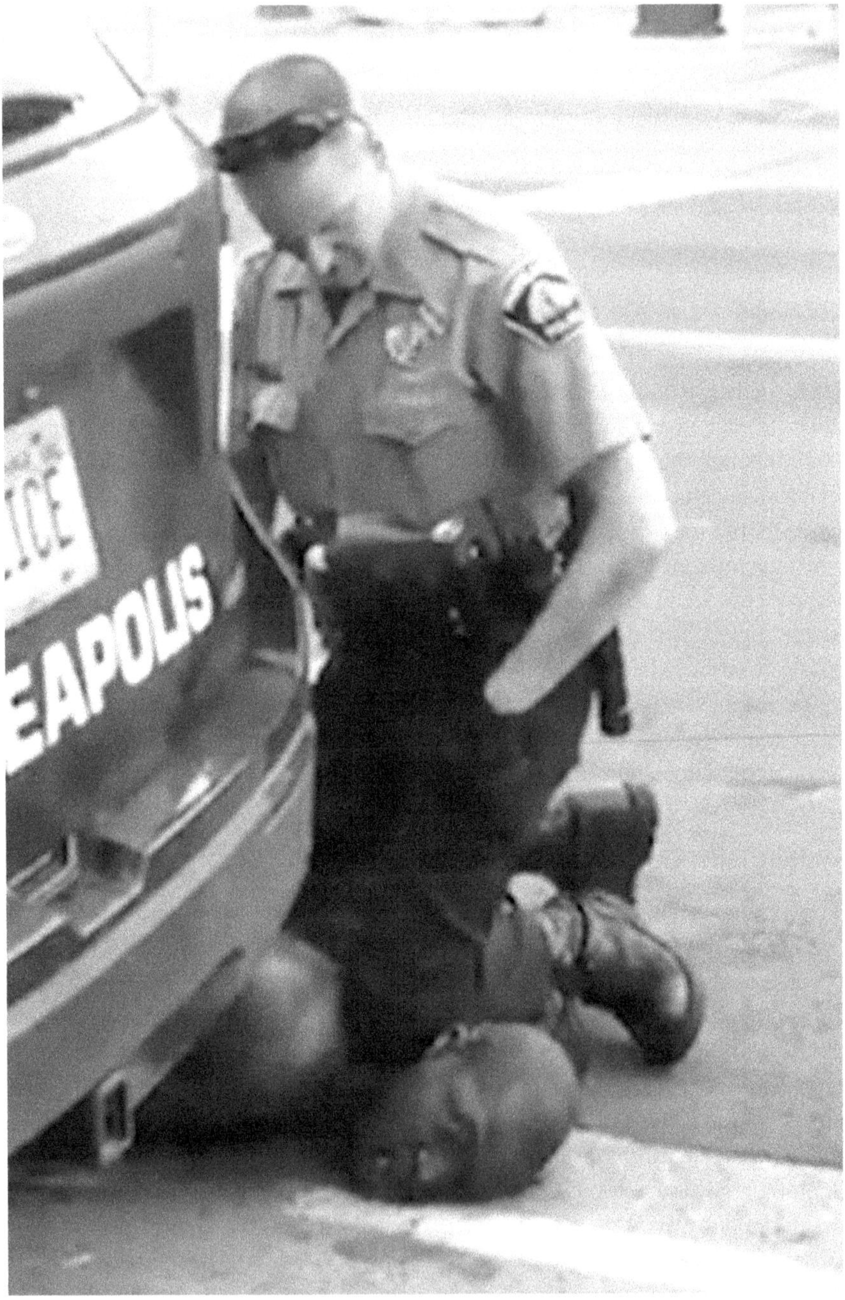

Fig. 9.1: Darnella Frazier, still from cellphone video of police officer Derek Chauvin with his knee on the neck of George Floyd, Powderhorn, Minneapolis, May 25, 2020.

While shooting, beating, or choking is the most common kind of police violence leading to death in the United States, in Australia, a culture in which guns are largely absent, "allowing to die" is a frequent cause: omission, inattention, and the refusal of care. When we view the video of Floyd's death, we see this "allowing" occurring as we watch, above all in the contrast between the voices of bystanders, including a nurse, calling for the release of pressure on Floyd's neck and officer Chauvin's studied indifference to the consequences of what he is doing. The video shook the edifices of not-wanting-to know. It roused righteous anger at what it seemed to show: that the naked face of systemic coercion, when exposed, could not care less, because it had become entirely confident of its own immunity from punishment, and from the effects of your impotent rage.

This murder of *this* person, made public in *this* way, seems to have sparked a fire already fully primed to ignite. The fragile social fabric of whole cities, of nations, was put at stake. The already existing world (dis)order became even more chaotic, which in turn inspired fresh modes of both repression and communality, with much confusion in between. In Portland, Oregon, angry protesters demonstrated each evening around the Federal Courthouse for much of the rest of the year. President Trump, a self-styled warrior who nonetheless retreats from foreign wars, followed the postcolonial playbook of bringing the war back home, and sent in federal troops. In response, the crowds continued to grow and their protests became ever more inventive, as they swiftly took back their city, often with the full support of local leaders. The threat of COVID-19 notwithstanding, they kept on protesting. With some rough justice, and against many provocations, it seems that some lower levels of governance within the United States at least were finding their ways to sovereignty.

Why did this particular video have such an impact? Some reasons are formal, inherent in the video itself. One is its length, 8 minutes and 46 seconds as posted. So much more sustained than a single photographic image. So slow, so steady, so not look away, especially when compared to the images flashing by one's usual screen scroll. Another reason is its unequivocal presentation of its content. A single, point-of-view shot is maintained for the duration. No technical lapses, visual blurs, digressions, external interruptions, or obstructions (despite officer Thao's attempts to stand in the way). A prone Black man's head is visible in front of a car wheel, twisting under the knee of a middle-aged White officer, who kneels the weight of his body on the man's neck. The man's voice, pleading for his life, can be heard clearly. Until it stops. As does, we soon see, his breathing. His eyes close. He ceases to move. Commentary from bystanders is continuous and consistent; voices criticize the officers and plead for the victim. The officer maintains his studied indifference, until paramedics ask him to move, so they can collect the body. He gets up, they haul it away.

Nothing to see here, their attitudes say. The video says otherwise: much to see here, too much for things to stay as they are.

The address is direct, personal. We, all of us, along with all of our differences, constantly look at videos on our cellphones, on laptops, and on television monitors aimed at us. They typically address us as a friend, a family member, an audience member, or a citizen, but mostly as a consumer. However affective the imagery is, we are physically distant and categorically distanced. Yet here, what we are seeing could happen to any of us. Any of us? Possibly. But there is no doubt that the violence depicted in the video will mostly, overwhelmingly, and constantly be visited upon those who are black. No Black person in America, no one victimized in other places where colonialism still reigns (which is most places), needs to be reminded of this. Extreme violence was the root economy of slavery, of modern subjection, and contemporary incarceration. Making this violence widely known through ostentatious public display was, and remains, essential to its effectiveness.

"Can you be black and look at this without fear?" In her 1986 work *Accused/Blowtorch/Padlock*, artist Pat Ward Williams wrote this sentence among many other despairing questions on the tar paper surrounding a sequence of photographs of a young Black man who had been lynched, blowtorched, and chained to a tree.[4] Such trauma has a long history, and it is not diminishing. Throughout the country, young Black men leave home every day wondering whether they will return unharmed or return at all. Based on long experience, their parents already know this fear. It finds eloquent expression in Ta-Nehisi Coates' letter to his adolescent son, *Between the World and Me*.[5] The killing of George Floyd, and the manner of it, sent the same, routine warning to African Americans: we who control things are watching you, and are ready to use force, including lethal force, if you step out of line. On a larger, national scale, it reminds Black viewers that, despite Barack Obama's eight years in power, despite *Black is King: Beyoncé*, Wakanda remains a long way off.

Fearful, angry, and resolute, Black looking has priority here. I cannot be its ventriloquist, although I will cite many of its authentic voices in the chapters to follow, including several commentaries on the George Floyd video. Allyship prompts a secondary question. How can you be White, brown, Asian, and look at this—without horror, disgust, anger, and, yes, eventually, fear? Doubtless, many could look at the video, or a few seconds of it, wonder what this guy had done to deserve police attention, then pass through a momentary regret at his accidental or "collateral damage" death before turning their attention to the next thing. Yet, many other White viewers, those whom the police, themselves predominantly White in most cities in the United States, are sworn to "serve and protect," suddenly see the unadorned truth about what the police do—it seems routinely, without a qualm—in order to serve and protect *us.*

(Now I am a ventriloquist of those *like me*.) Having the luxury of systematically forgetting the previous occasions on which we were shocked, we are shocked, again. But this time, for reasons we cannot immediately understand, this time, *this is too much*. Do we want to be served and protected *like this*?

More accurately, we *no longer* want this to be the price of our status quo. No longer? What has changed since Reconstruction, when White Americans, through some legal institutions (first the Democratic Party and more recently the Republican Party) and several illegal ones (the Klu Klux Klan), systematically, violently, undermined Black gains against the legacies of slavery? The Civil War goes on. In the image world, one of its battles is around the question of how to deal with the monuments to the Confederacy that populate several Southern cities, and with statues across the nation (and the world) that celebrate slave holders, from the most unrepentant (Andrew Jackson) to the occasionally ambiguous (Thomas Jefferson). As I write, many of these monuments are being removed—to museums, storage, or to the garbage—in Britain, the United States, and elsewhere.[6] Others are being repurposed (Fig. 9.2).

There is more at stake here. Slowly, as White viewers watch, another realization dawns. What if these police were to turn against (some of) us? What if they were to apply such methods—the constant patrolling, the stop

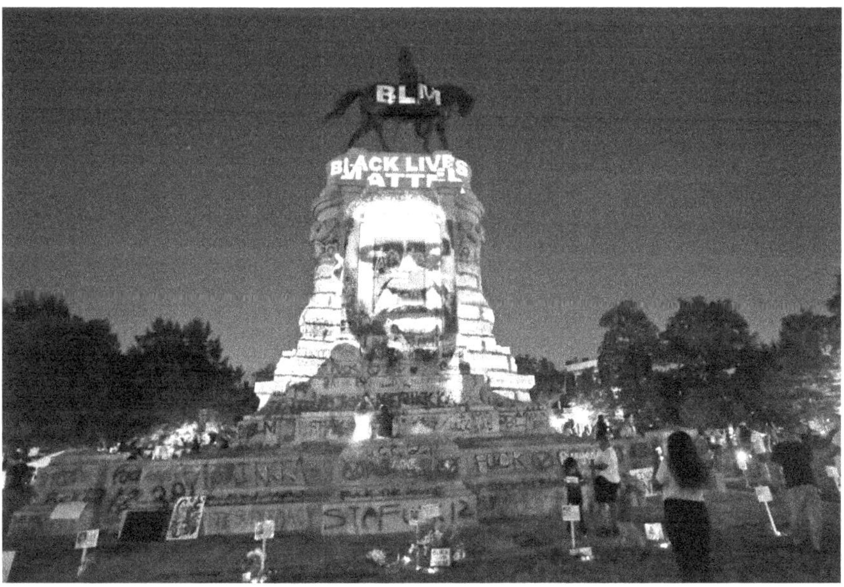

Fig. 9.2: Projection of BLM and Floyd imagery on Robert E. Lee statue, Richmond, Virginia, June 8, 2020. Steve Helber/AP Photo.

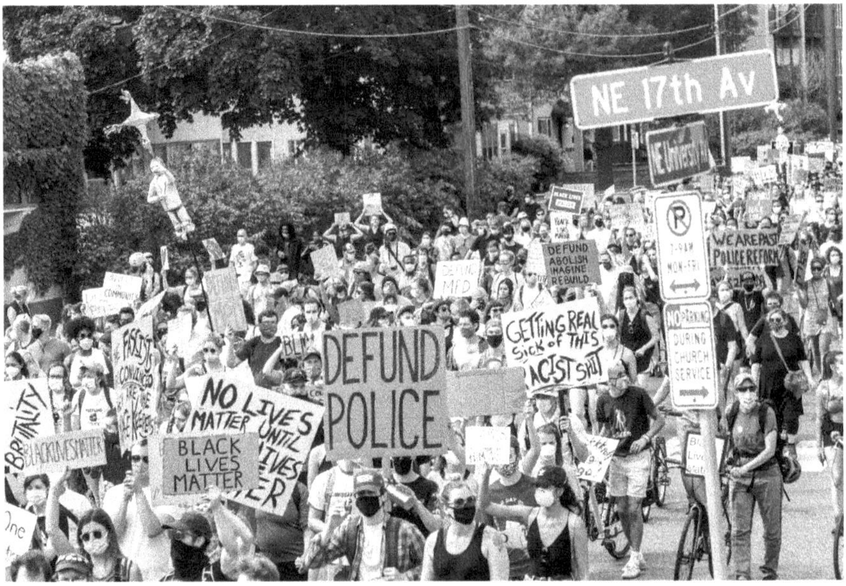

Fig. 9.3: Demonstrators march against racism and police brutality and to defund the Minneapolis Police Department on June 6, 2020 in Minneapolis, Minnesota, June 6, 2020. Photo: Kerem Yucel/AFP via Getty Images.

and searching, the quasi-military tactics, the arbitrary arrests, the demeaning ill-treatment when incarcerated, and, my God, the death-dealing—*to me*?

In the summer of 2020, support for Black Lives Matter in national opinion polls topped 50%, way above comparable figures for the mid-1960s, when Civil Rights for African Americans were signed into law. White involvement in protest and support for change toward racial justice is unprecedented. It is estimated that during the 700 anti-racism protests in the Spring of 1963, 15,000 people were arrested, many of them White. As 2020 unfolded, there were over 7,000 demonstrations in over 2,400 locations in the United States alone, involving an estimated 20 million people (Fig. 9.3). Most of these events, in their composition and behavior (over 90% peaceful), enacted the racial equity for which they are calling.[7] White allyship, however, is not only a matter of numbers on the streets, although it is importantly that. It is also a process of learning to cease to presume priority, of learning what it is to have one's concerns considered secondary.

Implicated Bystanders

The video of the murder of George Floyd was not made with the intention to communicate all, or even some, of these meanings. It is not a crafted representation. A 17-year-old schoolgirl happened to be there, on this ordinary street, outside this café, so she decided to film what was occurring in front of her, as you do. Among a small crowd, some of whom some had the courage to call out what was happening, she had the courage/fearfulness/shock lock to keep on filming. And to post to Facebook, as you also do. Videos on the platform receive on average 8 billion views each day. About 350 million photographs are uploaded each day—4,000 each second—by some among its 2.5 billion active users.[8] Yet no one, these days, is an innocent bystander, nor should we expect them to be. Floyd was murdered in the half hour following 8:00 pm that day. At 1:46 am the next morning, Frazier posted her video with the caption "They killed him right in front of cup foods over south on eighteenth and Chicago!! No type of sympathy </3 </3 # POLICE BRUTALITY." The Minneapolis Police Department website posted a notice entitled "Man Dies After Medical Incident During Police Interaction," with a short description which stressed that Floyd resisted arrest and stated that he died in hospital. To which Frazier responded at 3:10 am: "Medical Incident??? Watch outtt they killed him and the proof is clearlyyyy there!!"

Notes

1 Darnella Frazier's video, https://www.tmz.com/2020/05/29/george-floyd-killing-death-new-video-three-police-officers-derek-chauvin/.

2 For the June quarter of 2020, the total of imprisoned Aboriginal and Torres Strait Islanders was 2,325 persons per 100,000 compared to the national average of 201 persons per 100,000 adult population. See "Corrective Services, Australia," Australian Bureau of Statistics, posted September 17, 2020, at https://www.abs.gov.au/statistics/people/crime-and-justice/corrective-services-australia/latest-release.

3 See Human Rights Watch, "Australia: Act on Aboriginal Deaths in Custody," posted April 21, 2021, at https://www.hrw.org/news/2021/04/14/australia-act-indigenous-deaths-custody.

4 In the collection of the Whitney Museum of American Art, New York, see https://whitney.org/collection/works/8401.

5 Ta-Nehisi Coates, *Between the World and Me* (New York: Spiegel and Grau, 2015). And, from a mother's point of view in Elizabeth Alexander, "The Trayvon Generation," *The New Yorker*, June 22, 2020, at https://www.newyorker.com/magazine/2020/06/22/the-trayvon-generation.

6 Kirk Savage, "No Time, No Place: The Existential Crisis of the Public Monument," *Future Anterior*, special issue, *Ex-Situ: On Moving Monuments*, Winter 2019, 146–154. On the inventive, counter-monumental elaborations of official icons, see Ezra Marcus, "Will the Last Confederate Monument Still Standing Turn Off the Lights?" *New York Times*, June 23, 2020, Updated July 2, 2020, at https://www.nytimes.com/2020/06/23/style/statue-richmond-lee.html.

7 Peniel E. Joseph, Director of the Center for Race and Democracy, University of Texas, Austin, on *PBS Newshour*, October 28, 2020, at https://www.pbs.org/newshour/show/what-is-unprecedented-about-this-years-racial-justice-protests.

8 Usage measured by Omnicore on April 20, 2020, at https://www.omnicoreagency.com/facebook-statistics/.

Chapter 10

VIDEODEATH 1991 AND 2020: KING VS FLOYD

The video of George Floyd's murder entered an image-driven economy, one that is much larger and more complex than the image blizzard carried on Facebook, Instagram, WeChat, and similar platforms. While it was posted to YouTube, it quickly went viral on the other platforms and then was amplified by heritage media such as television and newspapers, in the United States and then quickly around the world. It soon proved to be the most impactful recent posting in a growing stream of such visual records, the grim inheritance of centuries of law enforcement exercised through excessive brutality. In the United States, the precedent that comes most readily to mind is the video of the beating of Rodney King by several officers from the Los Angeles police department in 1991 (Fig. 10.1). There are extraordinary parallels but also several significant differences between the two videos, the events they register, and the conditions of their reception. What might a comparison tell us about how the iconomy works, nearly 30 years later, in a society—indeed, a world—engaged in all-out image wars and mired in seas of misinformation and disinformation?

In the immediate and near aftermath of its making, the video of the beating of Rodney King had different valences in three related but, at the time, quite distinct contexts: on local and national media, above all on broadcast television, both free-to-air and cable; in the legal system, specifically a court in Simi Valley, in Ventura County, outside Los Angeles; and in an art museum, the Whitney Museum of American Art, New York, during its Biennial of 1993.[1] Today, by contrast, the George Floyd murder video counts in a media environment in which television is divided between several formats from free-to-air through cable to mobile phones and is just one among several other platforms, with multiple crossovers between them. Personal social media platforms predominate. Any image, any video clip, and every kind of information can be conveyed through them, with few constraints, although calls to impose some limits are growing louder as cultural and political divides widen in most societies.

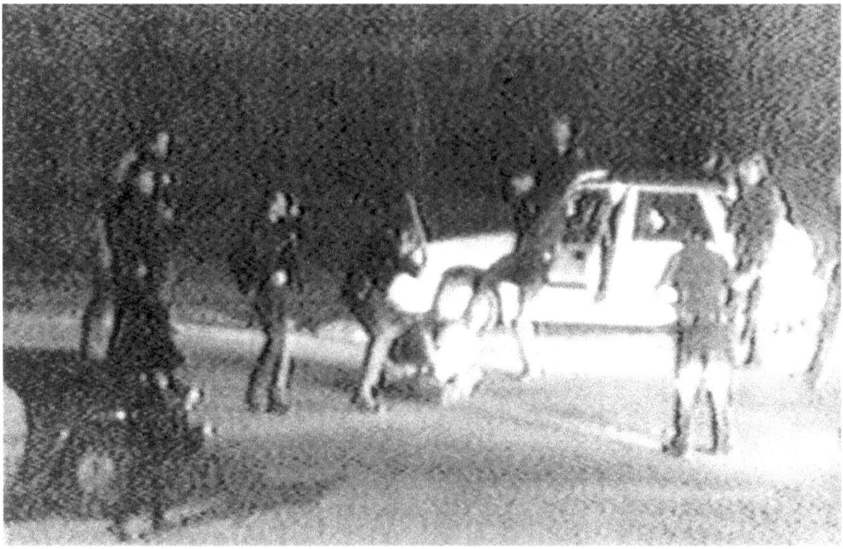

Fig. 10.1: George Holliday, Beating of Rodney King, Los Angeles, March 3, 1991, still from videocam recording.

After the video of Floyd's death was posted, the courts in Minnesota quickly came into play as prosecutors prepared criminal charges against the officers, all of whom were immediately dismissed from their jobs. Unlike the 1990s, however, there is no longer even a fragile consensus that the courts are the final arbiters of truth or dispensers of justice in such situations. Few are waiting on them to "provide closure." Protests against the wonton sacrifice of Black lives erupted straight away and spread worldwide. Unlike George Halliday's video of the beating of Rodney King, Darnella Frazier's video has not, to my knowledge, been shown in an art museum as an artwork, but many artists have responded to the murder and the events it has precipitated, and their work is beginning to appear in such places. We can also anticipate that her video and many other similar ones will be appropriated for artistic purposes, as such imagery has been for decades. In general, we can say that each of these contexts—mass media, the court system, and the artworld—has changed since the 1990s, and that many others have come into play. Visual imagery signifies differently now than it did then, even when similar content is being conveyed in a similar medium in what might seem closely similar situations. What, more exactly, are those differences? In this chapter, I will explore the differences as they manifest themselves in the courts and in public media.

The Specters of Simi Valley

The eventual re-signification of the video of the beating of Rodney King, during which its face value was transformed into an entirely opposite meaning, is a warning to those of us whose viewing of the death of George Floyd shocked us back into belief in the capacity of a visual image to be real. Film of King's beating was the product of chance and coincidence: On the evening of March 3, 1991, amateur videographer George Holliday had set up a Sony Handycam 8 mm video camera on his balcony to record the Los Angeles Marathon the next day; the beating happened to occur on the street below that same evening. Having been woken at 1:00 am by the sound of a police helicopter that was spotlighting the scene, Holliday found himself witnessing the culmination of a car chase. He began filming, zooming in from 90 ft away, after the initial violent arrest of two other people in King's car, but in time to capture the attacks on King. The video, which runs for 81 seconds, shows King, who had already been hit by two taser shots, receiving more than 50 blows and kicks, administered by four officers while no less than 15 others watch on.

While images of police brutality were hardly exceptional—in Los Angeles, they had sparked the Watts Riots in 1965—the camcorder was cheap, quick, and easy-to-use. Like cell phone videos today, it permitted amateurs to generate professional-looking results. Unlike cell phones today, however, they were rare. Film taken by body cams worn by police, now a widespread but by no means universal practice, was unknown in 1991. Prior to the ubiquity of the Internet, dissemination of footage depended on a public broadcaster. After the LAPD and CNN ignored Holliday's offer of the video, it was taken up by local TV station KTLA and aired the next day. The grainy black and white footage struck most who saw it as an unequivocal record of excessive use of force by the police involved, whatever the prior provocation might have been. It sparked local and national outrage at the brutality it depicted. Its widespread dissemination ensured that the officers would be prosecuted and that a trial would occur, neither of which were common in such situations at the time.[2]

Infamously, the apparent self-evidence of the video, on which the prosecution relied almost entirely, evaporated inside the courtroom when the officers were tried. To some degree, this was a result of moving the trial from Los Angeles, where the incident occurred and the jury might be expected to include at least some Black members, to Simi Valley, in Ventura County, where a jury was formed consisting of 10 White and no Black jurors. More determinative, perhaps, was that the video ran headlong into the convention that images of whatever kind could only count as "illustrative evidence," that is, were admissible only after being verified and interpreted by an expert witness.[3]

At the Simi Valley court, the expert witness was a police officer experienced in the interpretation of visual evidence. He and the defense attorneys showed selected clips, arbitrarily froze other sections, then projected sections of the video at varying speeds, often so slowly or abruptly that its actors became unreal figments. The narrative flow was broken into ambiguous fragments, then reconstituted into another story, driven by the threat posed by King to the white officers. Stilled images were characterized as showing King behaving in a "bear-like," "aggressive," and "combative" manner, as if possessed by a performance-enhancing drug (PCP). The evidentiary value of the tape itself was degraded by an artful but entirely legal disaggregation. As Louis-George Schwartz notes, this "effectively created a visual context which rendered the reality of what the police had done to King invisible."[4] Crucially, the defense lawyers argued that the televised versions omitted, on that basis that the imagery was too blurred, the first 13 seconds at the beginning of the tape. They argued that the first three seconds showed King stepping toward the officers with threatening intent, thus justifying their violent response thereafter as legitimate self-defense.[5] As I read it, it shows King attempting to flee past them, then him being beaten, relentlessly, as several senior officers looked on, approvingly. But many others, perhaps many millions of others, including the police officers involved and the jurors, saw what appeared before their eyes very differently.

Writing soon after, Judith Butler offered an incisive analysis, saying that to the jurors, the video was not about

> [...] simple seeing, an act of direct perception, but the racial reproduction of the visible, the working of racial constraints on what it means to 'see' [...] The attorneys [for the defense] proceeded through cultivating an identification with white paranoia in which the white community is always and only protected by the police, against a threat which Rodney King's body emblematizes, quite apart from any action that it can be said to perform or appears ready to perform. This is an action that the black male body is always already performing within that white racist imaginary, has always already performed prior to the emergence of any video. The identification with police paranoia culled, produced and consolidated in that jury is one way of reconstituting a white racist imaginary that postures *as if* it were the unmarked frame of the visible field, laying a claim to the authority of 'direct perception.'[6]

In Frazier's video of George Floyd dying, we do not see his body. The car obscures it. We do not see the other officers holding him down. We see only his head, his face, hear his voice. It is hard to assimilate what we do see to the format of a combat between equals, the (fictive) presumption that underlays any clash between two beings. It is hard to see the inherent violence in *this* unseen Black body, the criminality that he has always already performed, and that justifies that he be preemptively restrained whenever he appears in public, with whatever violence necessary, up to and including his death. What is literally shown can, to a degree and for a time, constrain what predisposition insists on seeing.[7] Yet, as will become evident when we discuss a *Fox News* analysis of footage from the video cams of the other officers involved, the specters animated by racism remain at the forefront of White consciousness in the United States. They are the specters of racial blindness, unconstrained.

Sounding the Image, Testifying

Framing, witnessing, and testifying. As we watch Frazier's video—transfixed yet resistant, our dread mounting even as we already know the outcome, our discomfort that we are watching someone dying turning into horror, sadness, and then into anger as we sense that we are witnessing a murder—the plain, simple power of what we are seeing drowns out most sound. There are some streets noises, there are Floyd's desperate pleas, there are the appeals from the few spectators to stop and the officers' orders to stay back. There are, of course, the voices in our own heads as we watch, each trying to fix some words, a name, and a descriptor, to what we are seeing. There is no voice over on the video, no overt discursive framing, and no one giving us their authoritative interpretation of what is going on. Yet, already framed is how all of us, Darnella Frazier excepted, would first encounter the video. In full on YouTube, as a portion, or a still, on our phones or screens or in print, in each case, it is quite literally framed by captions or by verbal description and commentary. The image, or imagery, never stands alone—although the particular force of this particular video is that its length does take those who view it, in silence, for its duration, as close as we are likely to get these days to such a state (I take to "stand alone" to mean that it stands, vis-à-vis us, as one other being in the world who stands always at once alone and with other separated yet inseparable beings).

"Can you be BLACK and look at this?"[8] For many viewers, especially Black viewers, silent experience of such a video is impossible: It already echoes with the sounds of sirens, flashing lights, the shouts, the urgent orders, the thuds of blows upon a body, the screams, and gunshots—remainders of several similar videos of thousands of all-too-familiar occurrences—every sound not just heard but felt, viscerally, on and in the witness's own body. Fred Moten reminds us of the other major moment in this recurrent narrative: the sounds of mourning the dead Black body, crying, keening, prayerful entreaty, wailing but mostly moaning, dying alongside the already dead, offering to die in their place, and hoping for resurrection. In the section of an essay on "Visible Music" entitled "Black Mo'nin' in the Sound of the Photograph," he discusses what he hears when he looks at the images of Emmett Till, laying in his casket at a funeral home in Chicago in 1955, his young face grotesquely disfigured by those who murdered him for allegedly whistling at a white woman.[9] *Jet* magazine ran several stories about Till, in one, the caption of close-up of the boy's face read: "Mutilated face of victim was left untouched by the mortician at the mother's request. She said she wanted 'all the world' to witness the atrocity."[10]

I will not reproduce this image, as I have noticed that most texts on these matters written by Black authors do not do so. I will follow their lead in showing only an image of Till's mother, Mamie Till Bradley, at the funeral where she insisted that her son's mutilated head be left exposed in the open coffin (Fig. 10.2). The event attracted 40,000 mourners. Images of it, such

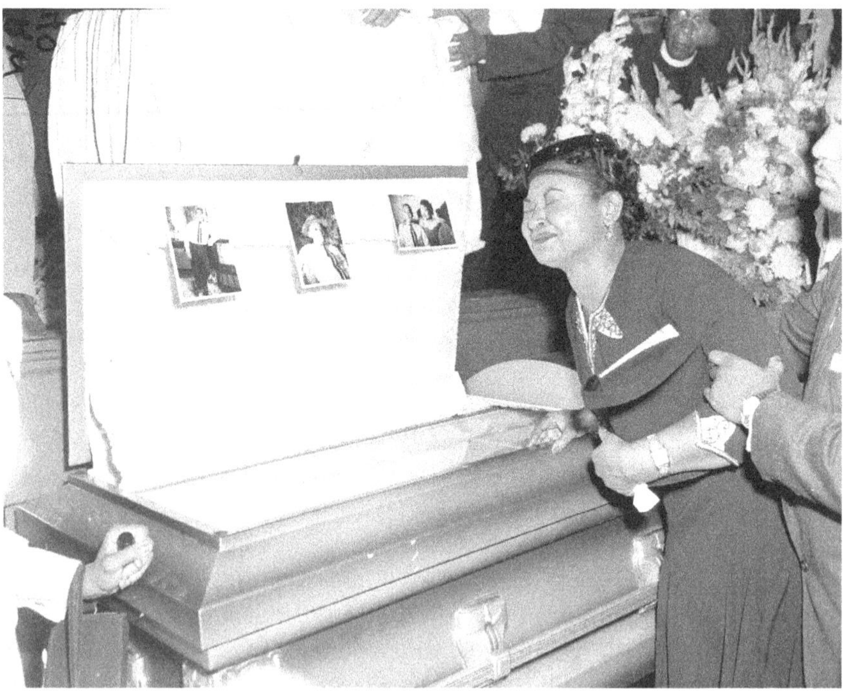

Fig. 10.2: Mamie Till Bradley at the funeral of her son Emmett Till, Roberts Temple Church of God in Christ, Chicago, September 3, 1955.

as this one, circulated widely. Moten underscores her agency in restaging of her son's death as a political act aimed against the closing-down that she knew was coming and was expressed in the acquittal of the murderers:

> How can this photograph challenge ontological questioning? *By way of a sound* and by way of what's already there in the decision to display the body, to publish the photograph, to restage death and rehearse mo(ur)nin(g). This includes a political imperative that is never far from an aesthetic one [...][11]

Mamie Bradley's action is widely credited with helping spark the Civil Rights movement that culminated in the following decade. She was herself a civil rights activist for the subsequent 40 years.

The hegemony that she was fighting against in 1955 swung into action again in 1991, as it does every time such images surface, including right now. It exercises its effort to determine what counts as truth through the seemingly "natural" fact that we encounter images, most of the time, as they are spoken about, usually in a tone of address that means that they are being spoken for. In a court of law, this is done standardly, as a required procedure, but it is a more general usage. Theodor Ringborg succinctly states the implications of institutionalized logocentrism, of what it is to be always spoken for:

> Testifying to the image names the practice of entering one's understanding of an image into discourse. It is to give voice to interpretation and ask to be believed. Faith in such testimony is in turn determined by the discursive space within which it is spoken. If an image never speaks for itself, and is always spoken for, then the video of King's assault in its three distinct discursive spaces offers the opportunity to reflect on the system of relations between image, viewer, and site. In doing so, it draws us towards questions not only of presentational circumstances and conditions of use, but also questions of who can speak in which spaces, what kinds of talk can and cannot be heard, and what conditions establish the possibility to make claims.[12]

In Simi Valley in 1992, the testimony that eventually rang out most clearly for the jurors, like a voiceover on a short, fast-paced, documentary film, and reinforced in explicit condemnation of King by the presiding judge, was that of police officers following their protocols when dealing with a (Black) man who had led them on a wild and dangerous car chase and was now threatening their persons as he refused arrest.

Injustice Normalized

The acquittal of the brutalizing officers sent out its own unambiguous message. Institutionalized power prevails, yet again, over visible evidence of the realities of everyday life in places such as South-Central Los Angeles, which exploded in rage, leading to 53 deaths, 7,000 arrests, and over $1 billion in property damage. Angry riots broke out across the country. Schwartz goes on to chronicle case after case—such as that of the strangulation of Eric Garner on a Staten Island street in 2014—in which what seems to be incontrovertible video evidence of excessive and often deadly police violence, now routinely recorded by police cameras as well as by independent witnesses, goes to court to die. He pinpoints the disjunction between then and recent times:

> In 1992, most scholarly responses to the video of King's assault focused on an effort to image the circumstances under which video evidence would lead to the conviction of violent police and the eventual prevention of police violence. Today, that thinking seems largely irrelevant, and the central question has become what to make of the widening chasm between legal and extralegal interpretation of these videos. Trials themselves, along with the entire justice system, have long since lost legitimacy as a search for the truth in the case of police violence. Outside the courtroom, as such footage increasingly triggers public interpretation and reaction in real time—before trials, before grand-jury findings—it seems destined to start more fires, which will burn hotter each time.[13]

This prophecy has come true. In recent years, the race war that simmered beneath the presidency of Barack Obama has smoldered ever closer to the surface. The accelerating accumulation of similar cases since 1992, however, did not seem change the overall equation. Until it did. The George Floyd video was a flashpoint. One among the several others in these partisan days but the one most relevant to racial repression. The race war is out in the open, dominating public discourse, flooding the iconomy, and rapidly reshaping everything it touches, showing it in a new and often shocking light.

Racial inequity prevails, in the United States as elsewhere, more evidently, in plainer sight, at the forefront of many more newsfeeds, Internet postings, and public broadcasts than ever before. Today, smart phones and surveillance cameras are ubiquitous, not least on the streets of an ordinary suburb such as Powderhorn. Cell phones make everyone into a ready recorder of anything mildly interesting, anything Instagram-able. They make us into potential witnesses to any unusual happening. As a 17-year-old schoolgirl,

Darnella Frazier exemplifies what it is to be an innocent bystander. But the readiness with which we post imagery of occurrences in our daily lives has qualified this innocence, this sense of being a disinterested observer. In parallel, the increase in police violence against African Americans in recent years, and the wider circulation of imagery of their excessive use of force, has increased awareness of the likelihood of its occurrence. We are less likely to be surprised bystanders. Some, indeed, are or became engaged observers: Ramsey Orta, who recorded the choking of Eric Garner, and Kevin Moore, who filmed the violent arrest of Freddie Gray that led to his death, began recording in the spirit of taking up their responsibility as citizen witnesses. Moore went on the become a member of WeCopwatch, an organization dedicated to this purpose.[14] Terri Weismann, who offers an acute analysis of Orta's and Moore's videos, concludes that they

> [...] reveal how the prolonged history of police brutality in the United States creates a system of durational incapacity that makes an ongoing awareness of death a way of life for black and brown Americans. Power is made visible on the body in these videos, on the body seen (Eric Garner, Freddie Gray, Rodney King, etc.) and on the body as imagined for the future or remembered in the past. In this way, I would further argue, the various ways that (state) power is pressed onto the body constitute part of the indexical mark that matters most in these witness videos.[15]

Did the sheer force of this indexical presence in Frazier's video, its unfolding for 8 minutes and 46 seconds, along with its ubiquity, make it less vulnerable to degradation as evidence when the cases against the officers who attended the incident at Powderhorn got to the courts in Minnesota? We will return to this question in Chapter 14 when we review the uses of visual imagery during the trial of Derek Chauvin.

Fox Fakes News

From those fighting to preserve the embattled status quo, reaction to Frazier's video was, at first, muted. It is, after all, hard to deny the obvious. As we shall see, even President Trump was, for a few days, unable to do so. But not impossible. In the United States, a leading warrior in the public opinion image wars is Fox News, which has mastered the art of disinformation, above all when it waves the banner of exposing "fake news."[16] On the August 3, 2020 edition of his much-watched show, Tucker Carlson took the occasion of the release of video footage from the body cams of the other police involved in the killing to mount a case that Floyd was, in fact, dying already, even

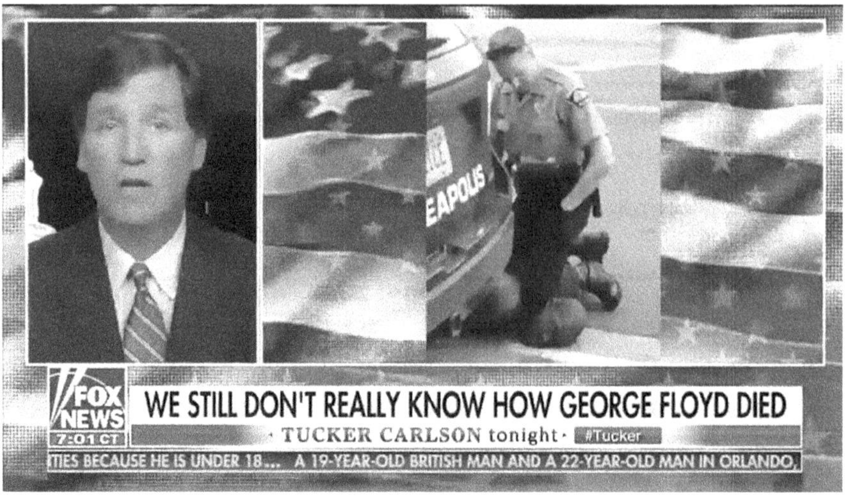

Fig. 10.3: Tucker Carlson Show, "We Still Don't Really Know How George Floyd Died," *Fox News*, August 3, 2020.

before the officers first approached him, that he, not they, was the effective cause of his own death (Fig. 10.3).[17] He set out to stage a reversal worthy of the poisoned legacy of the Rodney King video.

Carlson's setup, which I transcribe, is a masterful accumulation of fright wing tropes and rightward rebranding:

> On Memorial Day weekend this year, a man called George Floyd died in police custody in Minneapolis. America has not been the same since, may never be the same. In the months following, his death has been used to justify a nationwide convulsion of disruption, violence, and in some cases killing. And all of that in addition to unprecedented levels of political upheaval, a wholesale reordering of our most basic institutions. Floyd's death changed everything. It's a pivot point in American history. No matter what side you are on, that's very clear at this point.
>
> Yet with all of that about the significance of the event in mind, it's striking how little we know, months later, about how exactly George Floyd died. Because the story line is clear. Established news agencies say that it is a matter of factual certainty that Floyd was, in the words of NBC news and so many others, 'murdered' by a Minneapolis police officer. Politicians, both Democrat and Republican, echo that claim. Ideologues amplify it. According to filmmaker Michael Moore, Floyd was "Lynched by a cop's knee with a lynch mob of cops looking on."

> That certainly is a vivid image, but does it reflect what actually happened? [Cut to single image of Chauvin, hand in pocket with knee on Floyd's neck, surrounded by Fox stock image of a large US flag waving, and crawl below "WE STILL DON'T REALLY KNOW HOW GEORGE FLOYD DIED."] The short answer is we still don't really know how George Floyd died. The trial of the Minneapolis police officers hasn't started. We will know a lot more when it does.
>
> The media in the meantime aren't that curious about gathering further details. In fact, they are actively hostile to anyone who is. If you ask unauthorized questions, you will be banned from the Internet. The catechism has been written and it has been written in stone. George Floyd is a martyr, period. That's all you need to know. Shut up! But in America that's not good enough, it's not a real answer. In a free society, citizens have a right to know why things are changing so quickly. On what grounds are we dismantling police departments, rewriting curriculum, firing people from their jobs? What is the basis of this cultural revolution we are all living through?
>
> Once again, it may be some time before we can answer those questions with certainty. Maybe, we never will. We will probably debate them for decades. But more facts are always the first step toward establishing what the truth is. Finally, we have some more facts [...] Yesterday, British Paper *The Daily Mail* published video camera footage from the body cams of the other officers. Now, by itself, this video proves nothing, video cameras never prove anything conclusively. But this one does suggest quite a bit.

As he analyzes the video footage, disaggregation is Carlson's weapon of choice, followed by reinterpretation, all under the banner of objectivity loudly proclaimed and fearlessly pursued. Ignoring film of the officer holding a gun to Floyd's head as another opens the driver's side door of his car, Carlson says, "from the start, it is clear that this is not a typical law enforcement interaction"—whatever that might be. Instead, Carlson highlights one officer's question to the by now handcuffed Floyd: "Are you on something?" and reports that Floyd was later found to have fentanyl in his blood system, detailing the amount and concluding "More than enough to die of an overdose." He adds, "one of the symptoms of which, by the way, is shortness of breath." Noting that Floyd says "famously, that he is having trouble breathing, but says that long before the police officer kneels on his neck." He plays a clip of Floyd being shoved into the back seat of a police vehicle while shouting "I can't breathe" and "I am going to die," noting that this struggle goes on for about 10 minutes. Carlson says, "You can decide for yourself what you think of that video, and we hope you will, that's the whole point of our network, to bring you the facts and having you decide what they amount to." He gestures toward the more familiar images which show Chauvin kneeling on the neck of Floyd, now prone next to the police car—"what the whole world has seen before, that's the video that started the months of riots"—but does not show it. Instead, he switches to "But the question is why haven't we seen the rest of the video until right now considering all that happened next?" The answer he offers is that the Attorney General of Minnesota has been withholding it in order to enhance his case against the officers. Carlson plays a clip of an interview in which the man, an African American, seems to admit as much, while claiming to be a firm believer in "transparency, and the public's right to know." Carlson's final, ironic comment: "Right..."

More detail documenting the murder appeared as participants in the trails of each of the police officers revealed relevant material due to both legal obligations to do so and in their efforts to separate their liability from the pivotal act, Derek Chauvin's kneeling on the neck of George Floyd. A few days after Carlson's show, the transcript of the audio from the officers' cam recorders was filed in the Minnesota District Court.[18] It begins with employees of a convenience store, speaking to officers Lane and Keung, pointing out Floyd in his car as the gentleman who tendered what they believed was a fake $20 bill. The officers approach Floyd, one with gun drawn, ordering the occupants of the car to show their hands. Floyd says that he is sorry, that he did nothing, asks what he did wrong, then talks about being shot before by police, pleads not to be shot, says that he just lost his mother. His companion explains to police that Floyd is reacting oddly "because he's been shot before" by police, not because he is "drunk, or on something." Floyd also denies that, claims that he is scared, refuses to get in the squad car because he is claustrophobic, says that he is not resisting, that he just had COVID and does not want "to go back to that." All the while the officers, having restrained his hands behind his back, attempt to force him into their car. We read him saying "I can't breathe" five times to officer Lane before we hear the voice of officer Chauvin and Floyd is laid on the ground. At the point the transcript matches Frazier's video, Chauvin's knee is on his neck as the other officers kneel on his body, his hands cuffed behind him. Floyd's "I can't breathe" becomes a litany, repeated 19 times, interspersed with calls to his mother, pleas not to kill him. Soon he is silent. Spectators appeal to the officers to let Floyd up, they refuse. Lane and Keung ask whether they should roll Floyd over, Chauvin refuses. Keung tries to find a pulse, without success. The paramedics arrive, find no pulse, they try CPR. Meanwhile, in another parallel to Rodney King, the officers discuss whether Floyd is "on PCP," a body strength–enhancing drug, and note that a "weed pipe" was found in the car. They are already building a case that this death was caused by factors external to them. The transcript descends into exchanges between the police and paramedics about removing the body. The police discuss clearing the scene and leaving it. They do so.

When the transcript is matched to the 31 minutes of video released by the *Daily Mail* on August 3, 2020, and complemented by Frazier's video, a comprehensive picture of what occurred can be formed.[19] At the start, there is no indication of the police gathering evidence relevant to the accusation that Floyd passed a fake $20 bill in exchange for a packet of cigarettes. Nor of a presumption on the part of the officers that Floyd might not be guilty, and that their role is to conduct an inquiry before deciding how to act. Instead, he is approached by officers with raised voices and gun drawn, intent on restraining him as soon as possible, arresting him and removing him to the station as soon as possible. This scenario has become so normal in the United States that its inherent racism usually passes without comment. Nothing of what followed on that day is surprising. As soon as a weapon is flourished, the die is cast, death, already deeply anticipated, hovers ready at hand. In the Rodney King situation, the senior officer at the scene ordered the guns to be put away and the batons brought out, thus unleashing a lesser violence, yet one so intense it would have killed a weaker man. Nowadays, the guns come out early, and are often used, frequently to an excessive extent. In a war, everything is disproportionate. Directed at George Floyd, the murder weapons were multiple: racist presumption, a wavering gun, handcuffs, physical force, constant orders from a growing cluster of police, a halter restraint, the protocols of community policing in Minneapolis, a presumption of immunity, racist indifference to the rights of others, utter ignorance of human dignity, and a willingness to "let 'em die," all concentrated in the weight of a body through its knee bearing down on the neck of someone who has been rendered into an essentially worthless other.

Notes

1 These three valiances are insightfully explored by Theodor Ringborg, Testifying to the Image: The Video of the Assault on Rodney King as Evidence, as Event, and as Exhibition, PhD Dissertation, Goldsmiths College, University College, London, 2020. I had the privilege and the pleasure of being an examiner of this dissertation.

2 Neal Feigenson, "Visual Evidence," *Psychonomic Bulletin & Review*, vol. 17, no. 2 (April 2010): 149–154. On page 149, he remarks that "The police officers who beat Rodney King might never have been brought to trial were it not for George Holliday's videotape of the incident, and the jurors' verdict arguably turned on their interpretations of the tape."

3 See Tal Golan, "Visual Images in the Courtroom: A Historical Perspective," *Parallax*, vol. 14, no. 4 (October 2008): 77–89, at https://www.researchgate.net/publication/233073755_Visual_Images_in_the_Courtroom_A_Historical_Perspective. In his synopsis, Golan argues that one (good) reason for taking visual material as secondary evidence is that "human supremacy in the modern courtroom" is diminished by the plethora of "sophisticated visual technologies."

4 Louis-George Schwartz, "In Plain View: Video Evidence," *Artforum*, vol. 54, no. 10 (Summer 2016): 362–367, at https://www.artforum.com/print/201606/in-plain-view-video-evidence-60108.

5 A detailed account may be found on Wikipedia at https://en.wikipedia.org/wiki/Rodney_King. Book-length studies include Lou Cannon, *Official Negligence: How Rodney King and the Riots Changed Los Angeles and the LAPD* (Boulder, CO: Westview Press, 1999), and Rebecca Rissman, *Rodney King and the L.A. Riots* (Minneapolis: ABDO Publishing Co., 2014).

6 Judith Butler, "Endangered/Endangering: Schematic Racism and White Paranoia," in *Reading Rodney King/Reading Urban Uprising*, ed. Robert Gooding-Williams (Abingdon: Routledge, 1993), 16 and 19.

7 A Forensic Architecture type reconstruction by journalists working for the *New York Times*—who used imagery from multiple angles and sources to develop a clear story of the incident from the initial complaint that Floyd attempted to pass counterfeit money to the immediate aftermath of his death—was quickly compiled. See Visual Investigations Team, "How George Floyd Was Killed in Police Custody," *New York Times*, May 31, 2020, updated August 13, 2020, at https://www.nytimes.com/2020/05/31/us/george-floyd-investigation.html.

8 See the brilliant analysis by Elizabeth Alexander, "'Can You Be BLACK and Look at This?': Reading the Rodney King Video(s)," in *Black Male: Representations of Masculinity in Contemporary American Art*, ed. Thelma Golden (New York: Whitney Museum of American Art and Harry N. Abrams, 1994), 90–110.

9 Fred Moten, *In the Break: The Aesthetics of the Black Radical Tradition* (Minneapolis: University of Minnesota Press, 2003), 192–211.

10 "Boys Never Told Grandfather about 'Incident'," *Jet Magazine*, September 15, 1955, 8–9, pages reproduced at https://rosaparksbiography.org/bio/emmett-till/. Mamie Till Bradley is often identified as Mamie Till-Mobley, having adopted her third husband's name in 1957.

11 Moten, *In the Break*, 196.

12 Ringborg, Testifying to the Image, 10.

13 Schwartz, "In Plain View: Video Evidence," 367.

14 See https://wecopwatch.org/about/ and "Kevin Moore on the Inside Story of the Explosive Freddie Gray Video," *Democracy Now*. September 15, 2015, at https://www.youtube.com/watch?v=UibjjH0gpSs.

15 Terri Weissman, "Whose Streets? Police Violence and the Recorded Image," *Arts*, vol. 8, no. 155 (2019), 6, at https://doi.org/10.3390/arts8040155.

16 See, for example, Emma Vigeland for Young Turks, "Fox News' INSANE George Floyd Protest Double Standard," Rebel HQ, posted May 28, 2020, at https://www.youtube.com/watch?v=XjGsnnC3R9E.

17 Tucker Carlson, "We Finally Have More Facts Surrounding George Floyd's Death," Fox News Video, August 3, 2020, at https://video.foxnews.com/v/6178223265001#sp=show-clips. The video had been released earlier that day by *The Daily Mail* and posted to https://www.dailymail.co.uk/video/george-floyd/video-2227474/Video-bodycam-footage-George-Floyds-arrest-released.html.

18 GF police record 27-CR-20-12952, exported on June 15, 2020, filed August 7, 2020.

19 "Full Bodycam of George Floyd's Arrest Released," at https://www.dailymail.co.uk/video/george-floyd/video-2227474/Video-bodycam-footage-George-Floyds-arrest-released.html. See also the *New York Times* Visual Investigations Team reconstruction, note 7.

Chapter 11

THE CONTEST OF THE IMAGES

In the weeks after the George Floyd video became ubiquitous, it seemed in the United States that the multiplicity of forces contending for "the soul of the nation" were in all-out warfare. Within this confusion, two inchoate coalitions became most prominent. One was inspired to protest what the video revealed about the state of the nation and to urge for its healing based on full recognition of several intersecting rights. The other coalition, the Trump constituency, was, at first, stunned by the video. On May 29, President Trump made a video statement from the White House expressing the nation's "deepest condolences and heartfelt sympathies" to the family of George Floyd. He promised that all relevant Federal resources would join with local ones to make sure that "justice be served." Commenting on the video itself, he said, "A terrible, terrible thing that happened [...] we all saw what we saw, and it's very hard to conceive of anything other than what we did see. It should never happen, never be allowed to happen."[1] From someone (in)famous for saying about a Nazi-style rally in August 2017 by white supremacists in Charlottesville, Virginia—which led to the death of a protester—that "There were very fine people on both sides," this was a rare statement of conciliation. As the protests grew, however, the President's mood quickly changed. The constituency he headed sensed that the video's exposure of its dark and deadly underpinnings meant that the recognition it had won in recent years was in mortal danger.

The June 1 Pseudo-Event

On June 1, 2020, the Trump Administration came out fighting. Words and images were wielded, backed by as many sticks and stones as it could muster. The words were the President's avalanche of Tweets during the preceding days, including inflammatory evocations of the violent repression of Civil Rights protests during the 1960s ("when the looting starts, the shooting starts"), calls for governors to "dominate the streets," and threats to "bring in the Military," that is, the standing army of national forces, to do so.

Late on that day, as curfew approached, he delivered a "I am your President of Law and Order" speech in the Rose Garden, which ended with the odd statement "I am now going to pay my respects to a very, very special place."[2] Was he about to ascend into divinity? Or was this yet another voicing of his insane self-regard? We soon discovered that he was bent on generating a counter-image, one that would become an instant icon, intended to displace that of the sacrifice of George Floyd, an icon that was lighting up the media landscape in ways that was threatening to diminish his own electric aura.

Soon after finishing his speech, the President emerged from the White House and walked across Layfette Park, accompanied by a group including Attorney General William Barr, Secretary of Defense Mark Esper, Chairman of the Joint Chiefs of Staff General William A. Milley (in camouflage gear), a simpering Press Secretary, and some senior administration officials, including his daughter and son-in-law. Camera crews from several press networks circulated. As I watched live, I thought, "My God, he is going to front the demonstrators!" Reluctantly, I felt a momentary sense of admiration for someone confident enough, crazy enough, to take that risk. Then the political calculation: It would erase his cowardice in hiding in the bunker these past few days and the wildness of this threats during the early days of the protest. But no, I had overestimated him. On the advice of his daughter, son-in-law, and counselor Hope Hicks, in search of an image that would counter the by now notorious video of murder committed by someone on his side of the battle, he was leading his entourage no further than the steps of St John's Episcopal Church, on Lafayette Square, for a photo op (Fig. 11.1).

A performance which he bungled, standing awkwardly, and holding an unfamiliar bible upside down. There was no pretense of visiting the church for any religious purpose. Instead, he stood in front of the building, posing as a Christ-like defender of Faith against the disorder in the streets—*this close to the White House!*—that had forced this church to close its doors and batten its windows. The message to his base voters was clear: "I am doing this, and all that I might have to do in the coming days, for you." Doubtless, many of the Christian evangelicals and others who had made their bargain with Trump to overlook his faults for as long as he protected and promoted their values saw this as another confirmation that he was keeping his side of the deal. But the Episcopal bishop of Washington deplored the cooption of the church for blatant political purposes, as did the national leader of that church. The Roman Catholic bishop of Washington rejected Trump's repeat performance at a Catholic church the next day. Religious leaders across the country joined the chorus of dismay.

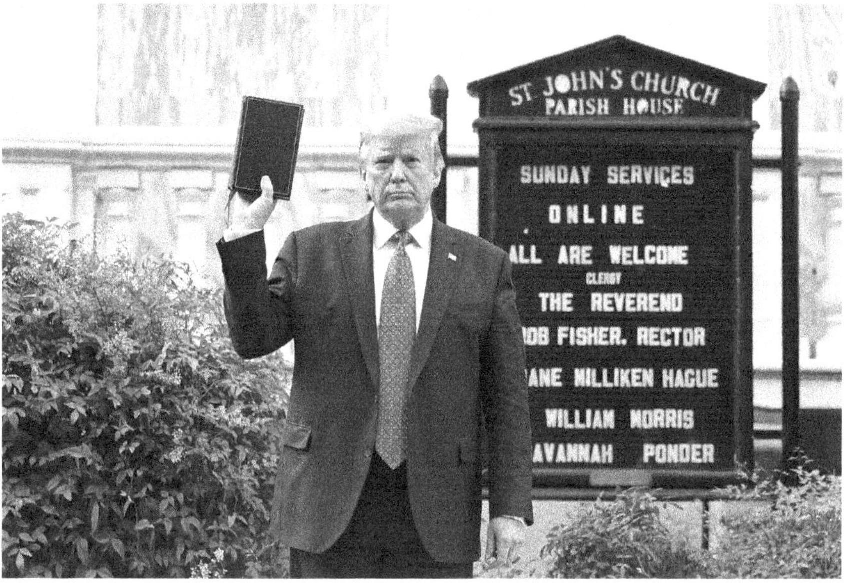

Fig. 11.1: President Trump holding Bible outside St John's Episcopal Church, Lafayette Square, Washington, DC, June 1, 2020. Photo: Brendan Smialowski/AFP via Getty Images.

Especially as it soon emerged that an extraordinary array of law enforcement, security forces, and quasi-military forces had been quickly assembled around the White House. They included the D.C. National Guard Military Police and regular soldiers, Park Police SWAT team and regular officers, uniformed U.S. Secret Service, FBI, US Marshalls, Drug Enforcement Administration officers, Arlington County Police on foot and mounted, and a specialist anti-riot squad, the Bureau of Prisons Special Operations Response Team. Some used tear gas, pepper balls, and strong crowd control tactics such as charges and rubber bullets to force demonstrators and media representatives from the public streets and spaces in front of and around the church (Fig. 11.2). By the next day, this abuse of the rights to free speech was dominating media reports, including film by news crews and other observers themselves subject to the violence of the clearance. Forensic Architecture-style reconstructions of the details of the events of the day soon followed, using a variety of visual footage and sound recordings.[3] While the White House distributed a brief triumphal video of the event to those organizing the reelection campaign, reports detailing its staged character, and its reliance on excessive force, spread quickly across national and international media.

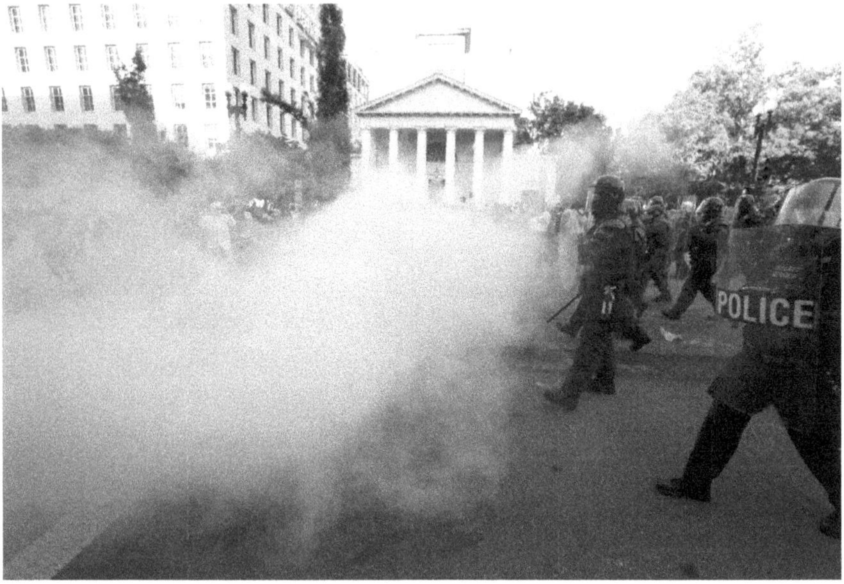

Fig. 11.2: Police officers in riot gear use tear gas to push back demonstrators near St. John's Episcopal Church, Washington, DC, June 1, 2020. Photo: Jose Luis Magana/AFP via Getty Images.

A crucial concern at the time was whether Trump would succeed in embroiling the US military in two contexts. One, defending the White House from those who might attack it directly, despite there being no public evidence of any concerted will to do so. Of more immediate concern was whether Trump would draw the actual military—as distinct from local police forces and the National Guard—into suppressing the protests that continued to grow in Washington itself, and in cities and towns across the country. These troops had been gathered in numbers at military bases outside of the city. Yet the use of riot control and military-style tactics for a purpose as banal as an opportunistic, campaign-style photo op—a misjudgment so blatant, and so quickly exposed to the widest public glare—must be counted as a factor in blunting whatever support the military establishment might have felt obliged to offer. Two days later, Esper ordered the troops outside the city to withdraw to their home bases, and the National Guard to stand down from the city. He and Milley disavowed Trump's intention to use the Insurrection Act, and retired generals Jim Mattis and John F. Kelly, formerly Trump's Secretary of Defense and Chief of Staff respectively, piled on in defense of the demonstrators' rights to free speech. As did several other major military figures. The threat of US troops acting against their own people in the national capital just outside the White House receded.

Instead of achieving a decisive victory in the image wars, the bungled photo op turned out to be a costly flop. So did the laughable efforts of Trump, on Independence Day, to position himself among the already bogus pantheon of presidents at Mount Rushmore. In case anyone doubted his commitment to fighting the image war, his speech was peppered with exhortations to resist the "angry mobs" that are "trying to tear down statues of our Founders, deface our most sacred memorials, and unleash a wave of violent crime in our cities," the "new far-left fascism" that uses "cancel culture" to attack "our beloved American way of life," this "left-wing cultural revolution is designed to overthrow the American Revolution." Against these dark forces and ignoring local tribal leaders who call for the removal of the Mount Rushmore memorial from their lands, Trump promised a National Garden of American Heroes, "A vast outdoor park that will feature the statues of the greatest Americans to ever live."[4] Including, it goes without saying, He who Would Make America Great Again. Just what that might look like was prefigured, on August 27, when the White House itself was turned into a prop for Trump's acceptance speech at the Republican National Convention.

From the inside, the Trumpian image regime seemed ascendent, approaching its apotheosis. From outside, however, it seemed ripe for all out contestation.

Diversity on the March

Throughout this period, counter imagery aimed at iconicity was constantly generated by those with opposing viewpoints. Immediately following the debacle at St John's church, Washington mayor Muriel Bowser ordered the renaming of the intersection in front of it "Black Lives Matter Plaza." Artist members of MuralDC, along with members of the D.C. Department of Public Works, aided by several volunteers, painted the words "BLACK LIVES MATTER" in capital letters in yellow paint along 16th Street for two blocks north of Lafayette Park.[5] A striking visual, it works well when seen from a drone camera (Fig. 11.3). It swiftly joined several other similar images that accumulated to be used as "set ups" in news and feature stories on television, video inserts in online stories, posts on social media, and (last and increasingly least) illustrations in newspapers. Together, these added up to an expansion, a strengthening but most importantly a focusing of already existing imagery of protest and demands for radical reformation.

This image regime found a fresh anchor in pictures of the "people's shrine" to George Floyd that emerged at the spot where he was murdered. The sidewalk, gutter and much of the street are covered in graffiti, flowers, and hand-painted signs. A mural portrait of Floyd's head and face, painted in black and white,

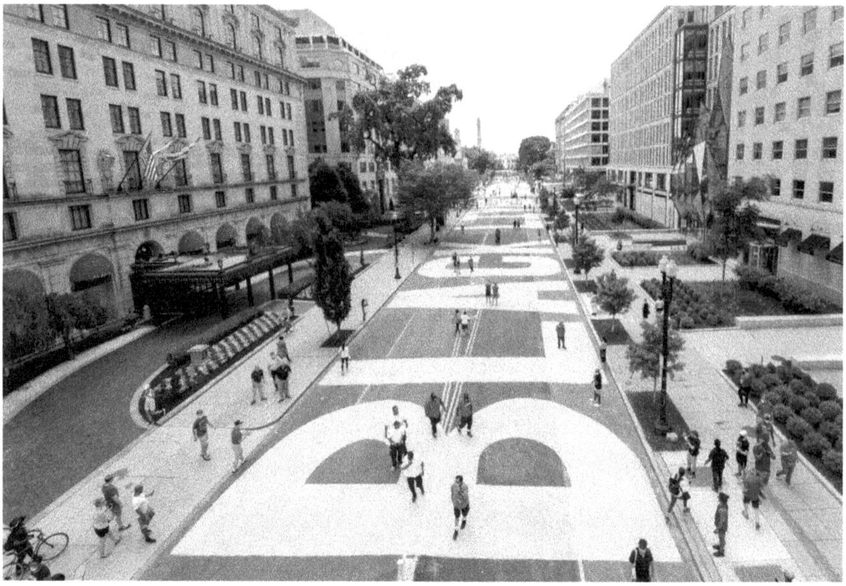

Fig. 11.3: Mural DC and D.C. Department of Public Works, BLACK LIVES MATTER, mural, 16th Street NW, Washington, DC, June 6, 2020. Courtesy of the Executive Office of the Mayor via AP Photos/Khalid Naji-Allah.

shows from an adjacent wall. Another adorns the wall at Cup Café: it shows the bust of Floyd, haloed by a sunflower which names the many others like him murdered by police, and saying, as if speaking from heaven, "I can breathe now." (Fig. 11.4) It was painted by local White and Latinx artists who have since apologized for leaping into that void without consulting their Black counterparts.[6] Such was the press of people coming to visit the site to pay their respects, to open their hearts, to try to learn, or out of curiosity, that the place has become a commemorative destination. The names of those killed by police in recent months and years are inscribed in various colors in large letters on the street surface. Led by the five killed in Minneapolis itself in the few months before George Floyd, it is a long litany, stretching the entire block. It, too, makes a powerful impression when a drone camera follows it slowly down its length and pulls back to see the skyline of the central city in the distance.

What we see here is a process that complements but also complicates the usual direction of iconicity, which is toward very few, often one, image or figure summarizing (and thereby banishing) all those similar to it, all those representing the same subject, place, event, idea, or attitude. Usually, this is a reductive process, familiar in propaganda campaigns, product branding, company logos, celebrity personas, and the signature style of

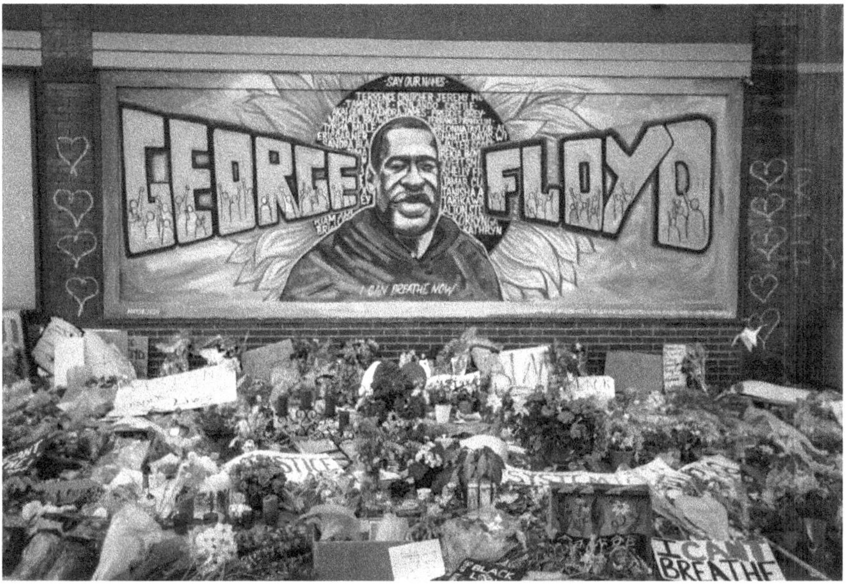

Fig. 11.4: The makeshift memorial outside Cup Foods where George Floyd was murdered by a Minneapolis police officer, June 2020. Photo: Los Angeles Times/ Jason Armond via Getty Images.

well-known artists. But the cultural logics of contemporary capitalism are in trouble these days, as the system proves itself incapable of managing its primal urge to creative destruction, while at the same time continuing to eviscerate governments, over-reward its leaders, and fall ever more conspicuously short of its promises to the rest of us. An imagery of diversity is called for: it is being created, on the streets and online, as we speak.

The commodity-celebrity-obsessed iconomy saturates our exchanges, all but the most private ones (into which it constantly intrudes). Several of its typical protocols were in evidence during this crisis. One is connectivity of content established through formal resonance. Mercifully, this works in both directions. A striking instance was NBA basketball star LeBron James' May 27 Instagram posting that juxtaposed an image of officer Chauvin kneeling on the neck of George Floyd with one of quarterback Colin Kaepernick kneeling during the playing of the national anthem before a game in order to protest precisely police violence and racial inequality in the United States. Kaepernick's contract with the San Francisco 49ers was not renewed after the 2016 season. Despite his outstanding skills, has not been able to find a place in any other NFL team. James' post was headed "This […]" above the image of Chauvin and "[…] is Why" over that of Kaepernick. The posting alongside reads: "kingjames. Do you understand NOW!!??!!?? Or is it still blurred to you?? #StayWoke." (Fig. 11.5)

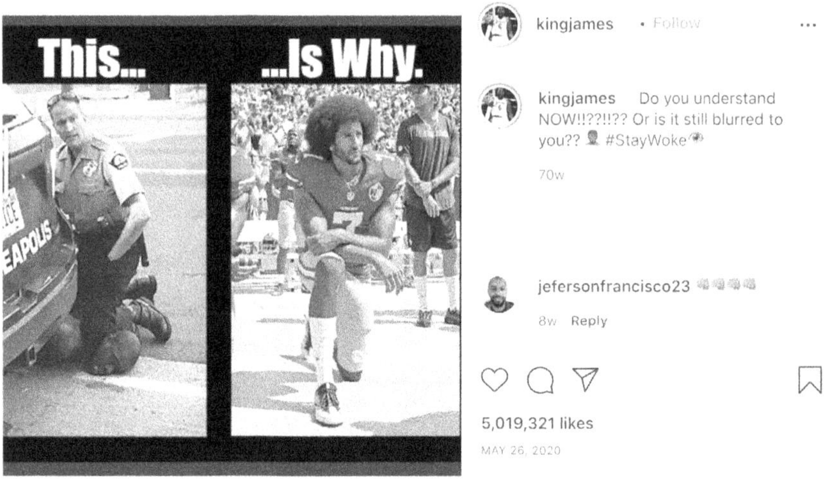

Fig. 11.5: LeBron James, "This … Is Why", Instagram post, May 27, 2020.

As neoliberal values increasingly infect the contemporary iconomy, imagery of the Black body falls more and more subject to a dichotomy based on economist alienation. Imagery of official violence directed against Black violators of the law, those designated lazy, criminal, and unruly, is matched by the high valuation of practices in which Black men and women visit extreme violence on their own bodies and minds to perform at extraordinary levels, especially in sports and entertainment. Imagery of these situations are spectacularized and commodified; producing them drives huge industries, and absorbing this imagery is a recurrent, peak experience in the lives of millions. Welcome to the surround-sound, HiFi cave, where our shadows are now in the highest possible definition. James' post exposes the master–slave dichotomy that is the infrastructure of this economy. His pairing connects the action of going on strike by one Black superstar with the enslavement unto death of an ordinary, out-of-work, Black man.

Concern that repeating the imagery of oppression can only serve to perpetuate it, which is true when people are simply clicking on likes and thumbs down as they keep on scrolling, should be nuanced by the ethical precision and the real-world effectiveness of actions such as this. Calling for ongoing acts of what she calls "contracirculation," artist Marielle Ingram remarks, "in this current moment, the circulation of images like the Floyd video doesn't merely commodify them into misplaced remedies for white guilt; it serves instead to build momentum to continue the movement. [...] the continual reappearance of certain images becomes a marker and reminder that there is work yet to be done."[7]

Black Lives Matter

It is no accident that the initial outburst of protest that followed the release of the video of the murder of George Floyd coalesced around three words: "Black Lives Matter." #BlackLivesMatter was established in 2013 by three organizers—Alicia Gaza, Patrisse Cullors, and Opal Tometi—as a response to the acquittal of the murderer of a young boy, Trayvon Martin. Oriented toward building "local power to intervene in violence inflicted on Black communities by the state and vigilantes," it became a national organization after the killing of Mike Brown in Ferguson, Missouri, in 2014. It is now an international network with more than 40 chapters. Black resistance has a long and much-storied history in the United States, but #BlackLivesMatter founders were particularly inspired to establish a leadership role in the struggle for "women, queer and transgender people, and others."[8] Their pursuit of an uncompromisingly intersectional outlook is a factor in the diverse composition of the protests during the months after the murder of George Floyd. It also underscores the continuing increase in numbers attending the protests, soon in their millions, and their spread to many places throughout the world.[9] When my first response to the Floyd video was published, among the images chosen by the editors as illustrations were two panoramic photographs of crowds assembled in protest. In one, the Occupy Wall Street protesters assembled in Zuccotti Park, Manhattan, in 2011, are overwhelming White; only one Black man is present. In the other image, a protest at Des Moines, Iowa, in late May 2020, a fierce intersectionality is on show.[10] "Others" now includes Whites, Hispanics, Asians, along with mixed and fluid identities of all kinds (Fig. 11.6). Outside the United States, "Black Lives Matter" signs are prominent among those being carried. Around them, local grievances are made manifest: in Australia, the struggle against the deaths of Indigenous people in custody continues to be vociferously and visibly protested on the streets of all the major and many smaller cities (Fig. 11.7)

In every place of protest, several demands are being made at the same time, together, in energetic harmony. Halt the systematic oppression of African Americans and other people of color, of those who wish to live differently from the heterosexual, cis-gender, patriarchal norms, and of those who are working to build a fair and just society, developed in harmony with the needs of the planet. Recognize the social value of such people because we are

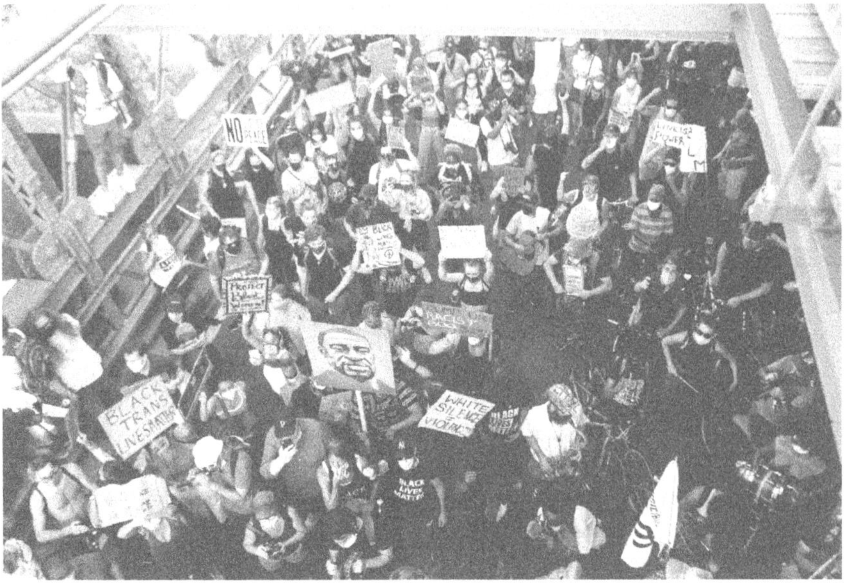

Fig. 11.6: Mel D. Cole, Brooklyn Bridge. July 25, 2020. Photograph courtesy of the artist.

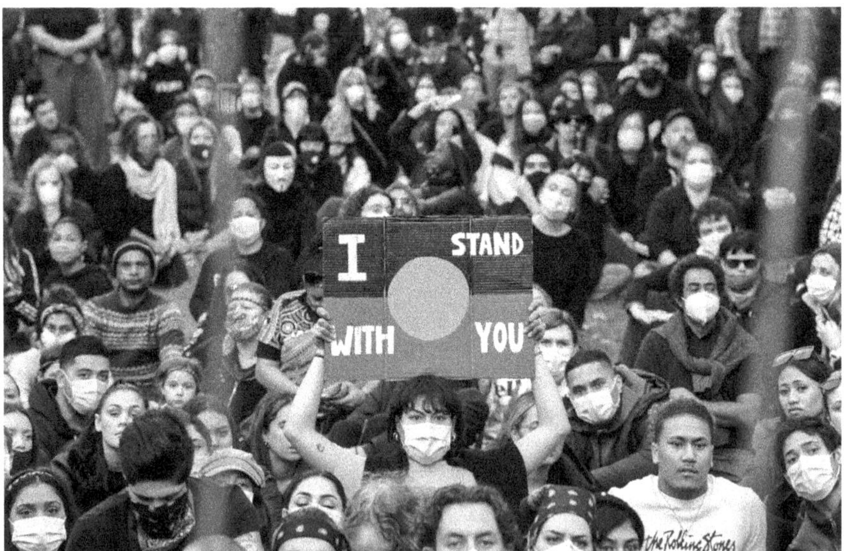

Fig. 11.7: Demonstrators attend a Black Lives Matter protest to express solidarity with US protestors and demand an end to frequent Aboriginal deaths in custody in Australia, Sydney, June 6, 2020. Photo: Saeed Khan/AFP via Getty Images.

the future, like it or not, coming ready or not. Take down the monuments to racists and colonizers. Remove violence from the management of everyday differencing. Begin from anti-racism as the first premise. Demilitarize the police. Focus them on serious crime. Shift the majority of resources to community services, affordable housing, medical care, disability. Deracialize the legal system, the education system, real estate, employment of all kinds. Reparate the damage already caused to those who have suffered, and continue to suffer, from historic colonization, including slavery and its continuing legacies. Decide what kind of policing is necessary *after* these problems are on their way to solution.

Monstrous Restraint

As we saw, Donald Trump's own brand, propelled by himself, and concentrated in his own appearance, built on his previous profile as a New York real-estate broker and a television celebrity. A confessed "media junkie," he is a creature of the 24/7 news cycle. He saw his primary role as President as ensuring that his image, his doings, his statements were always the trending topic on all platforms. For the most part, content is of lesser concern than mere, but constant, presence. Style is paramount: it centers on the image of him enacting the role of a rule-breaker who nonetheless always wins his battles against the rule-followers in the institutions around him. This is the basis of his appeal to the disenchanted voters who were the majority of his supporters in 2016 and since. As President, crucially backed by the Republican majority in the Senate led by his alter ego, Mitch McConnell (who presents, performatively, as everything Trump is not), it was, for four years, a winning strategy. The Supreme Court and vast tracts of the judiciary were populated with avowedly conservative judges; following Steve Bannon's call to "deconstruct the deep state," federal institutions were systematically eviscerated; major legislation and thousands of regulations introduced during the Obama years relating to health care, the environment and migration were compromised or annulled; foreign trade and international relations were arbitrarily disrupted in the name of "America First"; the United States surrendered its leadership role throughout the world, leaving gaps for the emergence (China) or reemergence (Russia) of other national powers; meanwhile, existing cultural, racial, and class divisions within the United States were exacerbated. The net result was an implosion of effective national governance: an executive branch gone rogue; the legislative branch, with the Republican-dominated Senate as the roadblock, largely failing to pass laws; while the Supreme Court, at the top of the judicial branch, now loaded with conservative appointees, mixes narrow judgements with increasing support for conservative causes.

Evoking the split screen of televised news, a newspaper front page, or an Instagram post, Fintan O'Tootle dramatizes the images wars of 2020 in these terms:

> [...] perhaps what defines this particular moment in America is its monstrous play on the idea of restraint. Citizens have a dizzying, sickening double vision. On one side of the screen, they see a show of violent restraint: George Floyd pinned down, trapped, immobilized to the point of paralysis while his life is squeezed out of him. The cry that echoes from the past through his voice and into the mouths of protesters on the streets—"I can't breathe!"—is the ultimate expression of the terror of absolute confinement. It was Eric Garner's cry too, when he was dying in a policeman's chokehold on Staten Island in 2014. What makes it so much more politically potent now is that on the other side of the screen there is the embodiment of absolute unrestraint, the president's unchecked exhalation of hallucinatory gibberish.[11]

Against this conjunction of deadly constraint and unhinged misgovernance, a huge, collective effort to imagine an equitable society premised on total anti-violence is what I see on the streets, in the composition of the crowds, in the slogans on their banners, in their costumes and performances, in the murals and graffiti that are transforming many neglected neighborhoods, in the monuments being deposed and those that are being proposed not in their place but in their own right, in the videos being streamed, and in the images being posted. Some early successes were already evident by late 2020. The agent provocateur induced violence, and the opportunistic looting (itself a form of DIY wealth redistribution), that marked some of the early protests had become negligible. Almost all violence was perpetrated by police, and even that had subsided, as increasing numbers of officers took the knee in support of Black Lives Matter. They came to understand what the protesters were saying to them. They also sensed that their jobs were on the line. In businesses large and small, community groups, universities and schools, and churches across the nation, anti-racism shifted from dutiful declaration to an active priority. In football leagues throughout Europe and in England, players wore Black Lives Matter insignia and took the knee before games. During the 2020–21 NBA and MLB seasons in the United States, every player and official did the same. When the killing got too much to bear, games were not played. Nonviolence was rediscovered and asserted in multiple ways.

The genuine diversity envisaged in the image regime based around protest and reform will, however, be in place only when coeval communality is achieved on local, national, regional, and international scales. No one expects this to be easy. We are in for many battles and a long war.

Notes

1 See https://www.youtube.com/watch?v=otqkKN-wdl8.
2 The White House, "Statement by the President," June 1, 2020, at https://www.whitehouse.gov/briefings-statements/statement-by-the-president-39/.
3 See especially, "A video timeline of the crackdown on protesters before Trump's photo op," *Washington Post*, June 8, 2020, at https://www.youtube.com/watch?v=-JxYmILDya0A. A detailed timeline may be found at https://en.wikipedia.org/wiki/Donald_Trump_photo_op_at_St._John%27s_Church. These events have propelled Wikipedia into becoming yet another platform for 24/7 news and events.
4 The White House, "Remarks by President Trump at Mount Rushmore," at https://www.whitehouse.gov/briefings-statements/remarks-president-trump-south-dakotas-2020-mount-rushmore-fireworks-celebration-keystone-south-dakota/.
5 For the back story of the mural's quick-fire creation, and initial doubts on the part of the Washington chapter of BLM which had not received what it believed was a fitting level of support from Mayor Bowser, see Robin Wright, "The Secret Project That Led to Black Lives Matter Murals Coast to Coast," *The New Yorker*, June 9, 2020, at https://www.newyorker.com/news/news-desk/the-secret-project-that-led-to-black-lives-matter-murals-coast-to-coast.
6 Sheila Regan, "Minneapolis art groups tackle equality in the local scene—and in the industry at large," *The Art Newspaper*, July 9, 2020, at https://www.theartnewspaper.com/news/minneapolis-arts-groups-reckon-with-inequality.
7 Marielle Ingram, "Contracirculation: On rewriting the terms of engagement with images of Black suffering," *Real Life*, June 29, 2020, at https://reallifemag.com/contracirculation/.
8 See https://blacklivesmatter.com/herstory/.
9 For a visual tracing of "How Black Lives Matter Reached Every Corner of America," see *New York Times*, June 25, 2020, at https://www.nytimes.com/interactive/2020/06/13/us/george-floyd-protests-cities-photos.html.
10 Terry Smith, "Videodeath: Powderhorn Explodes the Image World, June 3, 2020," Art Critics on Emergency, *AICA-USA Magazine*, posted July 6, 2020 at http://aicausa.org/magazine/videodeath-powderhorn-explodes-the-image-world.
11 Fintan O'Tootle, "Unpresidented," *New York Review of Books*, 23 July 2020, 27.

Chapter 12

IMAGE WAR, CIVIL WAR? JANUARY 6, 2021

The gathering of thousands of Trump supporters in the Capitol grounds at midday on January 6, 2021, transposed the image world of one of his rallies on to the main site of national governance. In the event, this was literally so, as the insurrectionary crowd was first formed and then fed by people who had assembled shortly before at the Ellipse, a stage on the Mall side of the White House, for a "Save America" rally. Trump's speech there was the final incitement to march on the Capitol to stop the certification of the Biden–Harris victory and, instead, secure his re-election.[1] Just in case the message was not clear, to the right of the podium from which Trump spoke, a gateway was erected with these words emboldened across its canopy: MARCH ON THE CAPITOL. Thousands did what they were told. Breeching the outer perimeters of the Capitol grounds by 1 p.m., the crowd found itself occupying the structures erected for the impending inauguration of Joe Biden. The Trumpian image world merged with the postcard site of US patriotism. The reinauguration of Donald J. Trump was prefigured. Supporters then swarmed the Capitol building (Fig. 12.1).

Inside, unaware of the tumult, the legislators began their certification process. Around 2:15 p.m., members of the Proud Boys militia led the break in through windows and the front door (Fig. 12.2). A few minutes later, the mob found itself in the Great Rotunda of the Capitol (Fig. 12.3). They had followed the unfamiliar passageways, brushing aside outnumbered and under-prepared officers. At times, they filed through crowd-control chords, as if they were on a guided tour. Then, they filled the huge hall with excited shouts, milled around in waves, taking selfies, posting to their friends and followers, waving their TRUMP flags and red MAGA gear, showing that they had arrived at the heartland. Some carried the metal bars they had used to beat back the police trying to keep them out of the building. Others covered their faces, half-aware that it might be smart to disguise their identity. Cell-phone videos show that soon the hubbub died down, voices were stilled, and the majority of those present stood in silent awe. They were surrounded

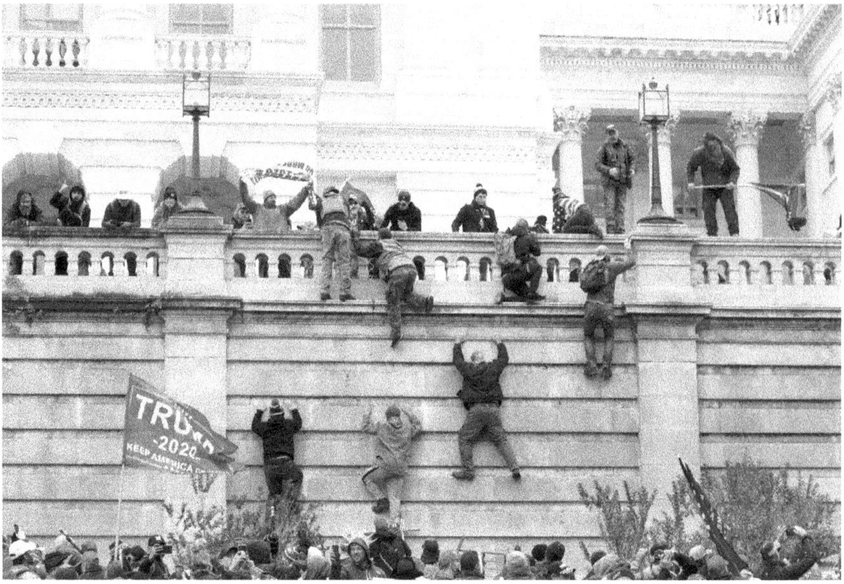

Fig. 12.1: Supporters of President Donald Trump climb the west wall of the Capitol, January 6, 2021. Photo: AP/ Jose Luis Magana.

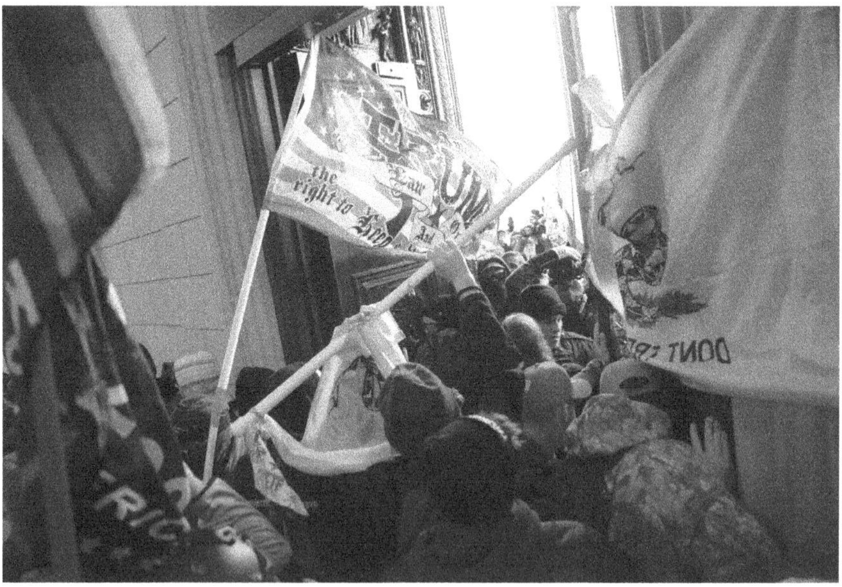

Fig. 12.2: Trump supporters break into the Central Building of the Capitol, January 6, 2021. Photo: Win McNamee/Getty Images.

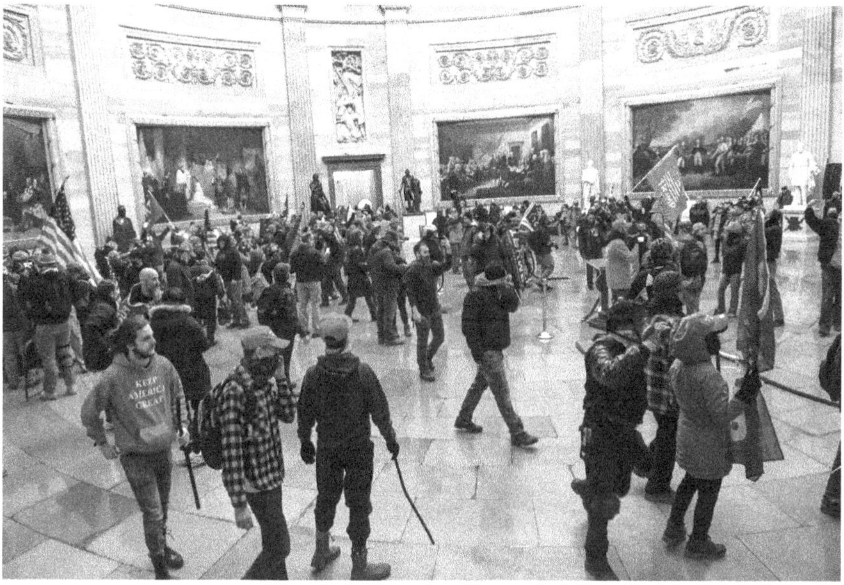

Fig. 12.3: The mob inside the Capitol, Rotunda, January 6, 2021. Photo: Saul Loeb/AFP via Getty Images.

by huge paintings, each of a scale and complexity few had seen before, showing the scenes of major battles to secure Independence and of historical gatherings that founded their United States. Between the paintings stood life-size sculptures of famous Americans, names from their history books, people who had walked these halls, who had made this space the place that it was. Above them hovered a majestic dome from which a gentle light descended.

The crowd kept replenishing itself, but soon thinned. Some people went off to join the hunt for the politicians attempting to steal their votes. Others wandered through other halls. Some sat slumped on the marble floors, stumped, wondering about what they had done and what to do next. Few had a strong sense of having committed criminal trespass. Instead, they felt that they had arrived at what they had been told was their spiritual home, the home place of the nation, the haven of true patriots like themselves, to the exclusion of all others. They believed themselves to be saviors of the nation's spirit, soldiers in the battle to prevent Democrats—and today, right now, the traitor Mike Pence!—from stealing its soul by falsely certifying a corrupt election. They had entered this sacred space, bringing with them their own image world. They *were* their image world, in dress, in their actions, in the icons they carried, in their own imaginations. They offered themselves to the gaze of these guardians of the national spirit, who did not look like them and, some perhaps slowly realized, did not recognize them for who they were.

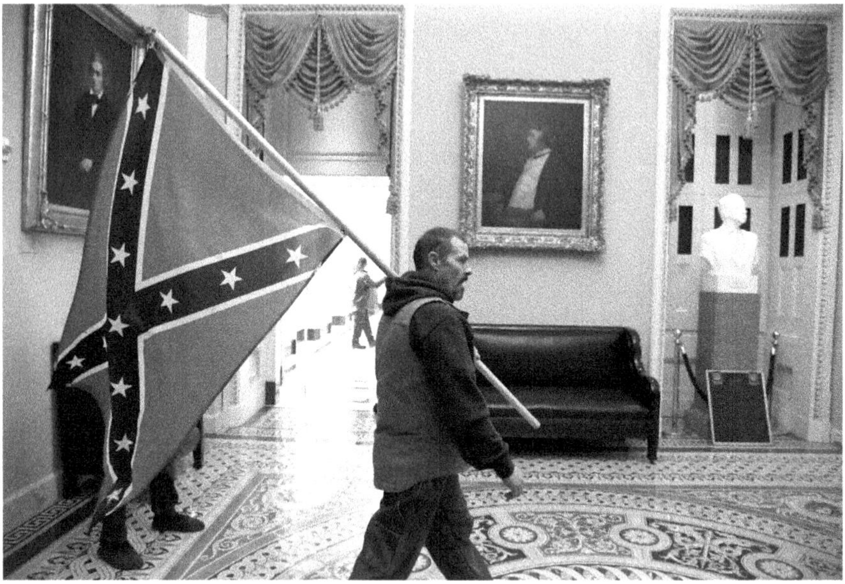

Fig. 12.4: Man carrying Confederate flag in vestibule outside Senate Chamber, January 6, 2021. Photo: Mike Theiler/Reuters.

The fissures between these image worlds, shifting gaps filled by degrees and kinds of mutual incomprehension, are embodied in the photograph of a man carrying a Confederate flag in the vestibule outside the Senate chamber (Fig. 12.4). Its bearer presumably aimed to convey his conviction that the Civil War had not been lost by the Southern states in 1865 but that, like Trump in 2020, they had been cheated, so that, in principle, the war still raged, and may still be won. Two days later, in *The Atlantic*, writer Clint Smith pointed out that the man happened to be carrying his flag past a portrait of Charles Sumner, the abolitionist Senator from Massachusetts, who, in 1856, had been attacked by a pro-slavery Representative Preston Brooks in the nearby Senate Chamber. Badly beaten by the golden head of Brook's thick walking cane, Sumner never fully recovered. A further coincidence is that the man portrayed in the painting behind the flag-wielder is John C. Calhoun, twice Vice-President in the early 1800s, who proclaimed slaveholding to be "a positive good." Smith traces the evolution of the design of the flag during the Civil War and subsequently. The photograph captures the moment of what is believed to be its first appearance in the Capitol Building.[2]

Initial reporting emphasized the most photogenic among the rioters, notably Jake Angeli, self-proclaimed "Shaman of QAnon," a standout for his costume—horns, bearskin headdress, shirtless, with hide overalls, his face adorned with red, white, and blue paint—and his penchant for over-performance. And the most improbable: Texas realtor Jenna Ryan, who livestreamed promos as she breached the Capitol doors. Only in America. Iconoclash of the Crazies meets Invasion by the Idiots. The suggestion here of harm being inadvertently caused by the harmless, an insurrection of the innocent (Senate Republican leader Mitch McConnell's defense of his voters), overlooks the planning that went into agitating the crowd, the quiet effectiveness of the thin line of militia as they snaked through the mob shouting on the steps, then broke through the doors and windows. Some, such as the "zip-tie guy," seemed prepared to take members of Congress hostage to stop the certification and keep their man in the White House (Fig. 12.5).

By early evening, the invaders had been cleared from the building. Soon after, legislators returned to their work. Over continuing objections by several Republican representatives, including several who had hours before been hiding out of sight of the mob, the election of Joe Biden and Kamala Harris as President and Vice-President was certified. Five people had died. Hundreds were injured, among them 136 police officers. Four officers subsequently took their own lives. On January 6, 2021, a pivotal battle with the image wars, had ended. What did it signify? What would be its aftermath? (Fig. 12.6).

Is the Second Civil War Already Taking Place?

Declaring that a war-like state prevails has become the metaphor of choice when rallying to combat the pandemic, when characterizing racial discord, and when attributing partisan politics to a clash of cultures. Some critical commentary warns that a second Civil War seems to be underway in the United States. It is occurring mainly as a clash of cultures, of performative contestations between opposing identities, within an iconomy intensely politicized by partisan divisiveness. Assessing such claims will be a major focus of this chapter. More broadly, expressions such as "the hunger wars," "the migration wars," and "the climate wars" are appearing in forecasts of the effects of failed states, natural catastrophes, and global warming. As class inequities manifest themselves yet again, on local and global scales, they have caused "the vaccine wars" between what used to be called "advanced" and "developing" countries. In each case, the lives lost, the lives at risk, make these claims plausible ways of highlighting what is at stake, but they fall short of encompassing the vast work that will need to be done to discover (I do not say re-discover, that chance has gone) states of relative peace within the battles ahead.

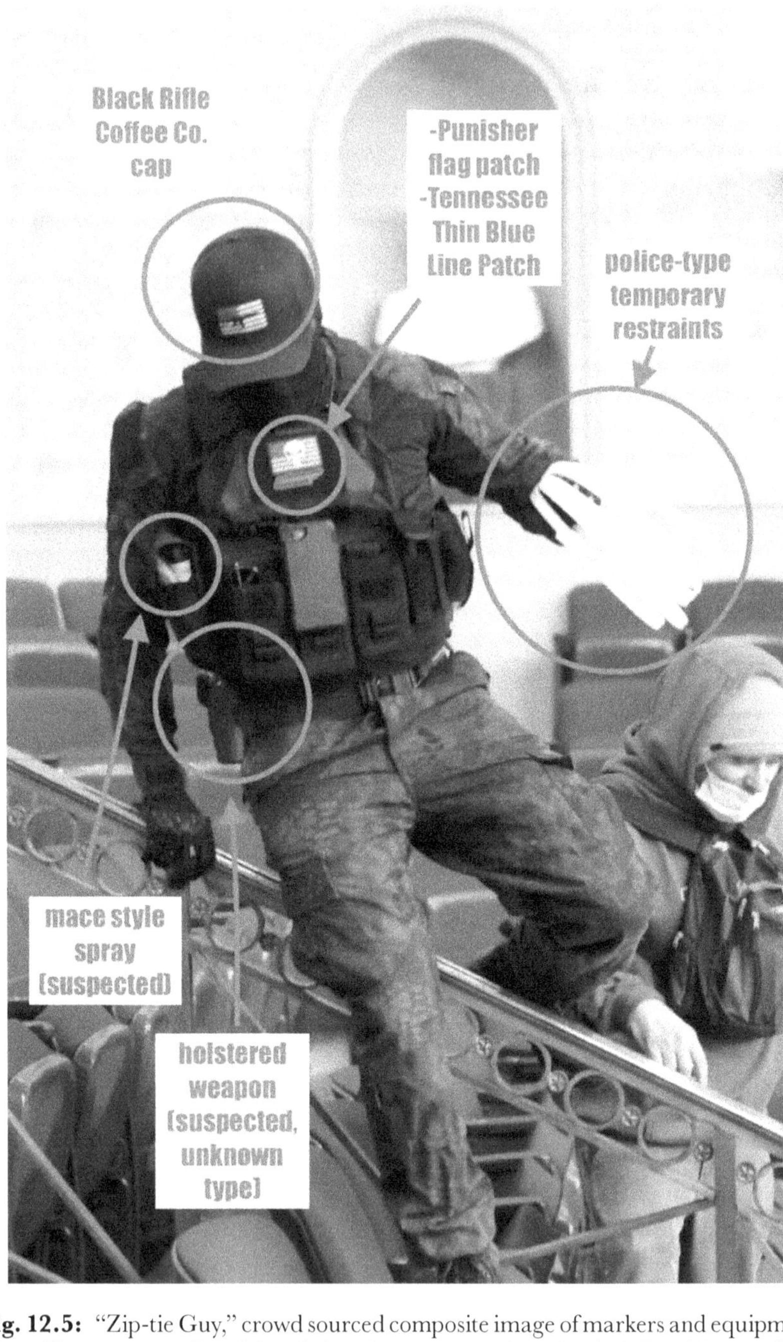

Fig. 12.5: "Zip-tie Guy," crowd sourced composite image of markers and equipment of pro-Trump rioter Eric Munchel in Senate Chamber, Capitol, Washington DC, January 6, 2021. From Twitter account of Scott-Railton, @jsrailton.com, January 8, 2021.

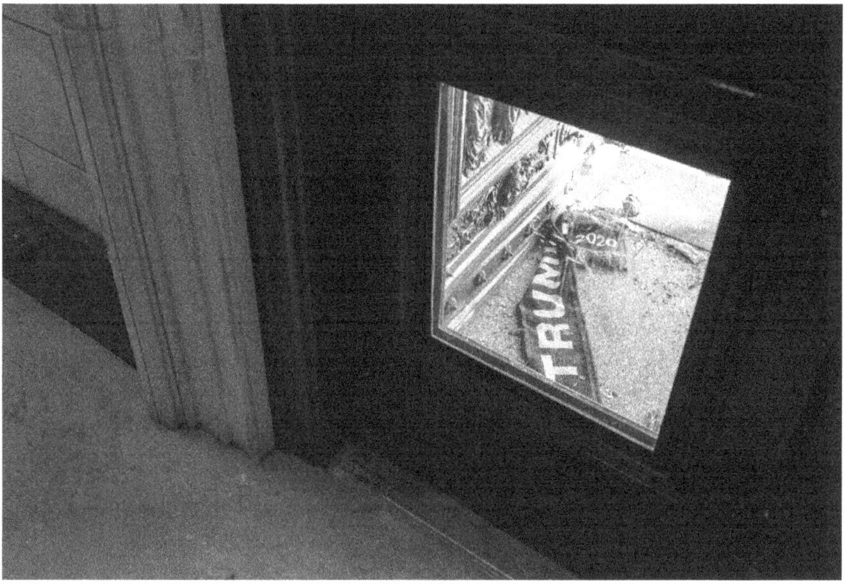

Fig. 12.6: A scarf left in the Capitol on Wednesday by a Trump supporter, January 6, 2021. Photo: Jason Andrew/The New York Times/Redux.

In an article entitled "Trench Warfare: Notes on the 2020 Election," sociologist Mike Davis offers this sobering assessment:

> We assume that times of great social upheaval and human peril produce equally dramatic political reactions: uprisings, counterrevolutions, new deals and civil wars. The one thing that most Americans agree on is that we are living in such a time, the greatest national crisis since 1932 or even 1860. Against a background of plague, impeachment, racist violence and unemployment, one party espouses a vision of autocratised government and a return to the happy days of a white Republic. The other offers a sentimental journey back to the multicultural centrism of the Obama years [...] Both parties are backward looking, solipsistic and unanchored in economic reality, but the first echoes the darkest side of modern history. The vote, held on a day when more than 100,00 American tested positive for Covid-19, was supposed to deliver a definitive verdict on Donald Trump. Indeed the President's increasingly frenetic attempts to delegitimize the election seemed to signal his apprehension of a Democratic landslide. In the event a projected 160 million votes were mailed in or cast in person, representing the highest turnout in 120 years. A stunning judgement was expected. Instead the election results

> are a virtual photocopy of 2016: all the disasters of the past four years have barely moved the needle. Biden eked out a slim victory, in some states with microscopic margins, that won him 306 electoral votes, the same as Trump four years ago.[3]

The casting of what turned out to be 155,485,614 votes (among them mine, as a registered Democrat in Allegheny County, Pennsylvania) in a country where voting is voluntary, and the steady and straightforward counting of these votes (despite intense pressure from Trump supporters looking for evidence of fraud), were celebrated by many as demonstrating that democracy was flourishing in the United States. Others read the turnout as expressing the anxiety of the warring parties that their opponents might prevail. Davis's close comparative analysis of results in the swing states, county by county, leads him to agree with descriptions of the two dominant parties as being like the armies in Europe during World War I, that is, gridlocked by "a mostly immobile line of battle and endless trench warfare."[4] The behavior of the parties reflects the broader national situation: "A powerful alignment of ideology, race and religion renders America's divisions unusually encompassing and profound. It is hard to find another polarization in the world that fuses all three major types of identity divisions in a similar way."[5] No surprise then that both sides of what is an increasingly divided yet mutually implicated society are increasingly open to the influence of their "Liberty or Death" brigades. Davis concludes that "Deep structures from the past have been disinterred during the Trump presidency and given permission to throttle the future. Civil War? Some [such] analogy is inevitable and should not be easily dismissed."[6]

On November 3, 2020, over 80 million Americans cast their votes for Joseph Biden. But 71 million kept holding their noses or had genuinely come to take Trump's claims literally. Seventy percent of those voters continued supporting him even as he insisted that his electoral defeat had not happened, that their house was being stolen from them. He repeatedly urged his supporters to converge on the capital on January 6, 2021, when Congress would convene to certify the election, and act to "Stop the Steal." Performative politics. The aesthetics of appearance. "Be there," he Tweeted, "will be wild."

Triumphalism within the Iconomy

Within an already intensely politicized iconomy, the most blatant imagery associated with the Trump brand was and remains unabashedly combative and triumphalist. Dark forces overcome. Trump as Rocky, as the Terminator, as a smiling Dark Vader, and as a Christ-like figure, magically making

America Great Again. When he became president, Trumpian triumphalism merged with the imagery of unequivocal patriotism: his visage glowed from the stars or from the stripes on the national flag, the word "TRUMP" stood out red on white and blue. He became, in his own words, "the best President of all" (with the possible exception of Abraham Lincoln). True belief in the United States and loyalty to Trump were one emotion, indivisible, under God. Opponents were demonized to become enemies of the nation: their names and images defiled and ridiculed. Enemies could be, and were, anywhere and everywhere: in the bureaucracies, on the streets, in the conference rooms of disloyal businesses, in foreign capitals, in the courts, in local government, in the universities of course, in the Democratic Party, and even among disloyal Republicans in the Congress. At the apex of this pile of denigration and glorification stood Donald J. Trump, constantly demanding and absorbing the admiration of members of his "movement." Occupying the symbolic centers of power, suffusing them with his imagery, was the name of the game.

At the same time, Trumpian triumphalism was embedded in chronic uncertainty. It entailed disguise, misdirection, and distraction. "Don't take me literally but do take me seriously." "Alternative facts." And was laced with defensive reversals. "Political Correctness." "Fake News." "Cancel Culture." Trumpian rhetoric was always transparent because bare faced was what he best knew how to be. And because it worked, often enough. Flatter, bluster, threaten (listen to the tapes). The hustle, the con, right out there on Fifth Avenue, now in the White House. What better way to convince them to keep sending in their dollars? A context character in *American Psycho* becomes Grifter in Chief. If you can make it in New York, where bluff is enough, you can do the same within the Republican Party, where cynicism and hyena-like opportunism came along for the ride. And have the same effect throughout the country, wherever someone can feel that they, in however small a way, could be part of this bigger game. Victims today could become the winners of tomorrow. The shadows on the cave wall become ever more dazzling, even as our chains become ever more visible and heavier.

Events and Processes

For a succinct description and an acute sheeting home of blame for the events of January 6, it is hard to beat that of Senator Mitch McConnell, speaking on February 13 at the second impeachment trial of Donald Trump:

> January 6 was a disgrace. American citizens attacked their own government. They used terrorism to try to stop a piece of democratic business they did not like. Fellow Americans beat and bloodied our

> own police. They stormed the Senate floor. They tried to hunt down the Speaker of the House. They built a gallows and chanted about murdering the Vice-President. They did this because they had been fed wild falsehoods by the most powerful man on Earth—because he was angry that he lost an election [...] There's no question, none, that President Trump is practically and morally responsible for provoking the events of the day. The people who stormed this building believed they were acting on the wishes and instructions of their president, and having that belief was a foreseeable consequence of the growing crescendo of false statements, conspiracy theories and reckless hyperbole that the defeated president keep shouting into the largest megaphone on planet Earth [...] This was an intensifying crescendo of conspiracy theories, orchestrated by an outgoing president who seemed determined to either overturn the voters' decision or else torch our institutions on the way out.[7]

Within hours, reverting to the moral cowardice mixed with ruthless self-interest that had characterized his past four years as the major power broker in Washington, McConnell voted to acquit on the grounds that Trump was not subject to impeachment as he was no longer in office. McConnell subsequently persisted in his stonewalling of every Democratic initiative while simultaneously doing little to resist the Trumpian takeover of his party. Yet, while civil wars require leaders, to attribute such agency to one man seems exaggerated—and, in McConnell's case, typically devious.

Some years from now it will seem remarkable that, throughout 2020, and into the early months of the following year, millions of people living in many countries woke up each day wondering what was happening with COVID and what would Donald Trump do, or mostly not do, about it. For four years, the infosphere had been filled by a daily diet of reports of events—events of world or national, often simply local importance—that were immediately matched by a Tweet from Trump or a report in several mediums of his reaction or likely reaction to it. I noted earlier that this one-two rhythm, at once exciting and enervating, shocking and tedious, went way beyond the attention that would naturally be paid to the sayings and doings of any president of the United States. As it turned out, the virus infected him personally. Yet, despite his staging of a Savior-like recovery, his narcissistic denial of the pandemic, and his abject failure as a national leader to manage it, were among the factors that led to his political defeat.

A crucial precondition of the events of January 6, 2021, was Trump's obdurate refusal to concede defeat in the November election. To this day, he rejects the overwhelming evidence that the total vote, the vote in swing states, and the vote in the Electoral College went against him. With several cases against him pending in New York courts, did he fear losing the protection of the Presidency? With all the "adults in the room" having resigned or been sacked, did no one remain to remind him of conventions and realities? Yes, but also there is this: In no edition of *The Apprentice* was it conceivable that anyone—not even the American people—might say to the boss "You're fired!" Perhaps this creature of celebrity culture—the celebrity's celebrity, brand-spanker extraordinaire, super-trender on Twitter, and, as President, dominant denizen of the 24/7 news cycle—believes what he says when he claims that the election consisted of the votes made and counted on November 3, that all other votes made before and after were fraudulently cast. He believes this because he is pressing the election through the same filter that everything else about the world comes to him: as an event, not a process. Events happen, at a time and in a place, which they fill as that which is most visible, most intensely felt, seemingly most world changing, then and there. They displace the preceding events. Trump's goal has always been to stay on top of events as they happen. He knew already that the best way to do that is to be the person who generates more events, and the anticipation of coming events, faster than anybody or anything else. To him, events play out according to a time-honored scenario, enacted in every episode of his television series. The all-conquering hero arrives with fanfare. He postures, he speaks. On script; off script. Images; gestures; voice. (Imagery is always multi-sensorial, time-taking, and performative.) Events unfold until he is ready to leave, a satisfied smile on his face. For four years, this indefatigable Master of Incipience succeeded. Until processes that take their time reasserted their power.

The lawsuits filed by the Trump Campaign and his motley band of supporters were attempts to create an event that would displace the election result, thereby bringing the election back onto the terrain where Trump had been the dominant player. This was not simply personal hubris, although it was obviously that, in spades. Nor was it merely the child-like delusions of one psychopathic narcissist, who talked his way into the Oval Office at a moment when an extraordinary conjunction of conditions made that possible, although it was obviously also that. It was what we might call image-world overreach. It takes media events to be more than pervasive, indeed ubiquitous, the main currency of spectacle societies. It believes them to be the most fundamental kind of event. This attitude is not confined to one person, however, "iconic." As Boorstin and Debord had predicted, the pseudo-event has become pervasive in contemporary iconomies.

Yet event enthrallment underestimates the power of process, which operates by the constant reassertion of similar, small-scale events, enacted within the framework of conventions, consensual or imposed. In the United States, the justice system, from lower courts to the Supreme Court, is designed to guard the conventions and the procedures necessary to uneventful evolution or, occasionally, exceptionally, speedier reform. The courts have the daily task of determining whether the existing legal processes have been properly followed in particular cases—in this case, the act of voting in a democratic system—based on the evidence about actions in the world that is placed before them. Lacking such evidence, the Trump lawsuits, in effect, asked these courts to perform an act what would take the form of a legal ruling, while in fact being a fabricated media event that would have the direct political effect of invalidating the elections and leaving Trump in the Oval Office. Most such attempts have, to date, failed, including at a Supreme Court stacked—as Trump himself candidly admitted—in anticipation of precisely this eventuality. While we should expect this in a democratic society, such expectations have proven fragile in several states within Europe (think Poland, Hungary, and counting), Africa, and South America in recent decades. And they have been under constant pressure in the United States, as Trump and his supporters within a Republican Party that has been almost entirely molded in his image, continue to try everything they can, in every sphere, to centralize power around him as its figurehead.

It should not go unnoticed that, on January 6, there were simultaneous assaults or attempted assaults on governmental centers in Washington, Louisiana, Florida, Ohio, Oregon, and Georgia. They were ill-planned attempts at insurrection, premature ejaculations that failed—in Washington, DC, spectacularly so—exposing the plotters (including the Wizard in the White House) and their guileless followers to prosecution, jail, and eventual impotence. Nevertheless, could it be that the occupation, however brief, signaled a future in which such a coup would be actual and could be made permanent? Stand down, stand ready. Wait for the call of the Leader. The Munich putsch of 1923 is a precedent. If not Trump, then someone less lazy, more competent, and more ruthless might be sensing an opportunity to lead their side to victory. The known candidates seem implausible, but then, in 2015, so was Donald J. Trump, and look what he did during his four years! In the meantime, his supporters avow, let us work tirelessly to prevent the possibility of elections being stolen again—that is to say, lost by our side of what will be, for the foreseeable future, a cultural/political divide in the nation. Trump himself was among the first to realize that the White nationalist agenda would reliably attract around 40% of voters, whereas modifications of it would dissolve this reliable rump. The trick then becomes how to reshape the electoral institutions so that this minority prevails against the majorities that the other side is likely to muster. Republican legislatures across the country picked up the pace of their gerrymandering and narrowing of voter eligibility laws. Throughout 2021 and 2022, Republican legislators in several states wrote laws that restricted the capacity of those likely to vote against them while at the same time making it less likely that election results would be arrived at without ambiguity, thus opening pathways to challenge the outcome if they lost.

Midnight in America, with all the lights full on.[8] The conditions are being created for demagoguery by default. What stands against this push?

Rebuilding America?

Despite constant simplification in all media and on their own part, the warring parties in the putative second Civil War in the United States do not form into readily discernible, largely self-defining, left–right divisions of political opinion. Among the formal political parties, both Republicans and Democrats have, for decades, prioritized the interests and the values of free market economies, largely in neoliberal terms. Obama's pro-Wall Street response to the 2008 global financial crisis was matched by Trump's only major legislative achievement: tax breaks for the wealthy. On the other hand, the Left has always had a considerable political presence in the United States, despite concerted repression, constant denigration by liberals, and its own self-defeatism. Yet its influence has been discontinuous, and—unlike in much of Europe, the (not so) United Kingdom, Australia, and elsewhere—its agendas have never been institutionalized in a major party that plausibly competes for national governance.[9] Bernie Sanders's strength as a "democratic socialist" candidate in the Democratic primaries for the 2016 and 2020 elections, and the support for Elizabeth Warren in the latter, were clear indications of a revival of progressivism. In both cases, however, an establishment contender emerged as the party's candidate, with Democrat electors sensing that the overall electorate was not yet ready for that much change.

Even before the 2020 election there were, however, deeper signs of the growing strength of progressive politics within the Democratic Party itself The capture of the Republican Party by right-wing ideologues and evangelical purists, a capture personified by Trump and entrenched by McConnell's leadership, made the need to compete on institutional ground obvious to many, especially many women, who had previously focused their energies on local activism. Self-identifying progressive candidates ran in record numbers in the 2018 midterm elections, with some, such as Alexandria Ocasio-Cortez and Rashida Tlaib, achieving significant success. In 2020, Jamaal Brown, Mari Newman, and Cori Bush were added to this list. Mirroring the Republican Party's shedding of its liberal wing in favor of hard-core, right-wing commitments, the Democratic Party has sidelined its reactionaries in favor of what is now a center-left agenda. A 40-year process, still in train. Key progressivist policies such as Medicare-for-all and the Green New Deal are present in all but name in the policy platform for which Joe Biden could claim a national mandate as clear as any recent president has won. Now that—in recognition of the outraged response to the killing of George Floyd led by Black Lives Matter and put into practice by focused organizations such as Stacey Abrams' Fair Fight Action—racial justice has been added as a priority, the possibility of a genuinely progressive political institution in the United States comes into view. Or, to be more realistic, a workable alliance between centrist, free market welfarism, and a populist progressivism might maintain itself for long enough to keep the Make America Great Yet Again forces at bay. As Nancy Fraser acutely remarks, "the future of the Biden compromise depends on its ability to make sufficient pro-working-class concessions to keep the left populists on board and to blunt the force of the right populists. Plus, it must also keep the investor class happy. Not an easy job."[10]

The $US 1.9 trillion American Rescue Plan, which passed through Congress on March 12, 2021, the 50th day of the Biden Administration, was touted by Democrats as the most progressive legislation since Lyndon Johnson's Great Society reforms of 1964. It is no secret that Biden himself compared his challenges to those facing Franklin Delano Roosevelt and saw New Deal scale reforms as the only viable solutions.[11] The 2021 Plan made direct payments to most Americans but was primarily targeted help to the millions of poor through tailored programs such as substantially increased child tax credits or basic child income for families with no taxable income, moves estimated to cut child poverty by 50%. Workers without children received tax benefits. The Affordable Care Act was significantly expanded, state welfare programs boosted, and unemployment relief increased. The Plan also offered some relief to those with student debt repayments, emergency rental relief to those in danger of eviction, and support to the homeless. Billions were provided for personal protective equipment (PPE) and for distribution of Covid-19 vaccines. Smaller initiatives had important implications: In what could be a step toward reparation for the historic legacy of slavery, black farmers received four billion dollars. Polls showed 70% of Americans in favor, including 6 in 10 Republican voters. Nevertheless, not a single Republican legislator voted for the Plan, claiming that it went well beyond direct relief from the pandemic as a health risk. They were right. While Biden touts the same bipartisanship as did Obama during his first term, he is not modifying urgently needed reformist legislation in the false hope of Republican support. Even some conservative commentators began to discern the dawn of a genuinely equitable mode of democratic governance.[12] But centralized reform on the massive scale necessary continues to face the occlusion of a nearly evenly divided polity, at least as that is expressed in elected representatives. Thus, major "Build Back America" bills on infrastructure—both physical and societal—stalled in Congress throughout 2021 and 2022, confidence in government by consensus shrinking a little each day.

Biden's Plain Style

The set designers for the Biden Administration concentrate hard on two or three thematics. Pairing the President with Vice-President Kamala Harris whenever executive orders are signed, and important announcements made. On the Oval Office wall, a large portrait of FDR centrally located, with busts of Martin Luther King and Robert F. Kennedy at either side, in contrast to his predecessors' preference for a bust of Winston Churchill and a portrait of General Andrew Jackson, destroyer of Southern cities during the Civil War and, afterward, as President, of Reconstruction.[13] Frequent visits to Biden's modest family home in Scranton, Pennsylvania, in contrast to Trump Tower, New York, Mar-a-Lago, Florida, and Trump-owned golf courses everywhere. The President as the leading partner in the expert business management of the pandemic and every other conceivable crisis (Fig. 12.7).

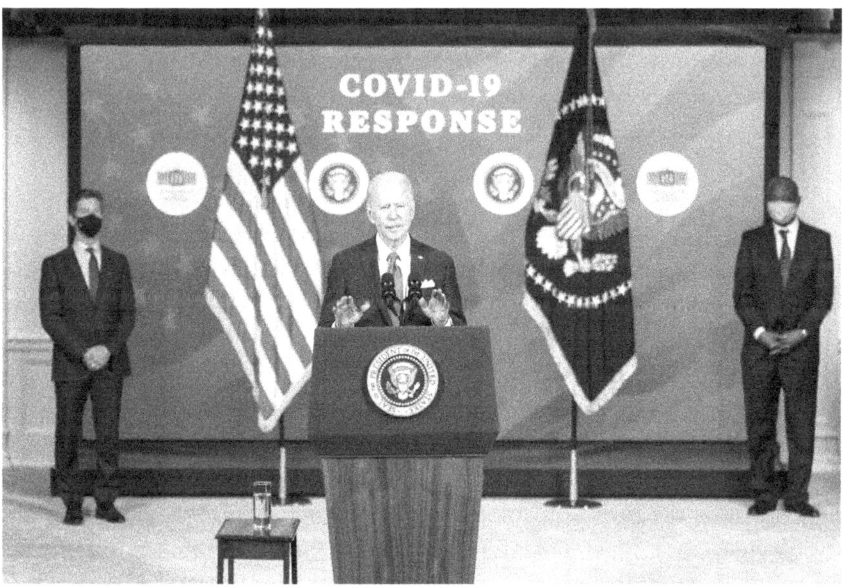

Fig. 12.7: President Joseph Biden with the CEOs of Johnson & Johnson and Merck on March 10, 2021. Photograph Adam Schultz/The White House.

The Biden rhetoric of straight talking laced with emotional appeals turns on hard fact truth-telling mixed with evocations of familiar, family-focused scenarios. His first national televised address on March 11, 2021, watched by 89 million, was presented in front of a corridor of state flags.[14] He began by evoking family photographs of life 12 months prior, before the virus was notified. The failure of his predecessor to deal with the pandemic was left implicit, but its toll was not. Biden read out the number of US deaths as of his moment of speaking: 527,726, more than the losses in the two world wars, Vietnam and 9/11 combined. Recognizing the psychic impact of enforced separation, he nonetheless deplored political division and personal anger, singling out hate crimes against Asian Americans. He quickly turned to celebrating America's ability to "find the light in the midst of darkness," declared that government's first job is to "tell the truth"—namely, that the virus is the greatest threat. War against it is not hyperbole, he averred, it is the primary task of "we the people." He detailed the virtues of the American Rescue Plan, outlined reforms to come, highlighted the accelerating vaccination program, while pleading with viewers to see themselves as working together, still following Centers for Disease Control rules, to build back the economy and defeat the virus. He pictured July 4, Independence Day, five months away, as a moment when all Americans could celebrate together, in their normal ways, having overcome "the darkest period we have ever known." The contrast with his unnamed predecessor's appetite for carnage was stark. "We," not "I." "I need you," not "I am." Empathy, not ego.

A necessary shift in political style. A plausible tone in the days before COVID-19 struck back with its Delta variant. Would it be enough to cool down the nation as it approaches the boiling point of full-scale civil war?

Opening the Doors of the White House

One further dimension of January 6 calls for consideration. As an action within a symbolic array, if imagined as a collage, the main thrust of the day can be seen as an attempt to fuse one white building—literally, The White House—with another, larger one: the Capitol. Occupied by Donald Trump—in Ta-Nehisi Coates' apt description, "the first white president"—the White House was the home of the Whitest forms of White rule and aspired to even greater racial purity. The politicians working at the Capitol are mostly White and have for decades been mostly concerned with securing or reforming the privileges of those they represent, although some are committed to affirmative action in their parties, their districts, and their lives, and work steadily to follow through on that commitment. Almost all the demonstrators who became an insurrectionary mob on January 6 were White. In a typical

American contradiction, most of the Capitol police officers who tried to contain them were colored. Picture these elements. How do they fit together? Can they be collaged, convincingly?

Pan out to a larger picture. Compare the police treatment of Black Lives Matter protestors with how the police responded to those who stormed the Capitol. There are of course factors on the ground specific to each time and place. Yet the overall difference is striking. Asked about this the following day, author Ibram X. Kendi was unequivocal: "My takeaway is that, yesterday, we saw in many ways, white privilege on display at the US Capitol. You have many people who are black, Latinx, who are Native, looking at what those white domestic terrorists were doing and were thinking that if they had been black, they would not only certainly have been arrested, but also people would have been killed."[15]

This civil war has been going on since slavery was institutionalized in the Americas. It is a significant subcurrent, among several others, within the broader divisions that are emerging and coalescing across the country. How might we counter this divisiveness? X. Kendi alerts us to one starting point: "What we saw, at the US Capitol, is part of us. That is who we are. It's not all of us, but it's part of us. In America, there's a long history of white domestic terror laying siege on American democracy. We have to own that and accept that, because that's the only way we can rid this country of it."[16]

In Chapter 13, I will explore how certain actors within contemporary image worlds, especially artists—the research and development agents within iconomies—are showing us some of the ways in which this might be done. It is turning out that Black artists are leading the way.

Notes

1 It has since emerged that Trump had accepted a legal fiction prepared by law professor John Eastman that Vice-President Pence had the power to declare the certification of certain electors invalid, announce a majority for Trump, and declare him re-elected. Later that morning, Pence sent a letter stating that he did not have "the unilateral authority" to do so. See The Editorial Board, "Opinion: Jan. 6 Was Worse Than We Feared," *New York Times*, October 2, 2021, at https://www.nytimes.com/2021/10/02/opinion/jan-6-trump-eastman-election.html. Drawing on evidence in Bob Woodward and Robert Costa, *Peril* (New York: Simon & Shuster, 2021), which also includes accounts of the efforts of General Mark A. Milley, chairman of the Joint Chiefs of Staff, to block what he feared might be attempts by Trump to create a state of emergency—including announcements about possible nuclear war or war with China—that would require him to stay in office.

2 Clint Smith, "The Whole Story in a Single Photo," *The Atlantic*, January 8, 2021, at https://www.theatlantic.com/ideas/archive/2021/01/confederates-in-the-capitol/617594/.

3 Mike Davis, "Trench Warfare: Notes on the 2020 Election," *New Left Review*, no. 126 (November–December, 2020) at https://newleftreview.org/issues/ii126/articles/mike-davis-trench-warfare?pc=1307.

4 Davis cites here William A. Glason, "In the Popular Vote, Why Wasn't Biden's Victory Bigger?', Brookings Institute, posted November 12, 2020.

5 Davis cites here Thomas Carothers and Andrew O'Donahue, "How Americans Were Driven to Extremes," *Foreign Affairs*, September 25, 2019.

6 Davis, "Trench Warfare: Notes on the 2020 Election."

7 Office of Mitch McConnell, Republican Leader, "McConnell on Impeachment," posted February 13, 2021, at https://www.republicanleader.senate.gov/newsroom/remarks/mcconnell-on-impeachment-disgraceful-dereliction-cannot-lead-senate-to-defy-our-own-constitutional-guardrails.

8 See Adam Shiff, *Midnight in Washington: How We almost Lost Our Democracy and Still Could* (New York: Penguin Random House, 2021). For pertinent remarks on Trump's evocation of the post-election period as "a temporal non-man's land" that has created a "great prairie of paranoia between what happened and what *really* happened" (Trump won), see Fintan O'Toole, "Democracy's afterlife," *The New York Review of Books*, December 3, 2020, 4-8.

9 James N. Gregory, "Remapping the American Left: A History of Radical Discontinuity," *Labor: Studies in Working-Class History*, vol. 17, no. 2 (2020), 11–45.

10 Nancy Fraser, "American Interregnum," *New Left Review*, Sidecar, April 20, 2021, at https://newleftreview.org/sidecar/posts/american-interregnum?pc=1331.

11 See James Bouie, "Joe Biden Knew He Was on to Something Long Before We Did," *New York Times*, March 12, 2021, at https://www.nytimes.com/2021/03/12/opinion/biden-covid-plan.html?action=click&module=Opinion&pgtype=Homepage.

12 David Brooks, "Joe Biden Is a Transformational President," *New York Times*, March 11, 2021, at https://www.nytimes.com/2021/03/11/opinion/biden-covid-relief-bill.html?action=click&module=Opinion&pgtype=Homepage.

13 For a review of the messaging in Oval Office art choices going back to John F. Kennedy, see Larry Buchanan and Matt Stevens, "The Art in the Oval Office Tells a Story: Here's How to See It," *New York Times*, May 5, 2021, at https://www.nytimes.com/interactive/2021/05/05/arts/design/oval-office-art.html?action=click&module=Well&pgtype=Homepage&section=Arts.

14 White House, Washington, DC, "Remarks by President Biden on the Anniversary of the COVID-19 Shutdown," March 11, 2021, at https://www.whitehouse.gov/briefing-room/speeches-remarks/2021/03/11/remarks-by-president-biden-on-the-anniversary-of-the-covid-19-shutdown/.

15 Interview with Ibram X. Kendi, "Police response at Capitol brings claim of 'white privilege'," *PBS Newshour*, January 7, 2021, at https://www.pbs.org/newshour/show/police-response-at-the-capitol-we-saw-white-privilege-on-display.

16 Ibid.

Chapter 13

WHITE ARTWORLDS/BLACK AESTHETICS

We have been tracing a contest of images within the United States that falls along racial, class, geographic, ideological, and party-political lines. Most of the time, these social divisions remain multiplicitous, not quite coalescing into the kind of generalized partisan divides and armed conflict that characterize full-scale civil war. Yet, the media campaigns orchestrated around Donald Trump, and the protests following the circulation of the video of George Floyd's murder, highlighted contrasting aspects of what might be called the cultural phase of such a war. So did January 6, 2021, when considered as a peak action within a concerted campaign by supporters of Trumpism determined to "Stop the Steal." In both cases, mass media events were staged with the intent of effecting direct political change. In the United States and everywhere else during recent decades, the game has changed. The iconomy has become intensely politicized. And politics has become intensely iconomic.

Control of the circulation of images has always been important in any struggle for political advantage. Today, their saturation of most aspects everyday life means that they also occupy its extraordinary moments, those that connect us or threaten to abruptly disconnect us. We have been tracing the kinds of control over image circulation exercised by the social media companies, by governments of all kinds, by certain religions, by legal systems, and by dominant economic agendas, notably that of neoliberal capitalism and its recent centralized, statist variants. In the previous chapters, we also tracked the widespread emergence of strategies of contracirculation, and of engendering diversification, especially among activists who are building campaigns that resist these systems and envisage alternatives. This chapter will focus on the contribution to these strategies of artists, particularly Black artists, working with these widely circulating images to show why and how Black lives matter.

The "Political" Biennial

In New York in 1993, George Holliday's video of the beating of Rodney King was exhibited in the Whitney Biennial of that year as a work of art. Curator John G. Hanhardt saw it as such, as formally aligned with the examples of contemporary avant-garde and experimental video that he was showing in his section of the exhibition. He believed, moreover, that this video "extended the definition of documentary," that it would push other artists working in that genre toward a more engaged, real-world practice. The video was, Hanhardt said,

> part of a whole body of work I am showing which focuses on an emerging practice within video to rethink the medium and address public issues [...] There's a long history of art showing us something about the world; the Holliday tape adds a new dynamic to that tradition [...] George Holliday has revealed something about the world, the police brutality that we have heard about but most of us haven't seen.[1]

Neither this degree of naivete about police beatings nor this kind of instinctive presumption as to art's social relevance and its inherent importance have much purchase these days. Yet, confrontations continue to occur when "something about the [real] world" enters an artworld. Some clashes are same old, many are new, and the borders between these worlds have developed different logics of hardness and permeability. What have these changes put at stake for artmaking, the curating of exhibitions, and the critical interpretation of both when the representation of Black lives not mattering is the matter at hand?

A chorus of condemnation—expressed by art critics with left, right, and center orientations—was visited upon the 1993 Biennial. Accusations of "political correctness" were matched by complaints as to the "poor quality" of most of the artworks. The de facto liberal position was this: Yes, art can and should, when necessary, allude to real-world issues, but not at the cost of artistic achievement/visual pleasure and not in the same, unsubtle ways in which politics is usually conducted. Almost all critics singled out the inclusion of the video of Rodney King being beaten as the step too far that conclusively demonstrated the bad faith of the curators involved. [2]

Writing in *The Nation*, philosopher/critic Arthur Danto offered the most cogent account of the conceptual issues at stake:

> Now, the King tape certainly demonstrated the power of images and at the same time the limits of art, for no work of art in recent (or perhaps any) time has had a fraction of the effect upon society that the King

> tape has had upon ours: The broken storefronts, the burning city, the many dead—to paraphrase Yeats—all unleashed not so much by an act of police violence as by the fact that it was recorded and shown. The images had the effect in part because they were not art, because they were the flat and uninflected effect of reality mechanically registered on videotape: It was the zero degree of visual and moral truth the world beheld; were it to occur to someone that art might have had something to do with it, the effect of the tape would be diminished. I can understand an artist seeking to borrow the power of the King images for, let us suppose, creative purposes of his or her own, the way Spike Lee sought to do with his appropriation of them in the opening sequence of *Malcolm X*. Lee put them into a work of art without making the tape itself into a work of art; and indeed nothing can or should make a work of art out of that tape. That would put us in just the wrong relationship to it. In fact, any relationship in which we are put to the images other than the relationship in which they put us to the event they transcribe and record is a wrong relationship. About the tape itself there is nothing to say. It may seem unjust that snow shovels, bottle racks, bicycle wheels and Brillo boxes can cross the line into museum precincts while this tape languishes without. Still, it is instructive that there is something that evidently resists being turned into a work of art.[3]

His reference to "snow shovels, bottle racks, bicycle wheels and Brillo boxes" evokes three works by Marcel Duchamp and the 1964 exhibition by Andy Warhol which, at the time, had provoked Danto to conceive his institutional theory of art. The gist of which is that the actual answer to the question "What is Art?" is whatever the community of language users committed to the making, dissemination, and interpretation of works of art (the artworld) says that it is.[4] At first, with his New York milieu as his model, he envisaged these communities as naturally open-minded, even avant-gardist, disposed toward accepting the most radical challenges to their presumptions and norms. Yet, the instant, almost universal rejection of the Holliday video—including by himself, now a member of that world—shocked him into realizing that "Institutionalism has its limits, and that the concept of art is not quite as plastic as recent turns in the history of art have led theorists to believe."[5] Artworld boundary marking, he discovered, could retreat as well as advance.

Beneath this debate about what kind of concept of Art was currently securing consensus, the grinding of the gears of a more intractable difference could be heard. Was not the argument over the admissibility of the King video as art an evasion of what the video so clearly showed before it got to the court in Simi Valley?

Reflecting on this exhibition a decade later, Danto was aware that the situation had changed, although a different kind of racism was at the forefront of his thinking. At a time when the photographs of the perverse degradation of Iraqi prisoners by US soldiers in Abu Ghraib prison had just been released, he recalled the earlier moment and asked:

> The 1993 Whitney Biennial showed the Rodney King tape, the appropriateness of which was contested on the grounds that it was not art, even though it was widely felt that the footage had already become part of American self-consciousness. And if one of the aims of the exhibition was to make this self-consciousness accessible, what image could do it better? I wonder whether the same is not true for the Abu Ghraib photographs, which might well be among the exhibits of the 2006 Biennial. My sense is that, hideous as the conduct they depict is, the Abu Ghraib photographs are powerful examples of how images can change what we are, and from that perspective they must from now on act as standards against which we can judge the political efficacy of art.[6]

What changed during the intervening years? As curator Theodor Ringborg notes in his acute analysis of the implications of the showing of the King tape and subsequent imagery of violence in art museums, the "ruminative museumgoer has given way to a 'civic spectator' who watches the image in order to view its conditions of fabrication and the new possibilities for intervening in what it frames."[7] He is evoking Ariella Azoulay's argument about the kind of "civil contract" elicited by widely circulated imagery of the kind we have been discussing. As she says, "A new spectatorial position has emerged within the museum, a position from which a responsibility to the sense of the image has coalesced with the responsibility toward the photographed. As a result, an influx of images of horror has transformed the museum into an alternative site vis-à-vis the media and its particular logic."[8] Indeed, at a time when most major newspapers and television channels in the United States would not show the Abu Ghraib images, the directors of some museums, notably the International Center for Photography, New York, and the Andy Warhol Museum, Pittsburgh, had the courage to do so, in an exhibition entitled *Inconvenient Evidence*.[9] Today, of course, the "civic spectator" is not confined to the museum: we are everywhere. But we are not the same, not "civic" in the same ways, and so we see things differently, and differently from each other.

What these examples have in common is that an image, or a body of imagery, intended for showing in a particular context other than an art one—and which, when shown, was highly effective on an overtly political level—appears in an exhibition in an art museum, where it is intended by its curators to be understood as setting, in Danto's words, "standards against which we can measure the political efficacy of art." Elision is everywhere in such situations, not least as an escape hatch. But so are some hard questions. Especially when we return to the concern of this chapter: What have social and political changes since the 1990s put at stake for artmaking, the curating of exhibitions, and the critical interpretation of both when the representation of Black lives not mattering at all is the matter at hand?[10]

Before the Law

In 2015, art historian David Joselit was provoked to pose a version of this question in an essay in *Artforum*:

> The failure in December 2014 of a Staten Island grand jury to indict the policemen who choked Eric Garner, an African American man accused of selling loose cigarettes on the street, delivered another kind of indictment: an indictment of post-Conceptual art. If the excruciating video of Garner seized and being relentlessly piled on by police could not convince a jury, how can forms of aesthetic critique based on research and visual evidence be more effective with a general public? While the life-and-death exigencies of American race politics should not be glibly equated with art's more distanced forms of engagement, proponents of visual politics would do well to learn from the Garner case.[11]

If "proponents of visual politics" include activists and "artivists," they have, surely, been aware of this situation for decades, as has every African American and many others as well. Why "post-Conceptual art" (left undefined: is it all the art celebrated in *Artforum*?) should fall under indictment by a Staten Island grand jury's failure to react to the Garner tapes is unclear. Nevertheless, Joselit's alarm led him to a version of the questions that concern us in this chapter. He expands it into a challenge to all art that would be in any sense "political":

> how can we account for the fact that the video of a police officer pressing his arm against Garner's throat—a document that could not have been less ambiguous—did not 'speak for itself' before the members of a grand jury? If such a visual artifact can so blatantly fail in the task of representation before the law, both politically, as the proxy for an absent victim, and rhetorically, as evidence, doesn't this present a challenge to how we define the politics of art?

In a previous chapter we explored the many reasons why visual documents, when exhibited and spoken for in a court of law or on a cable news channel, can be turned to mean the opposite of what they meant when made. Joselit is raising a parallel case, asking whether interventionist art, that aims to persuade by revealing a stunning fact, or many facts, about real world injustice (his example is the work of Forensic Architecture, which does the latter in the mode of multi-viewpoint, surround sound objectivity), can ever hope to succeed in securing its affects when "the general public" has become impervious to inconvenient truths wherever and however they are presented. The only kind of art that might do so, he suggests, is that exemplified by Pope.L's performances, such as *Eating the Wall Street Journal*, which was performed several times between 1991 and 2000 and restaged at the New Museum in 2010 (Fig. 13.1). Joselit's key point is that Pope.L does not *represent* the point he wishes to make, he *is* it.[12]

There are problems with the generalizability of Joselit's example: For most audiences, Pope.L's performances are understood as too literal to be art and too eccentric to be political. As well, to read them as entirely singular, turning as they do on "the particularity of individual bodies," is to

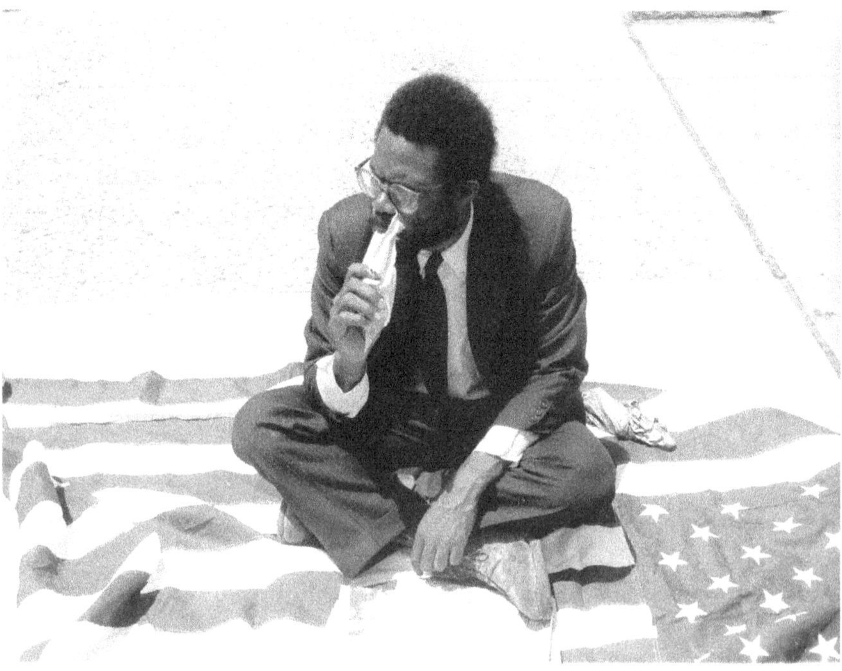

Fig. 13.1: Pope.L, *Eating the Wall Street Journal*, performance, New York City street, 1991. Courtesy Mitchell-Innes & Nash Gallery, New York.

rob them of the collectivity that is a necessary condition of any politics.[13] In this connection, it should be noted that Pope.L envisaged his "crawl" pieces—not least *The Great White Way, 22 Miles, 9 Years, 1 Street*, which entailed him crawling the length of Broadway on a skateboard wearing a Superman Suit—not only as individual performances but as public allegories to be carried out by groups of people.[14] Finally, Joselit's implied distinction between Forensic Architecture's "post-Conceptual" approach and the actuality of Pope.L's work indicates a limited read of conceptualism's legacy: If the former has inherited the strategy of building works around deep research into facts, and the inclination to do so to excess, then the latter inherits conceptualism's inclination to enact an idea in the world and, again, to do so to excess.[15]

Shaun Leonardo is among several artists who have reacted to the spate of police killings of young people of color, and who do so in ways that are both symbolic and actual. Since 2015, he has produced several charcoal drawings based on video imagery of the beating of Rodney King, and the killings of Trayvon Martin, Laquan McDonald, Freddie Gray, Walter Scott, Keith Lamont Scott, Tamir Rice, Freddie Pereira, and Eric Garner. In single images, pairings, or suites in sequence, shock effects are registered through blurred suggestions of partial shapes, as if the victim, and we, are catching glimpses of what is happening and where it is happening. Fragments of each setting cascade around us—a Los Angeles street, a children's playground in Cleveland, a jogging track in Florida, a Brooklyn shopfront, an inner-city sidewalk, some trees. Each place is instantly familiar from having been seen on television, and online, so often. We are in a partially blind panic. We know we are here and we don't want to be here, with this happening, spinning into its inevitably deadly trajectory. We are witnesses who cannot believe what we are seeing, who cannot see everything, and who strive to register details so we can report them accurately. In Leonardo's six drawings, we first see Garner being grabbed by unseen white forms; some arms and a capped man appear, grappling with his absent body; the setting comes into view as he is surrounded; then only the outlines of him appealing "I can't breathe!" can be seen; the entire scene is visible as he appeals again; finally, he and the officers become faint white shapes, the street scene resumes its normality (Fig. 13.2). Against the dumbing blur of the image flow, Leonardo is seeking "space within the tragedies [...] Literally, space within the image where we are forced to continue to look and to contemplate."[16] In 2018, he offered *I Can't Breathe*, "a public, participatory workshop and performance," in which he taught participants self-defense maneuvers, but also, with appropriate warnings, movements that led to moments when they would enact the exact physical exchange that led to

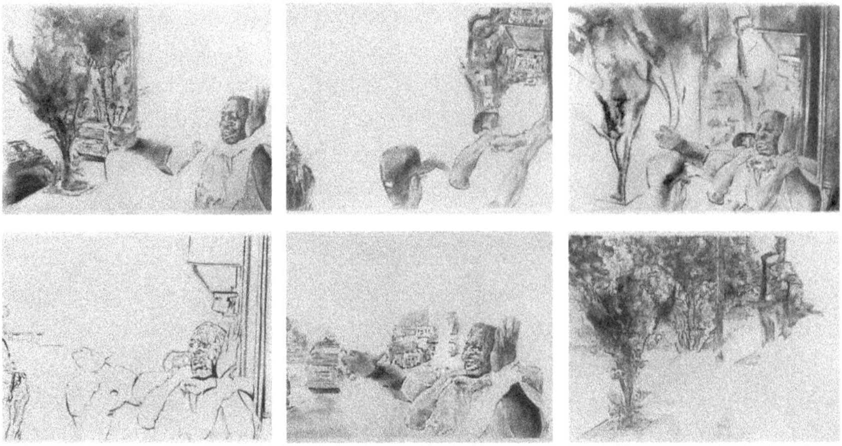

Fig. 13.2: Shaun Leonardo, *Eric Garner (Drawings 1–6)*, 2015, charcoal on paper, each 8.5" × 11". Courtesy of the artist.

the death of victims such as Garner. Watching this, or enacting it, means, he hopes, that we would "wear the trauma of Garner's death differently" than when we watch it on a screen.[17]

Something else not seen in Joselit's commentary is that work of this kind is driven less by the priorities of late modern and emergent contemporary art in general, although they are part of it, more by those of late modern and emergent contemporary "Black aesthetics." Does today's answer to his question, and the larger question we are asking, have its most vibrant life here, in this emergence, haunted by trauma and yet more impending death?

In *Troubling Vision: Performance, Visuality, Blackness* (2011), Nicole F. Fleetwood demonstrates that, in the United States and elsewhere in the West, the presence of Black subjects has always troubled prevailing regimes of visuality through the mere fact of their presence as distinct from the White preference that they be "seen through," remain in their place, and thus "invisible."[18] This relation also troubles—to paraphrase her argument—Black subjects as they come to occupy social positions that attract attention, in, for example, politics, business, entertainment, sports, or the arts. Many who do so become living icons, exemplary exceptions from White perspectives, pioneers of potential change for the better from Black perspectives. Some conform to the negative paradigm of hypervisibility (Michael Jackson's self-whitening), many flout it by flaunting their Blackness to deliberate excess (Malcolm X, Beyoncé, *Black Panther*), while others seek a middle path that emphasizes shared human experience (Oprah Winfrey, Barak Obama) or "non-iconic" ordinariness (Bill Cosby, Charles "Teenie" Harris). Still others, especially artists (Glenn Ligon, Kerry James Marshall, Deana Lawson, Arthur Jafa, and Paul Pfeiffer), leave markers of the racism that they must continue to fight against as "visible seams" in their productions. In every case, the "burden of representation" weighed, or continues to weigh, heavily. Fleetwood notes (in her italics) that "*seeing black is always a problem in a visual field that structures the troubling presence of blackness.*"[19]

The Sounds of Black Mo'nin'

Looking at the famous photographs of the infamously murdered Emmett Till, Fred Moten seeks to trace the trace of what is at stake there if we (asking if there is a "we" who can do this tracing together is the larger possibility to be traced in this asking) were to

> [...] look at it in the context of an aesthetics, look at it as if it were to be looked at, as if it were to be thought, therefore, in terms of a kind of beauty, a kind of detachment, independence, autonomy, that holds open the question of what looking might mean in general, what the aesthetics of the photograph might mean for politics and what those aesthetics might have meant for Mamie Bradley in the context of her demand that her son's face be seen, be shown, that his death and her mourning be performed.[20]

As befits the mobility of eyes/brain/feelings/body in this kind of looking, Moten seems to have in mind not one single photograph shot by a named photographer whose intention is primary, but instead at least six photographs shot by several photographers and reproduced in public media at the time and since. One was a family album photograph of the smiling young man, dressed up for an occasion in Chicago, before his fatal visit to relatives in Mississippi. Two others are close ups of his savaged head, as if recorded in a morgue. A third was taken by press photographer David Jackson in the funeral home: occupying the foreground is Till's upper body and head, distorted by a gunshot wound and bloated by three days under water, now turned white by the preparation solution. In the background, Mamie Bradley looks on, expressionless, as she is comforted by a male friend. These three images were reproduced in a double page spread in *Jet Magazine* in 1955, while similar ones appeared in the *Chicago Defender*, including one showing Till's upper body and head exposed in the casket.[21] A fifth image, a widely circulated Associated Press photograph, is a high-angle view looking down on some of the thousands who filed past Till's open casket. A woman mourner, dressed in white, turns to look up from her station at the head of the coffin, as if her name was just called by the photographer. She turns to see who is seeing from our vantage point. A look flashes across time. Finally, another image of the funeral, held in a Chicago church on September 3, 1955, and now the most widely circulated of them all, shows Mamie Bradley in a state of intense grief, being comforted at the side of the casket. We cannot see the body of Emmett, but two snapshots of him and one of him and her beaming with happiness are pinned to the underside of the open lid (Fig. 10.2). The gap between the boy as he hoped to present himself to the future and the brute reality of his battered body in the casket is exposed, without equivocation. Moten:

> Emmett Till's face is seen, shown, shone. His face was destroyed (by way of, among other things, its being shown: the memory of his face is thwarted, made a distant before-as-after effect of its destruction, what we would never have otherwise seen). It was turned inside out, ruptured, exploded, but deeper than that it was opened. As if his face were the truth's condition of possibility, it was opened and revealed. As if revealing his face would open the revelation of fundamental truth, his casket was opened, as if revealing the destroyed face would in turn reveal, and therefore cut, the active deferral or ongoing death or unapproachable futurity of justice. As if his face would deconstruct justice or deconstruct deconstruction or deconstruct death, though this infinite and circular chain seems too muddled, too crazy, too twisted and clotted, as if it, too, were in need of another cut, it was shown.[22]

At this point, Moten's deconstructive reading—precipitated by Mamie Bradley's performance, itself deconstructive, that uses photography as its medium—reaches a limit, absorbs itself, as he acknowledges. Then he writes on, as one must. He forges through a thicket of other writing about photography, death, and looking, as one also must, because he is not only performing a "Black aesthetic" reading of an instance of "Black aesthetic" performance (not just any instance but one of most paradigmatic ones), he is also finding the theoretical tools necessary to do so. And he is demonstrating their use *according to the same beat,* while flying solo *in the break.*

These photographs circulated a few months after the opening of one of the most famous and celebrated exhibitions of photography staged during the twentieth century, *The Family of Man*, curated by Edward Steichen for the Museum of Modern Art, after which it went on a worldwide tour. Among its 503 images, one of a lynched Black man was withdrawn before the exhibition opened on the grounds that response to it might confuse the positive message of shared humanity that Steichen intended to convey. It was one among several exclusions (imagery of class conflict, atomic radiation, propaganda, etc.)

spelt out in his open call to photographers worldwide to submit images for possible inclusion: "It is essential to keep in mind the universal elements and aspects of human relations and experiences common to all mankind rather than situations that represented conditions exclusively related to or peculiar to a race, an event, a time or place."[23] Against this "always and necessarily false universalism," Moten argues that Mamie Bradley's intervention was undertaken in the name of "a dynamic universality (which critically moves in, among other things, grief, anger, hatred, the desire to expose and eradicate savagery) whose organization would suspend the conditions of possibility of deaths like Emmett Till's, that the photo was shown, is seen."[24]

These conditions are not merely those that greater conceptual insight and enlightened social reform might amend. They are universals according to this sounding:

> Black Art, which is to say Black Life, which is to say Black (Life Against) death, which is to say Black Eros, is the ongoing production of a performance: rupture and collision, augmented toward singularity, motherless child, childless mother, heartrending shriek, levee camp moan, grieving lean and head turn, fall, *Stabat mater*, turn a step, loose booty funk stroke down my cheek, yellow dog, blue train, black drive. The ways black mo'nin' improvises through the opposition of mourning and melancholia, disrupts the temporal framework that buttresses that opposition such that an extended, lingering look at—aesthetic response to—the photograph manifests itself as political action.[25]

Above Till's coffin, behind a table covered in a white cloth, sat members of the church, with a microphone to one side. The church was filled with sounds of Black mo'nin', including that of Mamie Bradley. So are the photographs, and the artworks discussed in this chapter, if we are willing to share the discomfort, the work of "*looking through, with, alongside another*," which hearing the voices of the emergent "Black gaze" requires of us.[26]

Amazing Grace

Arthur Jafa's 7-minute video *Love is the Message: The Message is Death* (2016) manifests Black mo'nin' as itself, on its own terms, while at the same time working as a music video meditation on Kayne West's hip-hop/rap song "Ultralight Beam," which supplies its sound.[27] West's lyrics juxtapose passages of pure gospel with highly personal diatribes, of hopes for salvation riven by doubt, everything leavened with a repeated chorus: "This is a God dream," "We on an ultralight beam," "This is everything, Everything."

Recorded sound is sampled, while gospel singer Kirk Franklin, R&B singers The-Dream and Kelly Price, and Chance the Rapper sing significant passages, backed by a 10-voice choir. Sound swirls and drifts, as if being continually swept up and pushed forward from the same place, rushed and slowed down, looped and then doubled. In Jafa's video, the rapid editing of the images reinforces this sense of Black bodies constantly being beaten down and, in what seems the same time, unexpectedly arriving at rapture, only to hover there, on the cusp of deliverance, dancing, even while on the run. Recent film of police arrests, beatings, and other arbitrary interventions into Black lives resonate with historical imagery of the same actions during the 1960s. Clips from current television and film footage echo with extracts from D.W. Griffith's infamous *The Birth of the Nation*. Apocalyptical imagery abounds, from *Godzilla* to closeups of explosions on the surface of the sun. Yet, woven throughout are outpourings of Black American resistance and creativity, from Martin Luther King Jr. campaigning, Civil Rights protests, to extraordinary sporting feats, Serena Williams celebrating, Barack Obama breaking into *Amazing Grace*. The stirring chorus that ends West's song is visualized through the culmination of a James Brown performance, itself an apogee of Black vocality.[28] Jafa speaks of wanting to show the Black condition as an "abject sublime."[29] *Love is the Message: The Message is Death* does this, exactly (Figs 13.3 and 13.4).

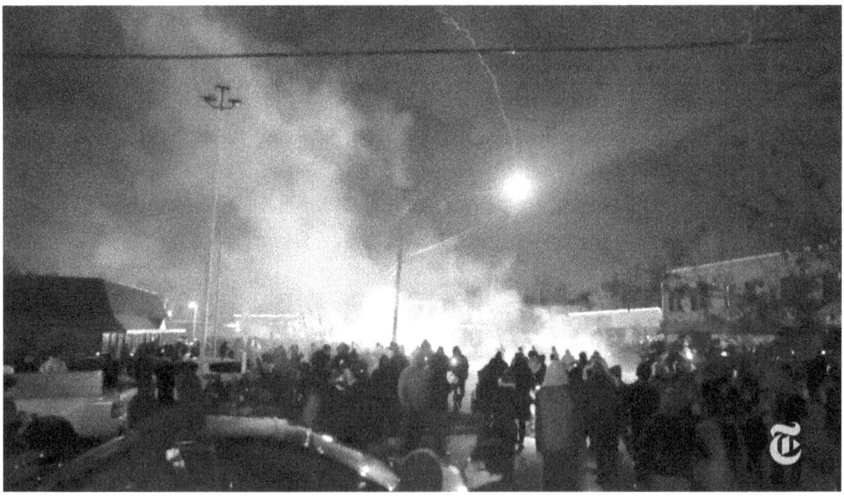

Fig. 13.3: Arthur Jafa, *Love Is the Message: The Message Is Death*, 2016, 7-minute video installation. Video still showing a crowd. © Arthur Jafa. Courtesy of the artist and Gladstone Gallery.

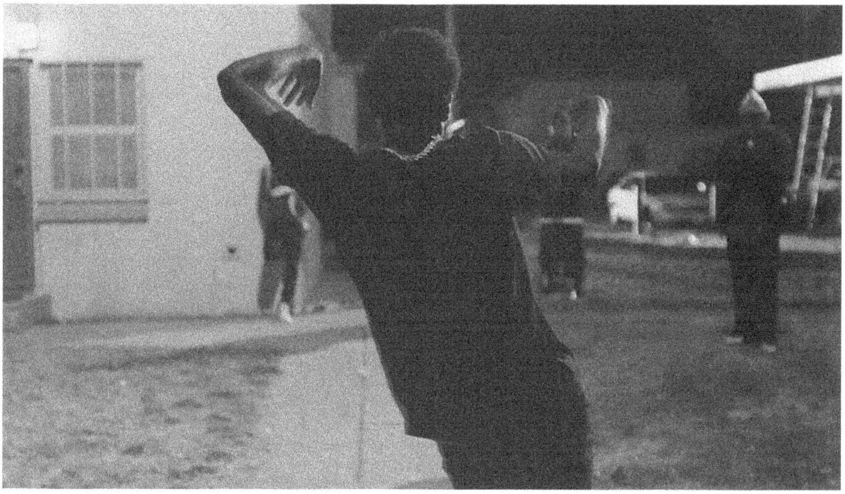

Fig. 13.4: Arthur Jafa, *Love is the Message: The Message is Death*, 2016, 7-minute video installation. Video still showing a youth dancing. © Arthur Jafa. Courtesy of the artist and Gladstone Gallery.

Jafa is explicit about addressing his work primarily to other Black people, saying that most art, and nearly every institution, simply presumes that it speaks to a White audience, so it is about time that White people experience the discomfort of not being addressed.[30] There are many layers in play here, some counterintuitive. For example: what would it be for a Black artist to show White people talking about their White blindness as if the judgement of the speaker by each Black member of the watching audience was situationally, naturally, presumed to count inestimably more than that of any (minority, incidental) White member?

A question of this kind provoked Jafa's 40-minute film installation, *The White Album* (2018), which shows more than 30 videos culled from Instagram, CCTV, and surveillance webcams interwoven with footage shot by him (Fig. 13.5). In a statement about the work, he explained

> One could say it's about the difference or distinction between 'whiteness' and 'white people'. Or perhaps, more bluntly, the difference between *bad* 'whiteness' and *good* 'whiteness'. The piece juxtaposes portraits I've taken of friends and found footage of 'whiteness' in action. Understandably, nobody wanted to be in the vicinity of all this *bad* 'whiteness' (footage of white supremacist and mass murderer Dylann Roof, among others). Participating definitely required a leap of faith on the part of my friends, who comprise a select group of (white)

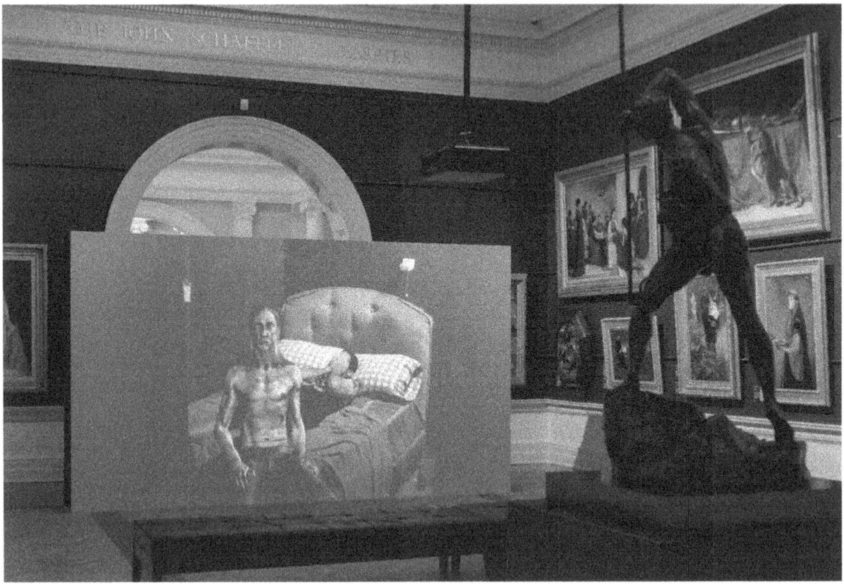

Fig. 13.5: Arthur Jafa, *The White Album*, 2018–19. Installation view for the 22nd Biennale of Sydney (2020), Art Gallery of New South Wales. Originally commissioned by the UC Berkeley Art Museum and Pacific Film Archive (BAMPFA). Presented at the 22nd Biennale of Sydney with assistance from the United States Government. Courtesy the artist and Gavin Brown's enterprise, New York/Rome. Photograph: Alex Robinson.

> folks (really important cultural or artistic figures) who I'd say have demonstrated an 'atypical' relationship to 'blackness'; a relationship I'd characterize as, not only progressive, but uniquely their own. They are offered up both for scrutiny and as points of identification; safe landing zones in the avalanche of (white) madness on display. For me, the question is: What is one to make of that which one cannot not know and that which one must, ultimately, unknow?[31]

The White Album opens with a full screen, in-your-face shot of Alex, the anti-hero in *Clockwork Orange*, mouthing his craziness. Later, blurred footage of aerial bombing of Iraq by US forces is intercut with that of the beating of white truck driver Reginald Denny by Black rioters during the uprising that followed the acquittal of the officers who clubbed Rodney King. Denny's eventual rescue by other Black residents is not shown. Iggy Pop's 2017 video *The Pure and the Damned*, performed by his zombie surrogate, is intercut with surveillance camera footage of Dylann Roof arriving in the parking lot and then calmly entering and leaving the Southern Baptist church in Charleston where he killed 12 Black worshippers. It is assumed that we recognize Roof and know that he did. The Iggy Pop video does not relieve us from the horror of imagining Roof's actions. Were Jafa to use the Floyd video, he might cut it against a sequence in *The White Album* in which YouTube personality Dixon White, a self-described "redneck," discourses for six minutes, brilliantly dismantling the illogics of White supremacism, albeit in a heavy Southern drawl and a sneering tone. Or with clip of a white girl (Honey Boo Boo) complaining, also at length, that Blacks and Hispanics are too sensitive about her earnest efforts to talk about race. And perhaps with the work's concluding passage: close ups, skin pore length, of his dealer Gavin Brown and a young woman gallery assistant in their New York gallery space.

Jafa acknowledged Cornell West's challenge to Black artists to show "What one cannot not know as a black person in America."[32] If Mamie Bradley exposed the beaten, bloated head of her dead son so that "they all could see what they had done," to show what White suprematism looks like when all the superstructures are stripped away, then *The White Album* might be understood as an attempt to show what one cannot, should not, not know as a White person in America. Since the video of the murder of George Floyd has declared its truths, that knowing extends to the world.

It should be obvious that Moten and Jafa answer Danto's and Joselit's question by reversing its terms and by reaching for a more "dynamic universality" that is also rooted in the particular contexts in which it arises. The Floyd video has already had the enormous impacts we have charted. It does not depend on a court of law for verification. Its impact may eventually be blunted, as the institutions close ranks against its implications. But it has done, and will keep on doing, its work. On its smaller scale, Jafa's work is having its impacts in its relevant settings, online, and in artworlds. For many years a cinematographer, especially of music videos, and experimental filmmaker, Jafa accepts the welcome he has had as an artist, including receipt of the Golden Lion Award for *The White Album* as the best work at the 2019 Venice Biennale. But he does not rely on such awards for his entire validation. His recent work is mostly presented as looped video installations intended for showing within gallery and museum exhibitions at, for example, the Museum of Contemporary Art in the artist's city Los Angeles. But it also, and inevitably, lives on YouTube.

It should be obvious that he is building, respectfully, on what he calls "the black body of work," not only the great cultural achievement that is the blues ("Black music is *the* music of the twentieth century") but also the work of many Black visual artists, including those who respond to the same "abject sublime" in similarly comprehensive ways: among them are Ulysses Jenkins, Adrian Piper, Kerry James Marshall, Lorna Simpson, Carrie Mae Weems, Kara Walker, Dread Scott, Henry Taylor, and Shaun Leonardo. John Akomfrah's epic video installations—treating the impacts of colonialism on Black bodies and natural phenomena—are a powerful British parallel to Jafa's concerns.[33] Some of these artists might also be building on the example of the few White artists who have sought ways to imagine the violence inherent in their whiteness. Artists such as Philip Guston, who did so along with some others during the 1930s, and then again, more definitively, in the late 1960s, when, almost alone among his peers, he painted his alter-ego as a hooded Klu Klux Klansman.[34]

The Black aesthetic that Moten seeks to theorize—a practice of *looking musically*, or, to put it another way, of "being the blues"—is, as we have seen, created by the work of Black artists such as Jafa. In its name, Moten wants to "challenge not only the ocularcentrism that generally—perhaps necessarily—shapes theories of the nature of photography and our experience of photography but that mode of semiotic objectification and inquiry that privileges the analytic-interpretative reduction of phonic material and/or nonmeaning over something like a mimetic improvisation of and with that materiality that moves in excess of meaning." The phonic material he has in mind here is jazz but also what a Black viewer hears when looking at images. He goes on: "This second challenge assumes that the critical-mimetic experience of the photograph takes place most properly within a field structured by theories of (Black) spectatorship, audition and performance."[35] The title of the chapter that includes the passages we are discussing is "Visual Music." This restructured, resounding field is the one that we are all now in, like it or not.

To date, few artists have used the George Floyd murder video within their work. An exception is George Gittoes in his film, *White Light*, which documents Black life on the South Side of Chicago from the perspective of a White participant observer who has embedded himself in a war zone. The film includes brief footage from several police murders of Black men, including George Floyd.[36] The most subtle usage to date is Marielle Ingram's three-minute film *Document 0* (2021) (Fig. 13.6). It opens with an intertitle: IMAGE CAPTURE: MAY 2019 and a voiceover announcing that "In Minneapolis, May 25, 2020, a man is arrested in his vehicle in front of a grocery store opposite Cup Foods." As the deadpan account of the unfolding events drones on, we see Google Earth images of the intersection showing people going about ordinary business, interspersed with film of the sky, as if we were on the ground looking up at it. As the voiceover narrates George Floyd's death, the screen remains blank, that is, black. Cut to the only picturing of Floyd in the video, the police officer's body cam of him being threatened with a pistol and asked to get out of his car. This is followed by two sequences of police officers standing over

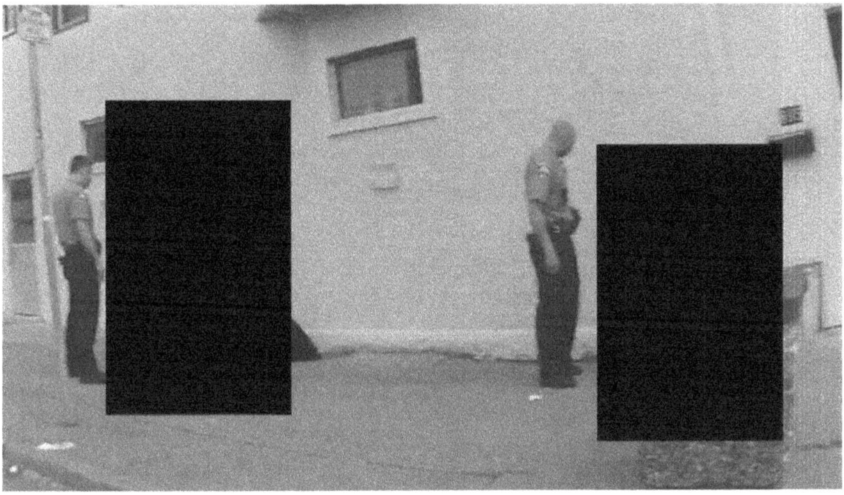

Fig. 13.6: Marielle Ingram, *Document 0*, 2021, 35mm film, 3 mins. Courtesy of the artist.

people on the pavement below who we do not see. Instead, vertical rectangles superimposed over those figures alternate between being totally black and carrying imagery of a group of Black kids playing a game of chase throughout the streets and buildings of their neighborhood. This footage is drawn from Charles Burnett's breakthrough film of the life of a slaughterhouse worker in the Watts neighborhood of Los Angeles, *Killer of Sheep* (1978). Ingram's voiceover: "It is true that one cannot escape from time, that time itself is but a window. The man, conscious but not moving, is untethered from time. As an image, conscious but not moving, the man implodes. An image unseen, he blocks out the world. What is an image untethered from time? A blackness, as unreal as ever." Lively, salsa-style music takes over as the pairing of standing police and black rectangles repeats. The black rectangles become animated, seeming to take on a life of their own. For the last minute of the video, the black squares are replaced by the children's game, which fills each rectangle then the whole screen. An evidently independent girl stands out among the boys. Their joyful game continues until the video fades to black.

Ingram reflects on her film in an insightful essay "What is an image untethered from time but blackness as primordial as ever?"[37] She explains that *Document 0* is a mediation on the use that artists such as Arthur Jafa make of the "aesthetic or logic of accumulation" as a form of contracirculation that responds to this dilemma: "What if, as we live with the internet and social media, the information overload has given way to the inability to image a new image—a phenomenological condition that has emerged from accumulation itself?" She was also inspired by Chris Marker's 1962 film *La Jetée*, in which the narrator calmly tells the story of the circumstances of his own death. Another precedent, especially in use of black screens, is Guy Debord's 1952 film *Hurlements en faveur de Sade* (Howlings for de Sade). But the main precedent is the widespread current use of pixilation and masking to block unauthorized content. *Document 0* aims to reverse all these usages: to evoke, instead, a George Floyd who lives in a manner quite other than the images of his death now circulating so widely on all media. Ingram suggests that he lives in a way that cannot be seen. She leaves us with an open question: "A thought experiment: at the end of black suffering, at the beginning and end of our world, what would it mean for stillness to become our primary mode of perception?"

Nirin, or, On the Edge

How might the imagery of violence—especially the kinds of violence occurring in the world today—be exhibited in art museums, places still shaped mostly by commitments to narrate the history of art and to prioritize the intentions of individual artists?[38] The short answer: show works by artists that explore the nature of this violence, works such as those of Arthur Jafa, Paul Pfeiffer, and Marielle Ingram which is built on an expanded history of what counts as art, and which enlarge the sense of what it is to have an artistic intention. A longer answer would argue for expanding the scope of such museums so that they show the artefacts of modern and contemporary visual cultures, not only the main streams and byways of modern and contemporary art. (This is something most already do when it comes to premodern periods.)

Not surprisingly, changes of this kind are not easy to make. The 2017 Whitney Biennial was again embroiled in controversy when curators included Dana Schutz's painting *Open Casket*, which drew on one of the photographs of the disfigured face and broken body of Emmett Till, the one showing his dressed upper torso and mutilated head. Several artists of color protested Schutz's assumption that she, a White artist, had rights that paralleled those of Till's mother; others defended her choice and rejected the condemnations as censorship, while still others (among whom I count myself) found that the application of her signature klutzy manner to *this* subject, however well intentioned, led inevitably to a painting that was, at best, half thought through and which, therefore, slighted its subject.[39] Two years later, the 2019 Biennale was swamped by the range of intersectional issues that continue to animate protesters today. It became the "Decolonize This Place!" biennial.[40]

From his first exhibition, "In/sight: African Photographers, 1940s to the Present," at the Guggenheim Museum, New York in 1996, the Nigerian born, New York and then Munich-based curator Okwui Enwezor gave powerful answers to the problematics of addressing in art exhibitions the violence inherent in racism. The vast violence of the European colonization of Africa, and the various, often violent, resistances to it, was a story that, he believed, required constant retelling in the West, if accountability was to be acknowledged, and, in Africa and its diaspora, if mourning was to be spared descent into terminal melancholia. Many of his pathbreaking exhibitions—from "The Short Century: Independence and Liberation Movements in Africa 1945–1994" (2001) to "Postwar: Art Between the Pacific and the Atlantic, 1945–1965" (2016)—included among their themes works by artists that wrestled with aspects of this unfinished business. He conceived an exhibition, "Grief and Grievance: Art and Mourning in America," for the New Museum, New York, hoping to open it before the November 2020 elections. (Due to virus-related delays, it opened in January 2021.) In a brief preface written shortly before his death in March 2019, he contrasted the travesty of Donald Trump conducting a campaign rally at Gettysburg to Barack Obama giving a eulogy at the church in Charleston, South Carolina, where Dylann Roof killed its pastor and eight members of its African American congregation. (The surviving congregation sang together and forgave him. Amazing grace.) Enwezor: "The crystallization of black grief in the face of a politically orchestrated white grievance represents the fulcrum of this exhibition […] With the media's normalization of white nationalism, recent years have made it clear that there is a new urgency to assess the role that artists, through works of art, have played in illuminating the searing contours of the American body politic."[41]

Like all Enwezor's exhibitions, the main points of departure are historical moments oriented back to the present: Jack Whitten's *Birmingham* (1964), Daniel LeRue Johnson's *Freedom Now, no. 1* (1963–4), Jean-Michel Basquiat's *Procession* (1986), and Nari Ward's installation *PeaceKeeper* (1995), set the tone. The broader narrative of Black experience in the United States is nuanced in Kerry James Marshall's *Momento* Series (2003) and in works by Melvin Edwards, Howardena Pindell, Ellen Gallagher, Henry Taylor, and Latoya Ruby Frazier among several others. Recent works such as Jafa's *Love is the Message: The Message is Death* (2016) are included, as are Kara Walker's subtle reflections on Obama's symbolic martyrdom, Cameron Rowland's relics of incarceration and exploitation, and Julie Mehretu's abstractions from images of current white suprematism. Performances by Rashid Johnson, Okwui Okpokwasili, and Tyshawn Sorey anchor each floor. We can hear Black mon'in', this expression of grief for such worthy grievance, this rejection of the politics of White resentment, as we look at each work in this exhibition and as we move, moved, between them.

Elsewhere, museums also opened themselves to consideration of these issues. From March to September 2020 at the Art Gallery of New South Wales, Sydney, the entrance foyer, the main galleries, and even the parts of the permanent collection galleries, were filled with works that were part of the 22nd Sydney Biennale. Curated by artist Brook Andrew and named "NIRIN" ("edge" in Wiradjuri, his Indigenous language), its theme was "Optimism from chaos drives artists in NIRIN to resolve the often hidden or ignored urgency surrounding contemporary life."[42] Works by Indigenous artists and artists of color occupied most of the spaces. Jafa's *The White Album* was installed in the collection rooms, built in the late nineteenth century, that house a suite of Victorian genre paintings. A more jarring contextual disjunction is hard to imagine, but the resonances were loud (see Fig. 13.5). Assemblages by Karla Dickens filled the vestibule of the museum, while banners by Kunmanara Mumu Mike Williams commanded the main ground floor space. This area also featured black and white, mural-sized photographs by Barbara McGrady, including one from 2015 of young women of Australian Aboriginal, Pacific Islander, and African American heritage, gathering, in casual intimacy, in Martin Place, the main commercial plaza in the center of Sydney, for a Black Lives Matter protest (Fig. 13.7).

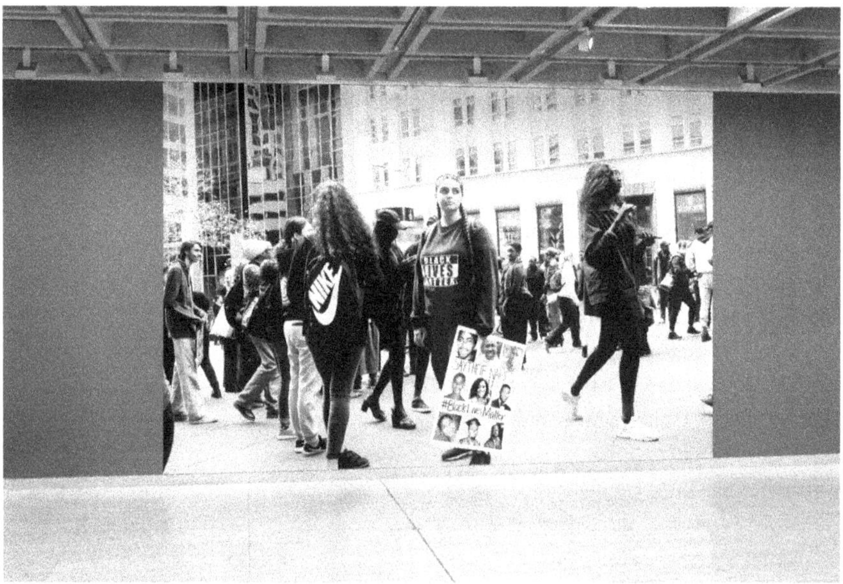

Fig. 13.7: Barbara McGrady, *Black Lives Matter, Martin Place*, 2015. Installation view for the 22ndBiennale of Sydney (2020), Art Gallery of New South Wales. Presented at the 22nd Biennale of Sydney with generous support from the Australia Council for the Arts. Photograph: Alex Robinson.

Sometimes, the gallery and the street can feel like the same place in that they seem to share the same challenges and possibilities. They are both nodes within the iconomy, where our minds and bodies can coexist, or exist alongside each other, against the grain of the prevailing circulation of images.

Notes

1 Cited in Suzanne Muchnic, "King Beating Footage Comes to the Art World: Art: George Holliday's tape represents 'a new way of seeing what is around us,' says the Whitney curator who chose it for the museum's Biennial," *L.A. Times*, March 10, 1993. See also Hanhardt's essay, "Media Art Worlds: New Expressions in Film and Video, 1991–93," *1993 Biennial Exhibition* (New York: Whitney Museum of American Art, 1993), 36–51.

2 See, for example, Robert Hughes, "Art: The Whitney Biennial: A Fiesta of Whining," *Time Magazine*, March 22, 1993, http://www.time.com/time/magazine/article/0,9171,978001,00.html, and Roberta Smith, "At the Whitney, A Biennial with a Social Conscience," *The New York Times*, March 5, 1993, https://www.nytimes.com/1993/03/05/arts/at-the-whitney-a-biennial-with-a-social-conscience.html. See also Hal Foster, Rosalind Krauss, Silvia Kolbowski, Miwon Kwon, and Benjamin Buchloh, "The Politics of the Signifier: A Conversation on the Whitney Biennial," *October*, Vol. 66 (Autumn, 1993), 3–27, and Charles A. Wright, Jr., "The Mythology of Difference: Vulgar Identity Politics at the Whitney Biennial," in *Theory and Contemporary Art*, eds. Zoya Kocur and Simon Leung (Malden, MA: Blackwell Publishing, 2005).

3 Arthur Danto, "The 1993 Whitney Biennial," *The Nation*, April 19, 1993, 533–536.

4 Arthur Danto, "The Artworld," *The Journal of Philosophy*, vol. 61, no. 19. (Oct. 15, 1964), 571–584.

5 Arthur Danto, "The 1993 Whitney Biennial," *The Nation*, April 19, 1993, 533–536.

6 Arthur Danto, "American Self-Consciousness in Politics and Art," *Artforum*, September 1, 2004.

7 Ringborg, Testifying to the Image, 116.

8 Ariella Azoulay, *The Civil Contract of Photography* (New York: Zone Books, 2008), 158. Azoulay's point about implicitly engaging the spectator as a potentially active moral witness, ethical actor, is prefigured in the work of the photo-essayists in *Life*, etc., not least in this context, Gordon Park.

9 See Michael Kimmelman, "Museums: Abu Ghraib Returns – As Art?" *New York Times*, October 12, 2004, at https://www.nytimes.com/2004/10/12/arts/museums-abu-ghraib-returns-as-art.html. Kimmelman was among the critics most forthright in their condemnation of the 1993 Whitney Biennial.

10 For a historical survey of the two main strategies deployed by museums in the United States when showing art by African Americans—ethnographic approaches that emphasis the artists' life or recovery narratives to rectify art historical omissions—see Bridget R. Cooks, *Exhibiting Blackness: African Americans and the American Art Museum* (Amherst, MA: University of Massachusetts Press, 2011).

11 David Joselit, "Material Witness: Visual Evidence and the Case of Eric Garner," *Artforum* (February, 2015) , at https://www.artforum.com/print/201502/material-witness-visual-evidence-and-the-case-of-eric-garner-49798.

12 Even though the performance exists for most who know about it in the form of a photograph of the event, that is, as a representation. This is unavoidable and does not void the quiddity, and the affect, of the original performance.

13 Point made in the critique by Paul Mullan, "On Joselit's 'Material Witness'," *Red Wedge*, May 4, 2015, at http://www.redwedgemagazine.com/conditions/on-joselits-material-witness. He also wonders about the relevance of Joselit's emphatic enjoinment that radical artists pay close attention to theories of "the hole," a recommendation that rings oddly in the context.

14 For comments by Pope.L on this aspect of his work and his *Foraging (Asphixia Version)* 1993–5/2008 being illustrated on the cover of *Artforum*, see Dan Duray, "William Pope.L discuss his Artforum cover at CAA: 'Leave Me Out of It'," *Art News*, February 17, 2015, https://www.artnews.com/art-news/news/william-pope-l-discusses-his-artforum-cover-at-caa-leave-me-out-of-it-3621/.

15 See Terry Smith, *One and Five Ideas: On Conceptual Art and Conceptualism* (Durham, NC: Duke University Press, 2017). Joselit expands his argument in an interview with David Andrew Tasman, "David Joselit: Against Representation," *DIS Magazine*, July 1, 2016, at http://dismagazine.com/discussion/75654/david-joselit-against-representation/.

16 Shaun Leonardo, *I Can't Breathe*, March 18, 2017, McColl Center for Art + Innovation, Charlotte, NC, at https://elcleonardo.com/videos#true-3. Leonardo's work has not been welcomed by some concerned viewers: Tamir Rice's mother objected to the showing of his drawings of her son's death at MOCA Cleveland, see Jasmine Weber, "Samira Rice, Mother of Tamir Rice, Speaks Out about Art Depicting Her Son after Cancelled Exhibition in Cleveland," *Hyperallergic*, July 8, 2020, at https://hyperallergic.com/573053/moca-cleveland-the-breath-of-empty-space/. On Leonardo's work, and that of other artists dealing with violence in America, see Nicole Scalissi, Something to see here: Staged Violence in Contemporary Art, PhD dissertation, University of Pittsburgh, 2019.

17 Leonardo, *I Can't Breathe*, as above.

18 Nicole F. Fleetwood, *Troubling Vision: Performance, Visuality, Blackness* (Chicago: University of Chicago Press, 2011).

19 Fleetwood, *Troubling Vision*, 4.

20 Fred Moten, *In the Break: The Aesthetics of the Black Radical Tradition* (Minneapolis: University of Minnesota Press, 2003), 198.

21 "Boys Never Told Grandfather about 'Incident'," *Jet Magazine*, September 15, 1955, 8–9, pages reproduced at https://rosaparksbiography.org/bio/emmett-till/. Footage of the funeral is included in the film *The Untold Story of Emmett Till*, directed by Keith Beauchamp for Till Freedom Comes Productions, 2005.

22 Moten, *In the Break*, 188–189.

23 Publicity notice, "Museum of Modern Art Plans International Photography Exhibition," 31 January 1955. Steichen Archives, Museum of Modern Art, New York, at https://assets.moma.org/documents/moma_press-release_325966.pdf?_ga=2.135258548.48044669.1607058852-273066670.1569185185. Among the copious commentary on this exhibition, see Allan Sekula, "The Traffic in Photographs," *Art Journal*, vol 44, no. 1 (Spring 1981): 15–25, and John O'Brian, "The Nuclear Family of Man," *The Asia-Pacific Journal*, vol. 6, no. 7 (July 2, 2008), at https://apjjf.org/-John-O'Brian/2816/article.html.

24 Moten, *In the Break*, 209.

25 Ibid., 209–210.

26 Tina M. Campt, *A Black Gaze: Artists Changing How We See* (Cambridge, MA: MIT Press, 2021), 8.

27 For Jafa's video, see https://www.youtube.com/watch?v=D1McJ8cci3Y; for West's, see https://www.youtube.com/watch?v=6oHdAA3AqnE. Jafa's direct debt to Moten is acknowledged in a conversation related to an exhibition at the Hammer Museum, Los Angeles, see "Arthur Jafa and Greg Tate," July 5, 2017, at https://www.youtube.com/watch?v=CAYSXam1vOA.

28 A powerful analysis of the work of Paul Pfeiffer and Arthur Jafa in these contexts can be found in Marielle Ingram, "Contracirculation; On rewriting the terms of engagement with images of black suffering," *Real Life*, posted June 29, 2020, at https://reallifemag.com/contracirculation/. See also chapter 6 of T.J. Demos, *Beyond the World's End: Arts of Living at the Crossroads* (Durham, NC: Duke University Press, 2019).

29 See above n. 7, "Arthur Jafa and Greg Tate."

30 See "In Your Face, Interview with Arthur Jafa by Carrie Scott," Showstudio, November 25, 2017, at https://www.youtube.com/watch?v=XAk0dk0IAWw. See also Arthur Jafa, "My Black Death," in Greg Tate ed., *Everything but the Burden: What White People Are Taking from Black Culture* (New York: Broadway Books, 2003), 244–257.

31 Arthur Jafa, "22nd Biennale of Sydney," 2019, at https://www.biennaleofsydney.art/artists/arthur-jafa/.

32 Ibid.

33 T.J. Demos offers a fine analysis of Akomfrah's epic work *Vertigo Sea* (2015) in chapter 1 of *Beyond the World's End.*

34 The postponement in September 2020 of a Phillip Guston retrospective by four major museums due to concerns that the artists' use of Klu Klux Klan imagery would be inflammatory became itself controversial. See Julia Jacobs, "Philip Guston Blockbuster Show Postponed by Four Museums," *New York Times*, September 24, 2020, at https://www.nytimes.com/2020/09/24/arts/design/philip-guston-postponed-museums-klan.html. Among much pertinent commentary, see Steve Locke, "Guston, Whiteness, and the Unfinished Business of the Vile World," *Artforum*, December 2020, who says of Guston's project, "That is what accountability looks like."

35 Moten, *In the Break*, 197.

36 See https://www.whitelight.film. In a series of works made in 2020 and 2021, Robert Longo addresses several of the topics we have been considering, from COVID to BLM. See https://www.pacegallery.com/exhibitions/robert-longo/.

37 Marielle Ingram, "What is an image untethered from time but primordial blackness forever?," *X-TRA*, posted September 28, 2021, at https://www.x-traonline.org/online/blackness-as-primordial-as-ever.

38 This is the main question posed by Ringborg, Testifying to the Image, where he insightfully examines it in relation to exhibitions he has curated and the program he is developing at the Bonniers Konsthall, Stockholm.

39 See Aruna D'Souza, *Whitewalling, Art, Race & Protest in 3 Acts* (New York: Badlands Unlimited, 2018), Chapter 1. Polar opposite positions were taken by Hannah Black, who argued for the painting's destruction, and Coco Fusco, who defended Schutz's (awkward) effort at allyship, and decried calls for the painting's destruction as censorship. For Black's "Open Letter to the curators of the Whitney Biennale," March 21, 2020, see https://www.artnews.com/artnews/news/the-painting-must-go-hannah-black-pens-open-letter-to-the-whitney-about-controversial-biennial-work-7992/. For Coco Fusco's statement, see her "Censorship, Not the Painting,

Must Go: On Dana Schutz's Image of Emmett Till," *Hyperallergic*, Match 27 and 29, 2020, at https://hyperallergic.com/368290/censorship-not-the-painting-must-go-on-dana-schutzs-image-of-emmett-till/. Schutz's account of her intentions and her response to criticism may be found at https://news.artnet.com/art-world/dana-schutz-responds-to-the-uproar-over-her-emmett-till-painting-900674. A succinct comment by Okwui Enwezor (*Artforum*, December 2017) may be found at https://www.artforum.com/print/201710/okwui-enwezor-72451. D'Souza's first chapter contains a comprehensive archive of responses, especially from social media.

40 See Terry Smith, *Curating the Complex and The Open Strike* (Berlin: Sternberg Press; Cambridge, MA: MIT Press, 2021), Thoughts on Curating series, ed. Steven Henry Madoff. The 2022 Whitney Biennial is, again, offered as a response to "these precarious and improvised times": see the curators' statement at https://whitney.org/exhibitions/2022-biennial#exhibition-about.

41 Okwui Enwezor, *Grief and Grievance: Art and Mourning in America* (London: Phaidon, for the New Museum, New York, 2020), 7. The catalogue includes essays by Judith Butler, Claudia Rankine, Elizabeth Alexander and others, and accounts of Enwezor's curatorial intentions by Massilimiano Gioni and Mark Nash.

42 Brook Andrew, "Curatorial Statement," Sydney Biennale 2020, at https://www.biennaleofsydney.art.

Chapter 14

THE TRIAL: AGGRESSIVE NON-VIOLENCE

As its aura of normality falls away, and its actuality becomes more widely exposed, police brutality against Black and colored minorities in the United States and elsewhere is coming into view as a form of white domestic terrorism. In contrast to the militias that dot the nation—which are rag tag until, on occasions such as January 6, 2021, they are not—this concentrated violence is organized, institutionalized, and, in principle and by community consent, regulated. Until it is not.

The images of violence unleashed on African American men and women that we have been considering may well be records of moments in an ongoing race war within the United States. If so, is a time of reckoning coming up soon, or is it already here? The intense politicization of the national iconomy charted in the preceding chapters seem to signal an acceleration in other long-standing social divisions, those based on class, geography, and ideology. But not evenly in each of these domains, and not along traditional lines. This is evident in the widespread support for Republicans by displaced industrial workers and by the divisions within the Democratic party between well-heeled elites and the working poor. Reckoning seems on the near horizon through whichever lens one looks. We have seen that imagery of all kinds has played several crucial roles within these scenarios. In this chapter, I will continue to track developments in the three image regimes we have been following, preparatory to offering some concluding remarks, necessarily provisional, on political iconomy today.

Judgement in Minnesota

Earlier I asked whether, when the cases against the officers who attended the incident at Powderhorn got to the courts in Minneapolis, the sheer force of the indexical presence in Frazier's video, its unfolding for 8 minutes and 46 seconds, along with its subsequent ubiquity on all communicative media, would make it less vulnerable to the kind of degradation that was visited upon George Holliday's video of the beating of Rodney King. Even today, the Federal Rules of Evidence, a document reviewed each year by the Supreme Court of the United States, offers no explicit statement about the ways in which courts should treat the visual evidence that comes before them.[1] If an injustice like that done to Rodney King was the outcome of the trials of Derek Chauvin and the other officers, an even more explosive reaction of outrage was primed to erupt, not only in Minnesota, but nationwide, and beyond.

In the event, the trials unfolded in ways that seemed to rehearse those that occurred in 1992, with both sides aware of the legacy of that and similar cases. Making their case against Derek Chauvin, prosecuting attorneys argued that the jury should believe what they saw in Darnella Frazier's video, that he had kept his knee on George Floyd's neck for those 8 minutes and 46 seconds—in fact, for 9 minutes and 29 seconds overall—and was therefore guilty of the crimes for which he had been charged: third-degree murder, second-degree manslaughter, and unintentional second-degree murder while attempting to commit felony assault. None of these accuse Chauvin of intentionally murdering Floyd. Instead, they charge that he did so while unlawfully assaulting Floyd, making him culpable of murder.

Defense lawyers had the task of convincing at least one juror that there existed a reasonable doubt that this was the case. They followed the Tucker Carlson playbook, arguing that video from the other officers' bodycams showed that Floyd resisted arrest, faked his responses to mislead police, was likely on drugs, had taken lethal doses of fentanyl, had underlying medical conditions—all these being more likely causes of his death than his handling by the police who were present, especially the actions of officer Chauvin. The judge advised jurors that the existence of other contributing factors to Floyd's death does "not relieve the defendant of criminal liability" for his central action of kneeling on Floyd's neck for so long. Defense lawyers also argued that Chauvin was following normal police procedures, a claim rebutted by the chief of the Minnesota Police Department, the chief trainer, and several other senior police in their testimony. Among the 38 witnesses called by the prosecution were police and external doctors and medical personnel, some with access to the body, all of whom testified that restraints on Floyd, above all Chauvin's pressure on his neck for that length of time, were the primary likely cause of his death. Of the seven witnesses called by the defense, two testified about Floyd's bellicose behavior during a 2019 arrest, others to his drug use, both leaving an implication that Floyd, a large man, was a violent, threatening addict. Although, remarkably, neither side explicitly raised race as a factor in anything that occurred, the subtext was obvious, again replaying an oft-used defense, fear of the unrestrained Black Man.

A few retired police and medical experts, without access to the body, offered opinions supportive of defense claims. Against the visual evidence of substantial police presence and a relatively few spectators, the defense further argued that the police were threatened by an angry crowd. Again, the racial subtext: These white police were risking their lives to subdue a seething Black neighborhood. Both sides closed their cases with detailed reference to the visual evidence. At this point, their analytical modes reversed those used in the King case: The prosecutors concentrated on what certain single, stilled images showed about Chauvin's actions and their impact on Floyd, whereas the defense urged jurors to attend to the purport of the entire range of imagery.

Regarding the wider role of visual media in the trial, there is the difference that, while proceedings in the King trial were filmed, drawings made, and reports presented on televised evening news, in 1991 the trail itself was not broadcast/streamed live, as it was in the Chauvin case. Viewers could see the judge, the defendant, and each witness giving evidence, but not the jury or the larger courtroom. Today, we expected a more immediate release of information, and with it, an appearance at least of greater transparency. Closer presence at the site of important events is also expected. As is a quicker definition of what is occurring. The King trial took just under two months to play out, at the end of which the jury deliberated for a week before acquitting the officers. Testimony in the Chauvin trial was complete within two weeks. The jury took 10 hours over two days to find him guilty on all counts. He was subsequently sentenced to twenty-two and a half years, which he appealed, but in December 2021 pleaded guilty to a charge of violating Floyd's constitutional rights by causing his death and was sentenced to 25 years in a federal prison.

While the trial was unfolding, National Guard troops surrounded the building to secure it from constant protestors. They were also deployed throughout the city. Some locals saw this as more evidence of the city preparing, at vast expense, to protect itself from them, far more than it does to protect them.[2] During the second week of the trial, a police officer in a nearby suburb of Minneapolis shot and killed a young black man, Duante Wright, in the front seat of his car as he sat alongside his infant child. At the time, the officer was training a group of police in how to conduct a traffic stop of a car not showing sufficient registration. She claimed to have mistakenly pulled her gun instead of a Taser. Meanwhile, police killings of black men and women continued in the city and around the country, as did demonstrations demanding justice for them.

The verdict against Chauvin sent a clear message to police: When the acts of those among you inclined to the exercise of excessive force become too visible, your presumption of immunity vanishes. To the legal system, it said: When realities are made plainly visible, evidence is to be taken as what it seems to be. To those seeking justice in such cases: This rare victory should encourage you, but it sets a very high bar for the accumulation of convincing evidence. And to those who demonstrated for so long: When you bring the spotlight of your appeals for justice upon those who have so flagrantly violated it, justice will be served and will be shown to be served. To all concerned, this message, inscribed on banners carried at marches in cities from Minneapolis to Sydney: THE WORLD IS WATCHING—so when it comes to interactions between us, act as if you, and we, are always visible to each other. Meanwhile, silent majorities across the country and around the world breathed a sigh of relief: The guilty verdict meant that large-scale social disturbance did not occur. The impending civil war had been postponed, at least for the time being.

Defund the Police?

Since the killing of George Floyd, the court of public opinion has been in active session. Several protesters reported being motivated in part by a desire to create a mediated context in which videos such as Frazer's will count as truthful, and count against the distortions of a system moving to protect itself. Demands that the killings of unarmed Black men by police stop, and that when they occur, the police involved be held accountable, are the driving voice of the protests. Justice for George Floyd, social justice for all African Americans, for us all, for justice itself. Yet, the killings did not stop. While most victims are White, African Americans and Hispanic peoples are killed in far greater numbers than their proportions of the population. During 2020, police killed on average one Black man or woman each week in the United States. Since 2013, less than 2 % of the officers involved have been charged with a crime, and 0.1 % convicted.[3] Meanwhile, Republican legislators around the country prioritize filling courts, from the Supreme Court to the Circuits and Districts, with strict law-and-order judges. Elected positions are similarly politicized. Protestors are finally asking about both the police and the courts: Are they reformable, or must they be reconceived from the ground up?

I am on board with what Judith Butler recently theorized as "aggressive non-violence."[4] She understands the scale on which non-violence must operate, and the kinds of combative force it needs to exercise, to be truly effective. Non-violence should become an alternative ethos and form for local, national, indeed international governance. Actually, and paradoxically, it needs to become a kind of policing, a shared securing of public safety that we all undertake, according to our abilities.

Imagine that: In every neighborhood in the world, and on a global scale, the goal becomes to protect our neighbors and ourselves against institutional, criminal, and personal violence by proactively serving and sustaining non-violence. This instinct swiftly blossomed at the very place that Floyd was killed. As flowers were laid, candles lit, murals painted, and mementos gathered, the intersection was closed and named George Floyd Square. A metal sculpture of a clenched fist, by local artist Jordon Powell Karis, arose in its center. Grieving neighbors patrolled barricades across the intersecting street, originally erected by the city to protect mourners and demonstrators, now with the goal of keeping the Minneapolis Police out. A temporary autonomous zone was created. It became the local center for symbolic demonstrations in favor of justice for Floyd and other victims of police brutality. Wisely, city police kept their distance. Its affairs are managed by a local committee of volunteers which, two years later, maintained a strong sense of community, despite the inconvenience to some businesses and a church within its confines and an increase in activity by gangs in the area and nearby.[5] It was here that crowds gathered to celebrate the verdict in the Chauvin trial (Fig. 14.1). In November 2021,

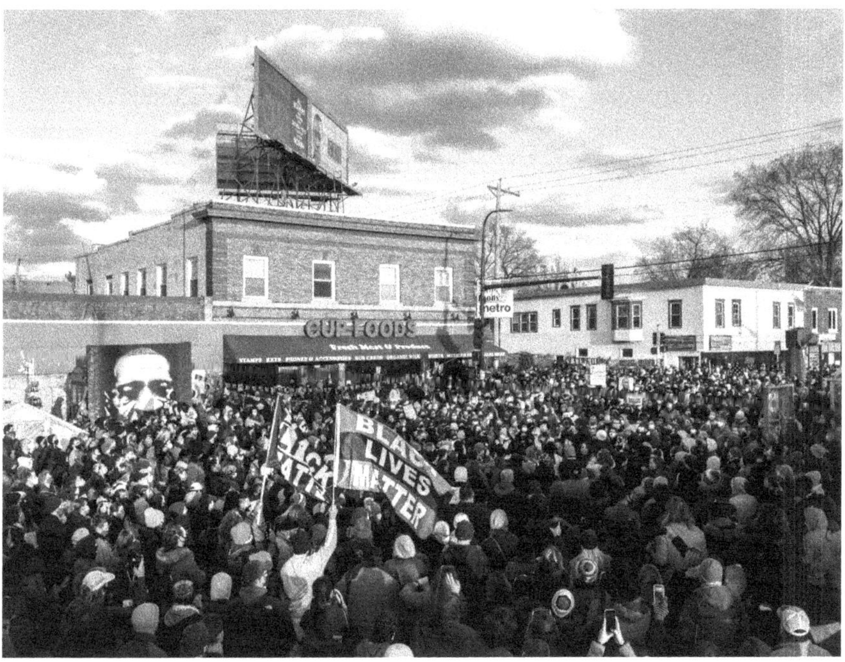

Fig. 14.1: Crowd gathers at George Floyd Square, Powderhorn, Minneapolis, after the guilty verdict of Derek Chauvin, April 20, 2021. Photo: Joshua Rashaad McFadden/The New York Times/Redux.

however, Minneapolis residents voted down a proposal to replace the police force with a larger, welfare-oriented Department of Public Safety.

The killing of George Floyd did not ignite a race war in the United States. It inflamed one that was in full swing but was conducted largely out of sight, with each eruption framed as an exception to what was widely portrayed as Black-on-Black violence occurring in neighborhoods bent on self-destruction. The video of his murder showed that police violence was systemic, indifferent to justice, autonomous, and thus a threat to all citizens. African Americans are still the big losers in this war, but there is, since the demonstrations, the coalitions of social movements, the growth of neighborhood governance, and announcements of support by the Biden Administration, more hope of positive change—one that must include appropriate reparations—than there has been since the false dawn of Obama's election in 2008.

On March 3, 2021, the House passed a Justice in Policing act named for George Floyd that reduces qualified immunity for police officers, prohibits racial and religious profiling, bans chokeholds and most no-knock warrants, mandates data collection on police encounters, and redirects funding to community-based policing programs.[6] Modified bills on similar topics can be expected as more and more elements of what is turning out to be a truly progressive agenda are put into place. On local levels, similar moves toward restorative justice were made: As the trial of Derek Chauvin began, the City of Minnesota awarded a significant sum to the family of George Floyd in compensation for their loss.[7] Evanston, a Chicago suburb, voted $10 million in housing grants to its Black residents. H.R. 40, a bill for national reparation for the impact of slavery, first proposed 30 years ago, was advanced by a committee of the House of Representatives. President Biden's "American Jobs Plan" co-opts then expands the commitment to infrastructure that Trump claimed as a priority but did little to create. It earmarks huge sums for job training, school investment, mortgage support, and business loans in Black, brown, and other "underserved communities," meanwhile replacing their lead pipes and reconnecting those divided by highways.[8] The realization that rebuilding infrastructure is indissoluble from bringing about racial justice underlies this plan.

This sentiment echoed in President Biden's speech welcoming the conviction of Derek Chauvin for his murder of George Floyd, remarks that bring us back to the theme of visibility as an essential tool for social change, for seeing why something needs to be done, and for checking that it is done:

> It was murder in the full light of day, and it ripped the blinkers off for the whole world to see the systemic racism [...] that is a stain on our nation's soul; the knee on the neck of justice for Black Americans;

> the profound fear and trauma, the pain, the exhaustion that Black and brown Americans experience very single day [...] So, we can't leave this moment or look away, thinking our work is done. We have to look at it—we have to—we have to look at it as we did for those 9 minutes and 29 seconds. We have to listen. 'I can't breathe.' 'I can't breathe.' Those were George Floyd's last words. We can't let those words die with him. We have to keep hearing those words [...] We have a chance to begin to change the trajectory of this country.[9]

Much certainly remains to be undone: not least, the damages wreaked upon individuals, communities, ideals of civil society, the environment, and international policy during the past four years. And much more needs to be done. Too few people link the civil warring we have witnessed simmering for years in the United States to the growing presence of guns and their concentration in the hands of police, gangs, militia, and fear-filled individuals. African Americans and other minorities see this link doing its deadly work each day. Action for racial justice should be joined at the top of the list by genuine equity for women and for all sexualities, alongside the need to act comprehensively against global warming, in the United States as elsewhere.

Unfriended, Banned, Waiting in the Wings

All such initiatives remain anathema to those committed to the social, cultural, and political agenda to which Donald Trump gave his name and which, for four years, was prosecuted through an image regime constellated around him, his doings, and sayings. In the weeks following January 6, 2020, Trump appeared for photo ops with the leader of the House Republicans, reaffirming his relevance to the 140 members who voted to reopen inquiry into the election result. He also continues to invite select groups of supporters to events at Mar-a-Lago during which millions are raised and traditional Republicans such as Senate leader McDonnell are excoriated. Twitter's November 2020 ban on Trump was a permanent one. YouTube announced that it would restore his account only when the threat of "real-world violence" reduces. Facebook did likewise. On May 4, 2021, Trump launched a new "communications" website, "STRAIGHT FROM THE DESK OF DONALD. J. TRUMP," that heralded him as a "Beacon of Freedom" and featured posts supporting Republican candidates committed to his agenda while excoriating those who few do not. Lack of interest led to its quick withdrawal. Compared to the saturation described in earlier chapters, this near invisibility is setting up expectations of a spectacular return. In October 2021, Trump formed the Trump Media & Technology Group and announced the creation of a "TRUTH Social" app. Such bang up promises, however, risk turning out to herald a whimper.

Looking back, were the Twitter, Facebook, and YouTube bans imposed on Trump on January 8, two days after his supporters invaded the Capitol, the most effective political tools of the season? His first order disseminators no longer available, Trump had to rely on email blitzes directed at committed supporters (again, with fund raising as the main goal) and on traditional tools such as issuing press releases on quasi-Presidential letterheads. Whereas during the Trump ascendency, heritage media companies felt obliged to act as amplifiers of these messages—on the grounds that they were reporting the Twitterspheric response to them as well as their content—this justification for reporting based on the weight of public interest no longer convinces even themselves. It was always a rationalization—indeed, from some perspectives, a kind of self-abuse. Discussion of the ethics of banning Trump displaces attention from strenuous Republican efforts to deny that the events of January 6 were what they were. Since then, within traditional media, some small-scale, dutiful reporting of Trump's announcements has occurred. During most of 2021, however, eyes were on the policy blitz emanating from the Biden White House and the obstacles it encountered in making its way through an obstructive Congress.

In the broader polity, aggressive non-violence likewise struggles to become the law of the land. As we saw, during the summer of 2020, the public spheres of 140 US cities were continuously occupied day after day, actions that—except for the looting, wanton property destruction, battling between extremist factions, and unnecessary provocation of police—enjoyed majority support from locals, from public media, and on much social media. At the time, hopes for large-scale change arose. Was this the turning of the tide? Would this be the moment to address the inequities so relentlessly exposed by the COVID-19 virus? These public spheres were being occupied on a scale, with an intensity and duration, that Occupy could only dream of in 2011. Was this, at last, after the Obama delay, the "US Spring"? The virus was already obligating several unexpectedly flexible political coalitions that aimed at building economic and social cohesion during the anticipated recovery. Yet, the partisan political divides were clear to see in the massive but also deeply divided turnout of voters in November 2020. The fact that the modest reformism of the Biden election agenda—coordinate the response to the pandemic, rebuild the economy, heal racial injustice, and address climate change—seemed, when the election was won, to promise a salvation from disaster showed just how precarious the situation had become.

Democracy at Stake in a World in Need of Rebuilding

What of the larger world picture? Today, democracies everywhere face a crisis of form that, for most, has become disabling: growing internal economic, social, and cultural divisions mean that the two-party—or government versus strong opposition—system, with a volatile heritage three centuries long, is, in many countries, fragmenting. These parties were, in most cases, already coalitions of convenience, formed to enable electable majorities. For much of the twentieth century, they regularly became large enough to govern for sustainable terms, and for the leading parties to operate as alternative governments with similar agendas, even during periods of great peril, such as war. Today, authoritarian leaders and populist demagogues promise to fix the fragmentation through the concentration of power in themselves and their close allies. Against them, genuine democracies face the challenges of governance through constant negotiation and coalition building between differences that may never form into majorities.

Within these world-scale transformations, a rebuilding of the currently disunited states of America may indeed be taking place, led by the liberal-progressive coalition that constitutes the Biden Administration and its supporters. Meanwhile, a majority of Republican voters—along with majorities of Republican representatives in the House and the Senate and in several state legislatures throughout the country—refuse to concede the 2020 election defeat, continue to support the Trump agenda, and remain willing to sacrifice representative government (by actively restricting voter access in Democratic-leaning districts and following a demagogue) if it means surrendering White supremacy. Trump continued to endorse Republican candidates who accept his agenda and attack the diminishing numbers who do not. Gerrymandering continues apace. Trumpist majorities in the Senate—and even, conceivably, the House in 2022—would open the way for his re-election in 2024. Worse still, a competent authoritarian could seize the opportunity. It remains to be seen if full-scale Civil War will be necessary for resolve these differences, or whether the rebuilding of democracy in the United States will work its ways through several smaller but pivotal battles fought within communities but with an eye on the larger issues, above all global warming.

This is true for the United States, as it is for democracies, and would-be democracies, everywhere. The image wars in other polities during 2020 and 2021 paralleled those in the United States, less for reasons of cultural dependence, more due to the fact of the global prevalence, the contagion, of their modes of contestation, their threat to community and the community building resilience that they called out and which everywhere, despite appearances, and against all odds, insisted on its fundamentality. In India, by mid-2021, COVID imagery dominated all communicative media as second and third waves of the pandemic raged out of control, and political imagery constellated around Prime Minister Modi's inability to manage balances between public safety, re-election rallies, religious festivals, and economic growth, while community campaigns protesting violence against women, against religious and caste discrimination, receded from view. But not for long. In Australia, where an "island fortress" against COVID was erected, the pandemic came to the fore as both an internal danger and an external threat, while political imagery was uncertainly driven by a Trump-imitating Prime Minister who struggled to spin all events to his electoral advantage. Yet, community campaigns for the fair treatment of women, against Aboriginal deaths in custody, and for local and global action on climate change continued to grow and to intersect.

Whatever the outcomes of these battles, and those like them, and whether they grow into full-scale civil wars, we can be sure that they will continue be fought, within world iconomies, as image wars of the kind that raged during 2020 and 2021. This remains the case, even as they join the recurrence of more traditional forms of image management, not least the constraints on media and the propaganda campaigns that are a crucial aspect of wars such as that unleashed on Ukraine in February 2022.

Notes

1 See *Federal Rules of Evidence*, 2020 Edition, at https://www.rulesofevidence.org. Feigenson (see above) reviews the research literature and finds widespread variation in the admissibility, interpretation, and impact of visual imagery in US courts.

2 See Justin Ellis, "Minnesota Values White Comfort More Than Black Lives," *New York Times*, April 16, 2021, at https://www.nytimes.com/2021/04/16/opinion/sunday/george-floyd-daunte-wright-minnesota.html.

3 See *Mapping Police Violence* at https://mappingpoliceviolence.org, which on October 28, 2020, highlighted that, so far that year, Black people were 28% of those killed by police despite being only 13% of the population, and that, since 2013, 98.3% of killings by police have not resulted in an officer being charged with a crime while of those charged 0.1% have been convicted. See also Todd May and George Yancy, "Policing Is Doing What It Was Meant to do. That's the Problem," *New York Times*, June 21, 2020, at https://www.nytimes.com/2020/06/21/opinion/police-violence-racism-reform.html?action=click&module=Opinion&pgtype=Homepage. Also Charles Mudude, "White Knee, Black Neck," *e-flux Journal*, #110, June 2020, at https://www.e-flux.com/journal/110/337358/white-knee-black-neck/. Tamika Mallory puts it unequivocally: see https://www.youtube.com/watch?v=m7-2qnaCQr4.

4 Judith Butler, *The Force of Non-Violence* (London: Verso 2020). See also Ibram X. Kendi, *How to Be an Anti*-Racist (New York: One World, 2019).

5 See, for example, Amudalat Adjasa, "'It's for the People': How George Floyd Square Became a Symbol of Resistance—and Healing," *The Guardian*, March 28, 2021, at https://www.theguardian.com/us-news/2021/mar/27/its-for-the-people-how-george-floyd-square-became-a-symbol-of-resistance-and-healing.

6 See https://www.congress.gov/bill/117th-congress/house-bill/1280.

7 Lisa Navratil and Maya Rao, "Minneapolis to Pay Record $27 Million to Settle Lawsuit with George Floyd's Family," *Star Tribune*, March 13, 2021, at https://www.startribune.com/minneapolis-to-pay-record-27-million-to-settle-lawsuit-with-george-floyd-s-family/600033541/. The family gifted $500,000 to Black-owned businesses at the intersection where Floyd was killed.

8 See https://www.whitehouse.gov/wp-content/uploads/2021/04/AJP-Racial-Equity-Fact-Sheet-FINAL.pdf. For commentary, see Nicholas Fandas, "House Panel Advances Bill to Study Reparations in a Historic Vote," *New York Times*, April 14, 2021, at https://www.nytimes.com/2021/04/14/us/politics/reparations-slavery-house.html.

9 See https://www.whitehouse.gov/briefing-room/speeches-remarks/2021/04/20/remarks-by-president-biden-on-the-verdict-in-the-derek-chauvin-trial-for-the-death-of-george-floyd/.

Part III

TOWARD POLITICAL ICONOMY

Chapter 15

ICONOMIC VALUE: AN ACCOUNTING

Images, economies—one so present but elusive at the point of exchange, the other so concrete at that point but so elusive in its circulations. In the first part of this book, I surveyed several ways in which the two terms had been thought together. With Indigenous management of sacred and secular "designs" as a control case, we traced a trajectory within Western thought that took these terms to be linked in fundamental senses when explanations of world being were required. Part II profiled contention within contemporary cultures, the politics of the iconosphere, the clash of images as different world pictures competed to be seen, to become as visible as others, more visible than them, with social being at stake. Our subject has been the current warring between image regimes, where they came from, and what critical theory offers to our efforts to understand them.

Does "iconomy" acutely name the plane upon which these phenomena are operating, and pick out their distinctive features in ways that we need to know now? Or does use of the concept blur distinctions that must be made—not least those between imagery and economies—if our current situation, and the pasts that shaped it, are to be fully and clearly grasped?

As we have seen throughout these chapters, to think in iconomic terms does both things—at times one, at other times the other, often at once, in rarely predictable ways. Given what we know about the nature of images and economies, this should be no surprise. Nevertheless, we have also seen that pairing the concepts "image" and "economy" has brought into view several aspects of both that usually remain invisible or implicit. Viewing them politically focuses on real-world relevance. Iconomics becomes iconopolitics.

Before attempting some provisional conclusions, and proposing some possible principles for iconomic thinking, some basic terms require revisiting.

By "image" I mean material images of all kinds, from single pictures through moving images, virtual imagery, and self-images to public personae, as well as mental images of many kinds, from dream imagery to social imaginaries. In none of these contexts does an image exist by itself. It exists in something which carries it and in the regard of someone or something that sees it.

And it exists always in relation to other images, similar and different. Images constantly cluster into imagery, flows of likeness and difference. As their reach expands and their impact deepens, they take on broader roles: they compose into world-picturing practices and, on the political plane, constellate into image regimes.

Images might be carried by things, or even appear to be entirely things, but they are always presentations of something which is absent. This is their definitive relationship to that which they represent and to us who take them as representations. It is a quality of images that make them difficult to see with precision even as we look at them—or, more precisely, at the vehicle that is presenting them to us. The experience of viewing a daguerreotype illustrates this situation: we first see a negative image of the subject, then the positive image, which appears only when we change our angle of vision by shifting our heads or the plate in our hands. It is as if the positive were a chance effect of the negative, and vice-versa, each caught in a glimpse.[1] Images in general haunt their representational vehicles in similar ways, less as a switching between physical possibilities, more as figures that their needing to be seen and our wanting to know brings into visibility as we look and think.[2]

This example comes from the beginnings of photography, with its presumption of an individual viewer caught in the moment of looking at an individuated image made with the aim of capturing someone, something, or some place at a moment in time. In principle, several viewers could look at this same, mechanically reproducible image. But they would do so individually, alone or as members of a definable public. Today, a more typical experience is one of seeing digitally generated imagery flashing up at speed, manipulable by us and by others on the feed, already massively manipulated by machine-managed, algorithmic processes that no human sees. We perceive the top layers of image arrays the operations of which we remain unaware, except for glitches, or when artists, especially filmmakers, imagine them for us. The discorrelation between the visible and the invisible elements of an image, present since Indigenous representation, returns in new forms.[3]

We have seen that "economy" has been understood in parallel ways. Historically, at the level of individual acts within a relatively narrow framework, for example, a personal ethics, a traditional family code, or a morality prescribed by a religion. This usage is now obsolete, but the practices are not. Economics is now commonly understood as the systematic exchange of goods and services that functions at both microeconomic and macroeconomic dimensions. The logic of lack is as definitive of exchange economies as it is of images. Capitalist commodification orchestrates yearning for things perceived as providing access to desired lifestyles, may fulfil that need if you can pay for it, but will strive to immediately precipitate further wishes of the same sort, at continuing, and accumulating, cost to each of us. "Attention must be paid"—as Willi Loman, in *Death of a Salesman,* insisted—to which we must add, "[…] and paid for."

When thought historically, ways of seeing and economies can be paired as adjacencies, as parallel formations that touch at specifiable points but remain on fundamentally different trajectories within the same social system or during the same period. Or their points of convergence can be the focus, raising the question of what these two fields have in common when viewed as interacting across time. The noun concepts "iconomy" and "iconomies" appear, and thus the adjectival qualities that might be named "iconomic."

As we have seen, "Iconomy" or a variant is used as the name of several internet and financial service providers in the United States and Asia. It is a brand for two design shops in Johannesburg. It is also gaining traction as the name for economies of several kinds—monetary, organizational, managerial, ethical, and aesthetic—that deal mostly in images, in which they are the primary units. The value established by them is the basis of their currency. "Iconomics" might also be an appropriate name for a discipline, or better, a convergence of interdisciplines, that examine the operations of actual iconomies. Finally, to act iconomically, in an iconomic manner, could also be an attitude, an approach, a way of doing things, a mode of behavior. In this sense, there would be parallels to behaving economically, or artistically. This, too, could be studied, be the object of historical, economic, academic, and artistic inquiry. The costs and benefits of these usages, however, remain subject to serious accounting.

A Brief History of Iconomy

In Part I, we tracked the trajectory marked within the history of thought when images and economies were conceived of in relation to each other. We saw that in each phase of this development, images and economies came into distinctive conjunction. They all work as political economies of one kind or another. These conjunctions haunted later ones, and they continue to resonate in specific ways.

In Chapter 1, I made the point that interpretations of Plato's Allegory of the Cave—the paradigmatic Western evocation of knowledge of the world arrived at through the showing and seeing of images—have sedimented into contrasting pairs: between appearance and reality; superstition and objective knowledge; lies and truth; mystification and revelation; the real and the ideal. Yet if we read it closely, in context, and with an eye to its contemporary relevance, we can see immediately that the allegory exceeds these dichotomies, that it mobilizes at least four educational economies, which are incompatible. We can also see that, nevertheless, they might become operational in the task of building a republic through the capacity for deception inherent in every image, through direct coercion in the real world, and from the sense within the polis of there being no other option. Or they might fail to do so—as, historically, they did.

In Chapter 1, I posited a quite other set of understandings of the relationships between seeing and knowing and of how they are organized as social protocols. Plato's drawing of light to dark contrasts between truth and lies, revelation and deception, reality and imagery, so central to the cave allegory, exist on a minor register within Yolŋu ideology, and in that of many other Indigenous peoples. The driving force shaping their worldview is the living presence of the Dreaming, the worldmaking activities of the Originary Beings and of the ancestors descended from them, an eternal recurrence that animates the material world around them and all life within it, always has done, always will do. As we saw, Indigenous processes of imagining are devoted to seeing through the physical world to the work of the Dreaming and to assimilating seasonal change and new phenomena to this double reality. Double vision, layered in time and space, not deception, blind belief, or bad faith. Similarly, historical events and current happenings are assigned places within the patterns of social relationships inherited from the Dreaming and valued accordingly. Adjustment, calibration, not either/or, true/false, one thing or the other option taking. Representation, too, is governed by these rules. There are images galore, including sacred ones to be used only in the right ritual ceremonies, seen only by those who are appropriately initiated. When it becomes politically necessary, however, certain images are tasked with conveying the powers of the ancestors to others. The correct way to do so is not always codified and often needs to be negotiated if the circumstances are without precedent.[4]

Because the sacred content is actually present in Indigenous representations, none are icons in any of the several senses of the concept that appear during the Byzantine iconoclastic controversies.[5] Explicit Biblical prohibitions against idolatry meant that no party supported the worship of icons in and for themselves. All would regard Indigenous worship as idolatrous. Yet the Christian multitudes—among them illiterates, and those from other language groups—venerated the images of the Holy Family and the saints. The church and the state needed to define the theological status of religious representation in a way that removed the taint of idolatry. Nikephoros, Patriarch of Constantinople, seized on an irreducible quality of every representation, that it presents an image of what is not there, that is always a resemblance of an absence. He turned this recognition into the basis of an organized form of worship, an "economy" in Greek usage that became an orthodoxy in Byzantine usage, at least during the reigns of iconophile emperors. As Mondzian explained, "The solution arrived at was the dual doctrine of the *image, invisible* (and thus beyond the charge of idolatry), and the *icon, visible*, and thus perfectly fitted to be placed at the center of a pedagogical and political strategy serving the temporal power of the church. [...] the multifarious, interwoven strands of divine *economy*, God's overall plan for the salvation of humanity."[6]

The regulated worship of images when kneeling and looking at an icon became a repeated personal practice, undertaken in the same manner as other believers, a regular enactment of shared patterns of behavior based on shared beliefs—an economy, a religion. As we saw, there are parallels in the observances of all religions. And in the ways in which states regulate economies, right down to the images that certify the tokens used at the point of exchange. The medieval stamping of coins with icons of Christ on the obverse, the emperor on the reverse, echoes in the money tokens used in modern nation states: on one side, national icons illustrate the state's authorization of its value as legal tender, while on the other, the icons evoke a higher authority underwriting all transactions, as if money economies were divinely ordained and managed through these circulating icons themselves.

Transposing this distinction between icons and images to modern economies based on the exchange of manufactured material goods, Marx made it clear that commodities worked in similar ways. Things made for practical uses became "queer," "mysterious" images. Commodities sung a chorus that enchanted workers, distracting them from the fact that the bourgeoisie, in their relentless thirst for surplus value on which they could turn profit, were creating a chaotic and oppressive world. Shown the reality of their situation, however, he urged that workers should unite to bring about a revolution that would create societies in which all exchanges between humans, animals, and things made or given by the world, were based on everyone and everything being what they seem to be.

Benjamin spot lit the siren song of commodities, the energy they put into presenting themselves as unique among others of their kind, as heralding a new, modern kind of value. Exhibitionary value accelerated the transformation of use value into exchange value, thus generating more surplus value than ever before. Mechanization had expanded the manufacture of material goods and sped up their circulation through markets. So, too, for images: their reproducibility meant that they were no longer grounded and accessible only through icons located in one place or through icons repurposed as works of art. Images were also in movement, in the form of widely circulating photographs and, especially, movies. Opiates of the masses, yes, and highly effective fascist propaganda. But also, as Chaplin demonstrated, windows into other lives, and into other possible forms of life, including communist ones.

The pressure is building up. Quantities are increasing. Images are becoming more visible. Overload is looming. It is already here.

Marx, Benjamin, Debord, Baudrillard, W. J. T. Mitchell, up to the most recent commentators, including myself—everyone thinking deeply about images begins from what seems to be the most self-evident fact arrayed before their eyes and across their imaginations: that of seemingly endless, seemingly unstoppable, "immense accumulation." For the thinkers named, the accumulation occurs in the form, respectively, of commodities, moving image arts, spectacles, signs, and pictures. We can add to this list the ubiquity of multi-platform social media, resulting in widespread immersion in ambient imagery, processes that I call "immediation." In each case, the kind of images that these thinkers saw around them seemed to be qualitatively new in kind, to have quantitatively increased, to be more intense or more subtlety pervasive in themselves qua images, and more central to the most significant social formations of their times. No surprise then that "saturation" has replaced accumulation as the descriptor *du jour* of image economies. Saturation of our lives, including therefore its economic aspects, as a direct effect of this tidal wave of images and their seemingly infinite spread.

But the accumulating force of the historical trajectory that we have analyzed strikes also, and more forcefully, from the other side of the image/economy pairing. It is the growth of modern economies, the creative destruction wreaked by capitalism, the controls exercised by the command economies, and the globalization of both, that have brought images to a prominence even greater than during the times when spectacle seemed to prevail. Neoliberal economism having become a pervasive ideology in contemporary life, it is no surprise that imagery of all kinds has become, to an overwhelming degree, economistic. Thus the egregious prominence of Iconomics Inc., as we saw in Chapter 6.

The techno-utopic quasi-metaverse prefigured in sites such as Second Life, and now actively pursued by Facebook (to the point of rebranding as ∞ Meta), merges both these trajectories, promoting them as if they were the historically inevitable unfolding of the future destined for all. No, they are a corporate strategy to universalize one company, a contemporary instance of the modern drive to monopoly that inspires all such organizations.

All of which precipitates, as we have seen at every turn, resistance to these changes, adjustments on the part of traditional economies (and iconomies), and the constant invention of alternative worlds. May they soon be realized, as time is running out.

Iconoclash

The chapters in the second part of this book are responses to three constellations of images that preoccupied personal and social imaginaries in many parts of the world, beginning in the middle months of 2020 and extending through to the present. Globally, the imagery clustering around the SARS-CoV-19 coronavirus as it became a pandemic. Within the United States, the events staged by Donald J. Trump across a variety of mediums and the response configured around Joseph R. Biden. Also in that country, the anger and activism unleashed by the viral circulation of the cell phone video of the murder of George Floyd, its activation of Black Lives Matter and associated protests. Viral imagery all, each became epidemic, then pandemic, by no coincidence during the national, international, and global spread of an actual pandemic. Like the virus itself, each spread in waves, mutating constantly, competing with other image clusters to stay alive and to grow in its host bodies.

There is beauty in most imagery, or an intriguing ugliness, as well as, at times, abrupt movements, and striking gestures—images must attract attention at first appearance. To persist, however, they must offer a certain assurance, a degree of comfort, and the promise of a future flourishing. They settle into a seductive array. Yet the viral imagery of 2020–2022 was underwritten by violence that was vast and deep.

The spiky blob is a paradigmatic viral image, paradigmatic of the virality of images today. An iconic image of an invisible, tenacious connector whose every attachment causes disease and death in its human host. As we saw, public health campaigns put huge efforts into making SARS-CoV-19 visualizable and into publicizing its effects. Mass media concentrated on tracking its impacts on everyday life, locally and around the world. Social media did the same, its inherent virality also an incessant warring between negative and positive messaging.

Burnishing the public image of Donald Trump was the primary activity of his election campaign, of his Presidency, and his time since. Its blatant iconomism, its brand-name Trumpialism, was right out there, for all to see. It marshalled all the resources of political iconomy that we have been distinguishing. Its violence was, and remains, multi-dimensional. Less visible is the everyday violence inherent in the exploitation, degradation, and incarcerations that political conservatism and Republican Party policy perpetuates. More obvious were the threats to the poor, racial minorities, undocumented immigrants, asylum seekers, the media, Muslims, and uncooperative foreign leaders regularly featured in Trump's speeches and at rallies. Highly visible were pseudo-events such as the Bible stunt of June 1, 2020, an enactment of the kind of nationwide military crackdown on protest for which he was calling. This violent edifice, with Trump as the Leviathan-like, sovereignty-seeking figure astride its apex, reached a spectacular climax on January 6, 2021. Having failed to achieve the instant victory they craved, the forces involved continue to believe in the Big Lie and prepare for battles to come. These are battles within image wars, wars within the iconomy, obvious manifestations of the political divisions within the United States, usually dubbed "partisan." They raise an equally obvious question: are they proxy prefigurations, the cultural phase, of an actual civil war to come? Or is the war already in progress? If so, is it really what it most evidently seems to be: a warring between regimes of imagery within a highly politicized iconomy?

In mid-October 2021 a transaction occurred that epitomizes the nature of iconomy in its most naked neoliberal forms. Digital World Acquisition Corp (DWAC) acquired Trump Media & Technology Group (TMTG). DWAC is an example of a relatively recent Wall Street invention known as special purpose acquisition companies (SPACs). Investors pile in money to a venture capital fund that has the sole purpose of acquiring a start-up—any start-up, no desired missions specified, no restrictions of what it wants to do—that looks likely to make lots more money. (Chimera of credit default swaps, the trick too far that precipitated the Global Financial Crisis, hover into view.) At the time, TMTG's only asset was plans for a social media site modelled on Twitter coyly named "Truth Social," with the aim of becoming "a rival to the liberal media consortium and fight back against the 'Big Tech' companies of Silicon Valley."[7] The sale to DWAC lifted its capital value from $875 million (not a penny of which was invested by Donald Trump) to $4.05 billion. The image that is monetized in this instance is, obviously, Donald Trump's self-image, itself a well-marketed, trademarked brand, including its accumulated history, its unending promise of more of the same, of the same much bigger and better. Of course, the partisan divides drive much of this investment, but most of it is money chasing more of itself.[8] As we have seen, this has been Trump's primary motivation all along. The US Presidency as the biggest con game of them all.

An example from the other end of iconomic spectrum, from inside what economists would call the R&D arm of the iconomy, from among the work of professional visual artists, the image innovators, the image refiners, an example of what seems a perfect convergence of the values of globalized capital and those of contemporary art. The "big photography" of Andreas Gursky regularly achieves spectacular sales prices, but that is just the most obvious meeting point. Nor is it unique to this artist, as it is an act performed routinely by market darlings such as Jeff Koons and Damien Hirst. More interesting is that Gursky persistently takes as his subject-matter instances of the transformations of the observable world that globalization has wrought. Supermarkets, stock exchanges, airports and shipping ports, international hotels, real estate developments in Dubai, an Amazon warehouse, piece workers, tract housing, worker hostel complexes, a rave site. Usually of substantial, sometimes mural size, each photograph combines several negatives digitally melded into an all-over image that maintains uniformly high definition. Bright lighting, intense color, high viewpoints, similar resolution, and panoramic spreads prevail. A world replete to the point of excess, lifted from the actuality of place to become a fantastical field on which everything is everywhere the same and equally available to everyone for all time. As Pamela Lee remarks, these technical and formal strategies precisely parallel how global capital works to "bathe all *social* relations in an ambient and overall wash."[9] From this perspective, the spectrum turns out to be illusory. There is no spread between opposite poles. Trump and Gursky are in the same place, and that place is everywhere.

Yet our discussion of the emergence of a contemporary Black aesthetic teaches us otherwise. The disjunctive, discordant, compositional strategies used by Kara Walker, Arthur Jafa, Paul Pfeiffer, Marielle Ingram, Deana Lawson, and increasing numbers of other artists spotlight the defiant yet constructive energy that can be found within even the most systematic and prolonged repression. The excellence of the performance of Black athletes, musicians, and artists is itself an act of defiance, repeated often. They display the creativity that is sustaining them now, inside their unfreedom. They learn from their predecessors, they dance together, they cluster in chorus. The enslaved joyfully sing of their impending freedom. Free jazz, improvisation, Black mo'nin'. Generative difference, not restrictive sameness, is right here to see. It, too, could be everywhere.

Contracirculation also drives the imagery of protest, as we saw in Chapter 11. Diversity on the march, a plethora of signs calling for concrete changes, but mostly in the signal sent by those multitudes who marched and are ready to do so again. Ephemeral shrines to the murdered that continue to flourish for months. And the constant work of contracirculation on social media: to blunt the brute weapons of the trolls, to deconstruct the old normal, to disseminate prideful difference as its own, independent, abnormal, flourishing.

Image, Images, Imagery; Icon, Icons, Iconomy

I have no interest in modelling iconomy on the same kind of principles, models, practices, laws, and examples that are outlined in introductions to any kind of formal economics. I have attempted to offer, instead, a historical genealogy and a deconstructive critique. What has it told us about the value of thinking iconomically?

In these reflections, we have benefitted from the identification of several kinds of value: use, exchange, exhibition, symbolic, as well as other given values, such as those that are aesthetic and political. Which leads us to ask: What does *iconomic value* look like? Where does it appear? What does its identification add to these insights?

A reminder. Images cannot be sensed, appear, become visible, or even imaginable, without being carried by a support. Likewise, and in parallel, they cannot occur, and certainly cannot convey meaning, unless they are part of a representational repertoire, that is, be items within a known and manageable set of like and unlike images, to which they can be matched and differentiated. In other words, be elements within a symbolic economy.

These observations remind us further that *imagery* is the medium under scrutiny here, the constellating of images into image flows, through small scale, medium density, and immense accumulations of historical inheritances and fresh differences. Iconomies are movements of images in concert, and out of tune, passages across a field that their movement delineates. An iconomy is a society-wide, regional, and worldwide aggregation of imaginaries that are in constant and inconstant flux. We have been asking what kind of system is this—if it is one? What are its repetitions? How does it change? What are its options for reinvention, for generating something new? How does it orchestrate differentiation? How does it surprise itself? In one question: how does what we might call *iconomic value* come into the world?

As I hope to have shown, most useful answers to these questions profile how, in the relevant instance, particulars become generalized, and generalizations condense into particulars.

The most obvious of these is the ways in which single images become singular, attracting the descriptor "iconic," that is, invested with significance in ways analogous to the worship of a religious icon. Iconic images are those widely recognized as representing specifiable generalities—that is, certain ideas, practices, places, peoples, events, processes, products, companies, historical periods, ways of life, nations, even entire categories of human experience.

In doing so, at the same time, they push aside other, similar imagery that strives to represent the same or closely similar ideas, practices, places, peoples, events, etc.

The iconicity of particular images is established through initial incarnation but mostly through insistent repetition followed by variation within a relatively narrow range. Differentiation is abhorred, but it does not disappear. It is the constant ground of resistance to iconicity's tendency toward exclusion.

Iconic images, when they gather sufficient force to become central to an image regime, displace imagery of *other* places, peoples, events, etc. that seek prominence in the visual field, the iconomy, the domain in which interests and forces of all kinds compete to be seen, to be heard within public discourse, to occupy the subjective imaginations of individuals and the imaginaries of societies.

This domain is mostly structured in ways that echo the dispositions of economic, social, political, and cultural power in any given society, in its region, and in the world geopolitical (dis)order. Disposition here includes top-down, bottom-up, lateral movements, and micro-powers.

I have paid some, but by no means sufficient, attention to the operations of imagery within the inner lives of individuals, the psychic economies that Freud strove to delineate, Jung to generalize, and so many since have been moved to elaborate. Aby Warburg's *Bilderatlas Mnemosyne*, complied between 1920 and 1929, also stands out as a profound attempt to map how humans have used images to manage our fundamental, civilizational need to differentiate, as he put it, between "the self and the outside world," and to populate "the interspace between urge and action" where the psyche does its constant work to this end.[10]

Images also flow through structures that have developed, over centuries, and become dedicated to making them visible, to exhibit them, and to attract attention to them. Among these: Festivals, carnivals, parades, theatres, public squares, meeting halls, shops, markets, trade fairs, expositions, museums, galleries, billboards, department stores, malls, cinemas, broadcast then cable television, screens of all kinds. The multiple exchanges across this ever-expanding but also always localized network operate as a totalizing but not universal exhibitionary iconomy.[11]

Specialist representational practices, such as the visual arts, have developed distinctive sets of platforms for the showing, assessment, interpretation, and circulation of their products. These are the nodal points of artworlds, or visual arts exhibitionary complexes.[12]

Most imagery within capitalist societies is, like all other forms of exchange, commodified. Most imagery within authoritarian societies serves as propaganda for the ruling order. Most imagery within theocracies articulates the ruling narratives of faith and belief. Currently, the implosion of dominant systems is inducing a spreading sense that factuality is wavering in its role as their common substrate, as the ultimate measure of their accountability. As we have seen, opportunism and authoritarianism see little loss in encouraging this trend.

Image regimes emerge, compete, some may achieve prominence, even predominance for a time, then they recede, not disappear but become residual, as others emerge to play through the same cycle. There is, however, nothing natural or regular or predictable about this: it is a matter of accumulated weight, of momentum, disrupted by contingency, always.

Against the grain, some modes of representation seek to reshape these hierarchies and counter-hierarchies into a plane of appearance that would approximate closer to a level playing field, using dispersive imagery to build diversity, concurrence and, at best, community.[13]

Within each of these tendencies, so many nuances, degrees and kinds of conformity, neutrality, dissensus.

World pictures, meta-geographies, and imaged mapping strategies. These have been surprisingly few: Indigenous Creation stories that register the actions of Originary Beings as an eternal recurrence in the environment as it is lived now; Babylonian cities surrounded by the rest of the world; ancient and early modern China as the Middle Kingdom; the Great Chain of Being in Medieval Europe; the genealogies of noble families; continents and oceans during the Age of Exploration; Encyclopedias and dictionaries; the centers and colonies of empires; Blue Earth; Google Earth; and, perhaps, The Stack.

Meta-pictures, hypericons, are also few. The *tabula rasa*, Plato's cave, Aristotle's wax tablet, Locke's dark room, Marx's camera obscura, Freud's mystic writing pad, Sartre's keyhole, Wittgenstein's hieroglyphic, Derrida's pharmakon.

And then, already from the beginnings, there are the several kinds of imagery mobilized by artists. They stand to each of these iconomic principles in relations of connivance or obliquity, or discordance and opposition. They prefigure iconomies to come.

So, to return to the question of whether "iconomy" acutely names the plane upon which these phenomena are operating, and picks out their distinctive features in ways that we need to know now. Or does use of the concept blur distinctions that must be made—not least those between imagery and economies—if our current situation, and the pasts that shaped it, are to be fully and clearly grasped? We have seen it serve both purposes, along with several more ambiguous ones. Still in active formation, political iconomy has become central to our contemporary condition. It therefore invites the kinds of historical location and critical deconstruction that I have begun to provide in this book. It anticipates the critique to come.

Notes

1 For an illuminating discussion of the centrality of the negative to all kinds of photography, see Geoffrey Batchen, *Negative/Positive, A History of Photography* (London: Routledge, 2021). For his remarks on daguerreotypes, see Chapter 7.

2 W.J.T. Mitchell, *What Do Pictures Want? The Lives and Loves of Images* (Chicago: University of Chicago Press, 2005).

3 See Shane Denson, *Discorrelated Images* (Durham, NC: Duke University Press, 2020). For discussion of what Harun Faroki named the "operative image" see the questionnaire and several chapters in "The Changing Ontology of the Image," ed. Jacob Lund, *Nordic Journal of Aesthetics*, vol. 30, nos. 61–62 (2021), at https://tidsskrift.dk/nja/issue/view/9283.

4 For the discussions among Yolŋu regarding the Bark Petitions to Parliament, see Nancy Williams, *The Yolgnu and Their Land: A System of Land Tenure and the Fight for Its Recognition* (Canberra: Australian Institute for Aboriginal Studies, 1986). On the panels see https://www.foundingdocs.gov.au/item-did-104.html. For analysis of the adjustments made by artists at Papunya to complaints from elders at Yuendumu and at Alice Springs that they had, in their paintings of the early 1970s, revealed too much secret knowledge, see Vivien Johnson, *Once Upon a Time in Papunya* (Sydney: University of New Souths Wales Press, 2010), Chapter 4 "The Problem of Secrecy."

5 In this sense, the title of the exhibition, *Icons of the Desert*, is misleading, but it was, of course, intended metaphorically, to evoke a loose association within the economy of publicity for art exhibitions. It was, therefore, iconomic *as a title*. See Roger Benjamin with Andrew Weislogel eds., *Icons of the Desert: Early Aboriginal Paintings from Papunya* (Ithaca, NY: Herbert F. Johnson Museum of Art, Cornell University, 2009).

6 Marie-José Mondzian, *Image, Icon, Economy; The Byzantine Origins of the Contemporary Imaginary* [1996] (Stanford: Stanford University Press, 2005), back cover summary.

7 See Trump Media & Technology Group, "Company Overview," October 21, 2021, at https://www.tmtgcorp.com/company-overview/.

8 See Stephen Bartholomeuz, "There's art but little substance in Trump's latest deal," *Sydney Morning Herald*, October 26, 2001, 23, and Michael Hiltzik, "Trump's latest deal to set high water mark for investment scams," *Los Angeles Times*, December 14, 2021, at https://www.latimes.com/business/story/2021-12-14/trumps-spac-deal.

9 Pamela Lee, *Forgetting the Artworld* (Cambridge, MA: MIT Press, 2012), 77. Geoffrey Batchen accepts this reading, while also noting that Gursky sometimes uses similar techniques to critical ends, in his *Ocean* series of 2010, for example. See Batchen, *Negative/Positive*, 87–88. We might add that Gursky occasionally attempts a direct photographic critique of globalized capital itself, through collaged images of political leaders and businessmen, such as his *Politics* series of 2020. These are, however, his least successful works.

10 See Aby Warburg, *Bilderatlas Mnemosyne-The Original* [1929] (Ostfildern: Hatje Cantz for the Haus Der Kulturen der Welt, Berlin, 2022), 9. See also https://warburg.sas.ac.uk/archive/bilderatlas-mnemosyne.

11 I discuss this is more detail, and in relation to Tony Bennett's concept of the modern "exhibitionary complex," in my EGS lecture of August 19, 2019, "Exhibitionary Times: Art against Spectacle," at https://www.youtube.com/watch?v=d8mvqnMat3M. One must not fail to acknowledge, simply because it has become canonical, the pioneering work on image economies by Marshall McLuhan, beginning with *The Mechanical Bride: The Folklore of Industrial Man* (New York: Vanguard Press, 1951) and including, of course, *Understanding Media: The Extensions of Man* (New York: McGraw Hill, 1964).

12 See Terry Smith, *Curating the Complex, The Open Strike* (Berlin: Sternberg Press; Cambridge, MA: MIT Press, 2021).

13 In "Defining Contemporaneity: Imagining Planetarity," *Nordic Journal of Aesthetics*, vols. 49–50 (2015): 156–74, I set out a planomenal framework within which these possible principles should be understood as located.

INDEX

Page no with 'f' indicates figure and page no with 'n' indicates notes.

www.ingramcontent.com/pod-product-compliance
Ingram Content Group UK Ltd.
Pitfield, Milton Keynes, MK11 3LW, UK
UKHW021837100926
8556IPUK00004B/402

9 781839 98435